JOHN H. STROUPE is Professor of English at Western Michigan University and co-editor of *Comparative Drama*, from which three volumes of comparative and critical essays have been published by AMS Press. Stroupe has published widely on O'Neill and on modern drama, has worked on the O'Neill Collection at Yale, and on the O'Neill-Commins Correspondence in the Commins Collection at Princeton.

CRITICAL APPROACHES TO O'NEILL

AMS Studies in Modern Literature, No. 17

ISSN 0270-2983

Other titles in this series:

No. 1. Richard E. Amacher and Margaret F. Rule, compilers. *Edward Albee at Home and Abroad: A Bibliography, 1958 to June 1968.* 1973.

No. 2. Richard G. Morgan, editor. *Kenneth Patchen: A Collection of Essays.* 1977.

No. 3. Philip Grover, editor. *Ezra Pound, the London Years, 1908-1920.* 1978.

No. 4. Daniel J. Casey and Robert E. Rhodes, editors. *Irish-American Fiction: Essays in Criticism.* 1979.

No. 5. Iska Alter. *The Good Man's Dilemma: Social Criticism in the Fiction of Bernard Malamud.* 1981.

No. 6. Charles L. Green, compiler. *Edward Albee: An Annotated Bibliography, 1968-1977.* 1980.

No. 7. Richard H. Goldstone and Gary Anderson, compilers. *Thornton Wilder: A Bibliographical Checklist.* 1982.

No. 8. Taylor Stoehr. *Words and Deeds: Essays on the Realistic Imagination.* 1986.

No. 9. René Taupin. *The Influence of French Symbolism on Modern American Poetry.* 1985.

No. 11. Clifford Davidson, et al., eds. *Drama in the Twentieth Century.* 1984.

No. 12. Siegfried Mews, ed. *"The Fisherman and His Wife": Günter Grass's "The Flounder" in Critical Perspective.* 1983.

No. 14. Arnold T. Schwab, ed. *Americans in the Arts, 1908-1920: Critiques by James Gibbons Huneker.* 1985.

No. 15. *Partisan Review Fifty-Year Cumulative Index: Volumes 1-50, 1934-1983.* 1984.

No. 16. Amy D. Ronner. *W. H. Hudson: The Man, the Novelist, the Naturalist.* 1986.

CRITICAL APPROACHES TO O'NEILL

Edited by
John H. Stroupe

AMS PRESS
New York

Library of Congress Cataloging-in-Publishing Data
Critical approaches to O'Neill.
  (AMS studies in modern literature; no. 17)
  Includes index.
  1. O'Neill, Eugene, 1888-1953—criticism and interpretation. I. Stroupe,
John H. II. Series.
PS3529.N5Z62726   1988   812'.52   86-47845
ISBN 0-404-61587-2

MANUFACTURED IN THE UNITED STATES OF AMERICA

Contents

Preface

Critical Approaches to O'Neill brings together twelve essays in honor of the Eugene O'Neill Centennial of 1988. The critical modes of the articles are deliberately various; each piece provides a different approach to the study of O'Neill's drama: archetypal, psychoanalytical, philosophical, textual, biographical, phenomenological, cultural, and through deconstructionist criticism, genre criticism, and traditional comparative methods. The essays have been chosen not only for intrinsic excellence and for their coverage of the desired works and figures but also for the ways in which they sharpen our vision and understanding of the plays of America's foremost dramatist.

The essays included in this volume are reprinted from *Comparative Drama*, with the exception of "O'Neill and the Creative Process: A Road to Xanadu," a reworking of material which first appeared in *Modern Drama*. Most of these essays were originally selected or solicited for publication with this volume in mind, for given O'Neill's stature and importance, there have been few anthologies of criticism, but five in the last twenty years: none employs critical approaches as a methodology to examine the O'Neill canon. I wish to thank Clifford Davidson and C. J. Gianakaris who provided assistance with these essays at their first stage of publication in *Comparative Drama* and allowed me to use the O'Neill material in this book.

John H. Stroupe
Kalamazoo, Michigan

Biographical Statements

EMIL ROY, Professor of English at the University of South Carolina at Aiken, has published some thirty scholarly articles, mostly on drama, and eleven books. His most recent text is *The College Writer*, 1986.

STEPHEN M. WATT, a member of the English Department at Indiana University, has published widely and is presently collaborating on two book-length projects: *Joyce and the Nineteenth-Century Irish Theatre* and *Essays on Nineteenth-Century Drama in Honor of Charles H. Shattuck.*

JOSEPH J. MOLESKI is an actor, director, musician, and critic. Currently director of his own public relations agency, he is working on several screenplays and a book on Henry James.

JOHN CHIOLES teaches comparative literature at New York University each fall and philosophy of culture at the University of Athens during the winter. His recent projects include the script of *Antigone* for the New York Shakespeare Festival; he is co-editor of a recent Greek issue of the *Journal of Literary Translation.*

LOUIS SHEAFFER is the author of the two-volume biography, *O'Neill: Son and Playwright* (1968), which won the George Freedley Award of the Theater Library Association as the best theater book of its year, and *O'Neill: Son and Artist*, winner of the 1974 Pulitzer Prize for biography.

JOHN H. STROUPE, co-editor of *Comparative Drama* and Professor of English at Western Michigan University, has published widely on O'Neill and on modern drama; he is co-editor of three volumes of comparative and critical essays published by AMS Press.

JAMES A. ROBINSON, Associate Professor of English at the University of Maryland, College Park, and author of *Eugene O'Neill and Oriental Thought: A Divided Vision*, is currently at work on a book about the father-son relationship in modern American drama.

MICHAEL MANHEIM, author of *O'Neill's New Language of Kinship*, is at work on a book tentatively titled *O'Neill's Transcendence of Melodrama*. He is Professor of English at the University of Toledo.

THOMAS P. ADLER is Professor of English and Associate Dean of the Graduate School at Purdue University. His most recent book is *Mirror on the Stage: The Pulitzer Plays as an Approach to American Drama*, 1987.

ALBERT ROTHENBERG is Principle Investigator of "Studies in the Creative Process"; Director of Research, Austen Riggs Center, Stockbridge, Massachusetts; and Clinical Professor of Psychiatry at Harvard University.

EUGENE D. SHAPIRO was a research associate on the project "Studies in the Creative Process" supported by the National Institute of Mental Health. He is currently a physician in pediatric practice.

MICHAEL HINDEN, Professor of English at the University of Wisconsin, Madison, is Chairman of the Board of Directors of the Eugene O'Neill Society. He has published widely on modern topics and is working on *Long Day's Journey Into Night: A Critical Study*.

The Archetypal Unity of Eugene O'Neill's Drama

Emil Roy

Seen from the inside the typical play by Eugene O'Neill recapitulates the ritual conflict of winter and summer, death and rebirth which both the early Greek and Christian drama inherited and extended. Found out in his lust for a forbidden love object, a son figure is expelled from his primal social group. In order to return and grasp his never fading Edenic vision of purity, he embarks on a quest pursued by inner and outer erinyes. As O'Neill has commented in his "Memoranda on Masks," "One's outer life passes in a solitude haunted by the masks of others; one's inner life passes in a solitude bounded by the masks of oneself." His dark voyage may take him inward through the spiraling entrails of the racial unconscious or outward through the labyrinthine windings of a Necropolis, figured scenically as an urban slum, ship, brothel or home. In his role as marked down prey, he vicariously enjoys the law-giver's power and endures the criminal's aggrieved sufferings. Finally exhausted but clear eyed, he achieves a blissful *Liebestod* with the long sought mother breast.

Most critics have recognized that O'Neill's career began with an early period of seascape realism, evolved through a most uneven middle stage of sometimes labored symbolism, and returned finally to the conventions of his beginnings. Yet the pervasive thrust of his drama is non-realistic and negative, sadistic and melodramatic, as Leslie Fiedler has characterized American fiction. Even when his plays deal with man's subjection to both his society and environment,

1

O'Neill places archetypal motifs in contexts which amplify their ironic implications in unexpected ways.

Like most poets O'Neill spreads the visualizable world out in mental space. He appears to conceive of his fictional universe as an emanation of his own rich and dynamic psyche. Friedrich Nietzsche's observation regarding symbolic map making in *Thus Spoke Zarathustra* could just as validly have come from O'Neill, whom he profoundly influenced: "For each soul, every other soul is a hinterland. . . . For me—how could there be an outside of me? There is no outside. . . . The center is everywhere." J. H. Raleigh has denoted sea and land, city and farm as O'Neill's basic pairs of antithetical settings. However, his scheme overlooks the dialectic of repugnance and desire which provides the essential dramatic conflict. As in the seasonal ritual play, O'Neill's action begins in a bright, sun-lit and rationally organized world, moves into a dark, nighttime world of dreams and passionate disorder, and *may* return to the normal world. At his most obvious he exhibits his paternal-maternal, sterile-fertile antitheses through his protagonists' pendulations back and forth, in and out. He moves between Greco-Roman, mask-like Mannon house and anchored ship *South Winds*, battlefield and marriage bed in *Mourning Becomes Electra*, house and barn, "hard" New England and "soft" California in *Desire Under the Elms*, the palace of the present and the nightmarish Great Forest in *The Emperor Jones*, ship's boiler room and urban labyrinth in *The Hairy Ape*, and men's saloon and women's home in *The Iceman Cometh, Touch of a Poet* and *Hughie*, among others.

On one side is a man's world, dominated by a series of selfish, magnetically attractive, and powerful old patriarchs who rule over the minds if not always the wills of their families. Even in their absence or after death, such men as Ephraim Cabot in *Desire*, Abraham Mannon in *Mourning*, and James Tyrone in *A Long Day's Journey Into Night* maintain a dramatic presentness. Like the folkloric dragon guarding a hoard of buried treasure, each of these father figures identifies his potency and well-being with property, often epitomized by something hidden in it. Thus Cabot claims that he resides God-like in his farm's stones, Orin Mannon jibes that his father the General "was no good on an offensive, but would hold a position until hell froze over," and James Tyrone comments, "The more property you own, the safer you think you are." Since O'Neill has stressed the Biblical precursorship of his patriarchs, the property in which their power has been ensconced becomes a disguised representation of the same desexualized body of the mother that the Garden of Eden was for Jehovah (a suggestion of Theodore Reik's); it is both repository and defense against repressed incestuous desires for the mother. Ironically, O'Neill's "fathers" use their wives like their lands, as objects, expelling their male progeny when they threaten their hegemony. These paternal overlords are the ones who establish the plays' atmospheres of competition, of aggression, of having to pay a price for everything.

At an opposite pole is a woman's world of romance, folklore, and love, full of riches and bounty, and giving. It is usually identified with Melville's early sea novels and, as in· Nietzsche, with the Blessed Isles of Greek mythology. Although O'Neill's characters conceive of the Islands as geographically remote, they are their spiritual counterparts of the mythic World Navel, with a fatal and sacred quality which his questors cannot resist. At the center of this paradise is a magic fountain or well which incarnates mirror-like the child's desire for maternal reunion. Nearby are its familiar spirits, the uninhibited natives who tempt frustrated puritans into unbridled sexuality. As Orin Mannon tells his mother Christine, "I had read and re-read [Melville's] book *Typee* about the South Sea Islands. . . . The whole island was you." The Blessed Isles never appear, however, at their most untainted and naive, with the possible exception of *The Fountain*. Even there the maternal spring is jealously guarded against voyeuristic intrusion. The play's pervasive Oedipal concerns emerge in the first scene where the Moorish minstrel Yusef is murdered near a fountain by a religious fanatic. Challenged to a duel by his rival Vicente, Juan threatens to "prick him in the thigh" and is sent off in disgrace with Columbus. When he finally discovers the hoped-for fountain of eternal life in Florida after many vicissitudes, he is ambushed by Indians. Only when he is near death from his wounds does he achieve a vision of the long sought "form of Beatriz . . . as if rising from the spring," finally uniting them. As projections of a spontaneous upwelling of passion, a re-capturing of lost creativity, these realms are literally unattainable except in dreams on the breast of a virgin mother as in *Moon for the Misbegotten*, in a state of drunken fraternality in the early sea plays or *Iceman*, or in regression to the state of child-like dependency that climaxes *All God's Chillun* or *More Stately Mansions*.

Originally the mother was the whole world, and since the human spirit seeks intuitively to perpetuate the union of child and mother, the O'Neillian protagonist embraces a mirror-version of himself in order to embrace her. The innocent camaraderie of adolescence extends past childhood the kind of chaste and undifferentiated love which is threatened by the onset of mature sexual passion. At its purest, this comradeship links two young men, often brothers, whose homoerotic conflicts are marked by an unusual closeness: "You and I ain't like most brothers," Andrew tells Robert Mayo in *Beyond the Horizon*, "always fighting and separated a lot of the time, while we've always been together—just the two of us. It's different with us." Similar feelings also bind Simeon and Peter in *Desire*, David and Ezra Mannon in *Mourning*, and Edmund and Jamie Tyrone in *Long Day's Journey*. Their closeness is often stressed by the hostility of a third brother whose parentage is clouded: Eben, Adam Brant, and Eugene. Even more frequently, ordinarily predictable rivals are paired off, like Yank and Driscoll in *Bound East for Cardiff*, Edmund Darrel and Sam Evans in *Strange Interlude*, and most of the bums populating Harry Hope's saloon in *Iceman*. O'Neill also pairs idealistic but guilt-ridden neophyte with an older cynical neurotic, on the pattern of *Henry IV* and *Don Quixote*, drawing together Don Parritt and Larry Slade in *Iceman*, Erie Smith and Hughie (both of them in *Hughie*), and Phil Hogan and Jamie Tyrone in *Moon for the Misbegotten*. In a psychological variant on the Elizabethan twinship motif, O'Neill even introduces characters who appear to be opposite but identical halves of a disintegrating personality. They are Dion Anthony and William Brown in *Great God Brown* and John and Loving in *Days Without End*. Since they are not really identical (the same person), but merely similar, their homoerotic desire to merge with one another is properly seen as a defense against fear of the loss of identity. As Dion Anthony protests, "Brown loves me! . . . because I have always possessed the power he needs for love, because I am love!" Such characters compulsively invoke delusions of imminent self-fulfillment, warding off guilt, intimacy, or despair in dramatic versions of Eric Berne's "pastimes."

Although the dominance-submission roles may be veiled in commercial terms, as when Smithers complains to James that "I done the dirty work and I was worth money to you," the binding tie is often viewed as a mystic or religious link. "I got a hunch that when I lost Hughie, I lost my luck," the gambler Erie Smith laments. In effect, each member of the pair avoids self-hate by receiving love of self from another, drawing emotional sustenance from him. Each builds a symbiotic relationship through exaggerated protests of admiration, tokens of friendship, and apparently uncritical acceptance. In the strongest attachments, each builds a self out of the other to replace a self no longer satisfying, as when the Negro Joe Mott says in *Iceman*: "White folks always said I was white." This desire to escape entrapment within a false behavioral skin is not confined to racism. By controlling another's reactions, he labors under delusions of superiority. Not only is his pipe dream of success received by another with apparent credulity, but the patent fraudulence of his partner's pretensions is seen to be damaging, making him less threatening. As Jamie tells Edmund Tyrone, "Wanted you to fail. Always jealous of you. . . . But don't get the wrong idea, kid. I love you more than I hate you." *Iceman*, however, demonstrates most graphically the murderous hatreds underlying the stagnation of drink, pipe dreams, and casual friendships. While the bums swing erratically between submission and repudiation, Hickey plays analyst to their analysands. But at the same time he attacks their delays, self-delusions, and obsessive ruminations, he must adopt similar tactics to protect his own secret against Slade's ever more effective probings. And while the traumatized Slade must resist not only Hickey's demands for self-revelation and Parritt's tacit pleading for condemnation, Parritt threatens to confess not too little but too much. In more abstract terms, such pairings give rise to conflicts between the poet and businessman, farm and sea, drink and love, with the same dialectical tension pervading all.

Noting O'Neill's repeated references to his characters' dreamy eyes, S. K. Winther has concluded that they live in two worlds, one the outward world of physical reality, the

other a world of unfulfilled and passionate desire. Many of
his characters do possess the "glittering eye" of Coleridge's
Ancient Mariner, the archetypal token of the alienated artist,
the *poète maudit* cursed with a blessing of supernatural
insight. Fated to know their own psyches well, their uncanny
prescience penetrates others' defenses as well, especially
through the eyes. This quirk may stem from the recognition
of her disillusioned family that Mary Tyrone's dilated pupils
signified a resumption of her debilitating drug habit in *Long
Day's Journey*. The calls to adventure which beckon the
hero usually assume the form of visions, therefore,
projections on the cosmos of what Joseph Campbell calls
"the feminine attributes of the first, nourishing and
protecting presence." After Simeon Cabot recalls his dead
wife's "hair long's a hoss's tail—an' yaller like gold!" Peter
cosmologizes the associative cluster as "Gold in the sky—in
the West—Golden Gate—Californi-a—Goldest West!—fields
o'gold!" These calls affect the young male as romantic
appeals to masculine self-assertion, affirmations of total
freedom, a resolution to cross barriers, abetted by female
sexuality: "I wanted to be by your side in danger, in the
vigorous life of it all. I wanted to see you the hero. . . . I
was dreaming about the old Vikings," Captain Keeney's wife
tells him in *Ile*. The voyeuristic impulse underlying this
voracious appetite for the cosmic maternal emerges in the
peculiar character of O'Neill's many eavesdropping scenes
which in dreams are linked to "primal scene" fantasies. The
child imagines his parents engaged in intercourse, but with
himself taking the paternal role in disguised ways. Thus
Eben and Abbie Cabot's gaze penetrates even the wall
between their bedrooms in *Desire*, Lavinia Mannon
fantasizes her mother's lovemaking with both her father and
Adam Brant and is observed in turn by her brother Orin on
the South Seas Islands in *Mourning*, and in *Dynamo* Reuben
Light observes Ada Fife from a hedge while watched in turn
by his mother, to cite only a few examples. The compulsive
regularity of these scenes is not only symptomatic of
O'Neill's interest in the drama, which draws together the
exhibitionist and voyeuristic tendencies of actors and
audience. They also comment negatively on a society forced
to find substitutes for its own barrenness in the lives of
others, particularly children, thus robbing them of their
separate existences, in effect destroying them.

Although the neurotic as R. D. Laing has described him needs to be seen by others to convince himself he is real, the very fact of being visible exposes him to attack. In the Mannon house even the portraits follow the family members with accusing eyes, and the picture of Parritt's betrayed mother Rosa torments him in *Iceman*: "Her eyes followed me all the time. They seemed to be wishing I was dead!" Characters are not only victimized by the felt hostility of others. They are also tormented by their own supersensitive perceptions turned inward, while being simultaneously projected outward on the cosmos as a kind of "black sun." "I hate the daylight," Orin complains, "like an accusing eye," which may echo a question in O'Neill's first surviving play *Abortion*: "Are you sure society is not suffering from a case of the evil eye which sees evil where there is none?"

If the son acts on his resolution to cross barriers erected against his desires, he usually encounters a paternal threshold guard, a dramatic version of the deceitful figures who people folk mythology. Occasionally he is actually benevolent, like Phil Hogan in *Moon*. Pretending to guard his daughter's virginity and his pigs' health, he actually sets up Josie's seduction and breaks down the fence around his neighbor's ice pond, turning it into a pig wallow. Or he may masquerade as a type of divine conductor, like the timorous Long who cautions Yank against violence while promising to initiate him in *The Hairy Ape*, or the caretaker Seth Beckwith who tricks a crony into entering the "haunted" Mannon house on a bet. Or his function may be ambiguous, providing his charges with liquor which is the paternal substitute for a mother's milk, putting her out of reach of the jealous sons. Whenever the infant Jamie had a nightmare or stomach ache, Mary accuses Tyrone, "your remedy was to give him a teaspoonful of whisky to quiet him." And Harry Hope provides the same remedy on a grander scale. Usually, however, he literally controls his ward's freedom and spontaneity with lock and key. Old Macomber locks his daughter Muriel away from Richard Miller in *Ah, Wilderness!* in a comedic version of Danae's vain sequestering from Zeus, Yank Smith is jailed, James Tyrone locks up his liquor supply, and Rocky Pioggo somewhat ineffectively guards both liquor and room keys in *Iceman*. Since the thresholds mark the boundary between adolescent servitude and adult independence, paternal light and

maternal darkness, the Cerberus-like guard is usually eluded
at dawn or dusk. Escapes usually occur at evening, deaths
when the sun rises.

The success of these guardians is manifested in the
plethora of dead children around the premises, innocent
martyrs forever excluded from attainment of their visions.
Since for many of O'Neill's parental figures, the child is a
vessel of potentiality which renews the parent's vitality,
quarrels within his Strindbergian marriages often center upon
a child: his parentage or legitimacy (*Desire* and *Iceman*),
whether or not the child should be conceived (*Strange
Interlude, Long Day's Journey*), whether the child should
survive or not in the womb or after birth (*Abortion*), whom
the child loves most or is most loved by (*Beyond the
Horizon*), whether a child should be ostracized or driven out
(*Dynamo*), or who killed the child (*Long Day's Journey*).
Although births of sons give fathers a burst of new vigor
displayed by Cabot's dancing and fighting at his birthday
party, the departure of an heir threatens the parent with a
loss of his life-force, even death. Ironically, the curses with
which he attempts to forestall this eventuality invariably
recoil upon his own head. Although Darrel tells Nina
typically in *Strange Interlude*, "You've got to give up
owning people, as if you were God and had created them,"
parents faced with their sons' departures replace all positive
feelings of affection with a child's furious rage and oral
aggression. Cabot calls down "heaven's wuss cuss" on his
errant progeny Simeon and Peter; Edmund and Jamie feel
the weight of their mother's accusation that the birth of one
brought on her drug addiction and that the other fatally
exposed the dead Eugene to measles, and *Iceman* culminates
in Slade's demand that Parritt "Get the hell out of life." In
most cases, the father does not long survive his son's
banishment. James Mayo dies soon after his son Andrew's
departure, Captain Bartlett collapses when his son Ned
ridicules his dream of buried wealth in *Where the Cross is
Made*, and Sam Evans dies of a stroke the moment his
"son" Gordon's rowing team crosses the victory line in
Strange Interlude.

Since the true nature of the maternal fruit sought by the
hero is made acceptable to his waking consciousness by the
process of displacement, the object of his quest manifests
itself to him literally as well in such plays as *Gold, Desire,*

and *Marco Millions*. As in the Midas story, it turns to dross at the moment of attainment. Bartlett's gold ornaments are proven to be paste and brass, Cabot's buried cache is stolen, and Marco loses his idealism. Innumerable equivalents appear, including Orin Mannon's accusatory book, Phil Hogan's hoard of bootleg whiskey, or Richard Miller's bundle of pornographic letters. Or it may even be a receptacle of spiritual *mana* such as the crucifix John Loving at last reveres in *Days Without End*, the "immaculate conceptions" in *Desire* and *Strange Interlude*, Ponce de Leon's fountain or even Lazarus's gift of eternal life.

Cursed with an insatiable yearning like the mythic Tantalus, O'Neill's hero may either be rewarded for his pains by a shattering glance from the Gorgon's head or be forced to endure the torment suffered by the usurpers deluded by Ariel's banquet in Shakespeare's *Tempest*. Once he glimpses what he so eagerly desires, rather than being permitted to sink dreamily into a Bower of Bliss, he instead experiences a moment of revulsion, a realization that everything he does is tainted with the odor of flesh. Self-identified with the hated father, he is reduced in an instant to brute male sexuality. The idealized self-concepts of Yank Smith and Ezra Mannon are identically shattered, the first by Mildred's scream, "Oh, the hairy ape!" and the other by being forced by his wife to appear "a lustful beast in my own eyes." Underlying the taboo against looking, as in the legend of the Medusa's head, is the prohibition against viewing the mother sexually. Further displacing the association from eyes to mirrors, Hickey rejects a mirrored face "without the old false whiskers," and Ponce de Leon recalls, "Always the mirror in the spring showed me the same loathsome blighted face."

O'Neill's deep fear of the conflict between a sexually aggressive female and a passive male extends the mirror-spring imagery toward poison-metaphors, a counterpart to the Siren calls to turn back. His duplicitous females may substitute drugs for a lover, driving Mary Tyrone to sleep apart from James, or manage the same effect with "poison"-pen letters. In *A Wife for a Life*, a faithless wife rejects her husband for his best friend in a telegram, and Richard Miller is given away twice by women's letters in *Ah, Wilderness!* Ezra Mannon, of course, is literally poisoned by his wife Christine in *Mourning*. In many plays, therefore,

O'Neill intensifies dramatic equivalents of the primitive belief that the sight of oneself was a premonition of death.

Man's hopes of ever attaining his goals are mocked most literally in the early plays, many of them built around actual or imminent disasters at sea: the voyage of the ammunition-laden S. S. Glencairn (*In the Zone*), the collision and sinking of the S. S. Empress (*Warnings*), the sinking of Bartlett's ship and subsequent loss of another ship (*Gold* and *Where the Cross is Made*), and Captain Keeney's ice-bound Whaler (*Ile*). Not only is the questor adrift on a sinking vessel, icebound, lost aboard a raft, hemmed in by fog, or confronted by indifferent, malevolent, or despairing companions. He may cry out for help without being able to hear the answer; if he hears possible rescuers, he must remain silent lest he doom them too; or he sees succour destroyed before his eyes, dashing hope with it. The danger lies both within as madness, disease, thirst, or loss of hope and outside as submarines, circling sharks, fog, and icebergs, armed and desperate companions. But worst of all menaces is the sure to be shattered illusion of salvation, of help nearby. Most of these ironies are compounded in *Ile*, whose catastrophic climax coincides with Captain Keeney's simultaneous discovery of a school of whales to fill his long-empty oil tanks, a way out of the entrapping ice floes, and the irruption of his wife's wild madness.

The road of trials upon which O'Neill's hero embarks not only drives him toward the fulfillment of his desire, but defines the obstacles to it. The quest-motif is archetypally shaped by Christ's gathering of disciples, a messianic, rebellious, and perfervid aim. At every turn, however, he hears the lulling call of the Sirens tempting him to abandon his journey. Yet O'Neill's recurrent quests of men in flight from women spiral through a fallen world as if through the entrails of a huge beast, attempting both to rise and resist falling deeper. To crystallize his rebellion against patriarchal tyranny, the hero establishes a brotherhood, a group whose tyrannical leader is egocentric enough to represent the collective ego of his followers. With the exception of such plays as Milton's *Samson Agonistes,* Shaw's *Saint Joan*, and Eliot's *Murder in the Cathedral*, messianic figures have been rare in the English-language drama. In the early *Moon of the Carribbees* series and middle romances, O'Neill's use of such leaders has mainly stressed a sense of human remoteness and futility. Except for *Iceman*, where individuals momentarily stand out from the unenlightened chorus, his hordes are microcosmic but faceless. They are usually aggregates of automatons roused from torpor only by sadistic hunts for a scapegoat.

However, such leaders as Yank Smith, Brutus Jones, and Theodore Hickman come across as charismatic though confused types of *alazon* or imposter. Unlike Lazarus and Marco Polo, who never interact convincingly with the societies they confront, these have fled a highly competitive, more typical outside world to a secluded "island" community because they cannot accept men as they are. Like the hero of romance, each of them seeks a magic weapon with which to slay the dragon holding a malign sway over the wasteland. However, Yank quests in vain for the dynamite whose counterpart, the silver bullet in *Emperor Jones*, has already lost its efficacy unknown to Jones through the taint of money. And in *Iceman*, which closely parallels the plot of *Lazarus*, Hickey's efforts turn the wine of the bums' Feast of All Fools into water, a demonic parody of the Marriage at Cana miracle.

Although the settings of such plays as *Hairy Ape* and *Emperor Jones* place two worlds in conflict, one idyllic and paradisaical and the other full of injustices and anomalies, the societies which strike the cowed hordes as unharrowed hells appear utopian to their leaders, at least initially. Each of the messianic leaders has not only an overwhelming wish to be all-important in his world, but an uncanny gift for spotting and exploiting others' weaknesses, a set of satisfactions which James Tyrone seems to have derived at least fleetingly from his stage roles. Moreover, the reversals which dash these men to destruction from heights of influence resemble practical jokes which have backfired. Lacking any desires they can call their own, they tend both to envy the realness of their victims' feelings and to despise their delusions. Having been suddenly inspired to invent a magic charm and foist himself off as a god incarnate, Jones is destroyed by being taken *too* seriously at his own fraudulent self-estimate. And although Hickey intends to de-intoxicate the bums from their illusions, his therapy destroys instead of cures. While Yank Smith had at first believed he had been acting on his own initiative, he becomes painfully aware that he is totally subject to the wills of others. At his best, O'Neill's calculated ironies convey his image of modern man as both criminal and persecutor, victor and victim.

The *agon* or contest between two friends or brothers over a woman or her mythic equivalents, such as fame or wealth, generally culminates in the "victory" of the weaker and their inevitable separation. The more aggressive of the pair usually embarks on an outward business-oriented quest, while the more passive and poetic of them is immobilized, frozen into a dream, often drawn obsessively into books as an escape. The female who so tantalizes their sexuality is usually blonde, dressed in white as the ambiguous color of purity, and possessed of neither vitality nor integrity. A version of the archetypal sex temptress appearing as Duessa in Spenser or Eve in *Paradise Lost*, she is the "light" counterpart of O'Neill's dark, sensual and maternal figures. At O'Neill's most complex, these roles are combined within the same woman who experiences them as incompatible self-concepts. Mary Tyrone, for instance, pendulates between fantasized roles of the virtuoso pianist receiving the adulation of an audience and as a nun withdrawn to a secret place. The motifs re-emerge in her marriage to James Tyrone, who embodies in her eyes both the idealized Count of Monte Cristo who is pure but available to all, or real and her own, but soiled and sexually repugnant. The rival who enters the embrace of O'Neill's *femme fatale* is neither better nor worse off than he who rejects it. Both are doomed, especially after they discover that it is their conflict and not possession she seeks.

As two homoerotically attracted men can neither admit their passion nor belong to one another, they instead possess a woman in common, an arrangement Continental critics have termed the "unnatural triangle." In *Great God Brown* it is neither the "pure" Margaret's person nor the "prostitute" Cybel's that counts for Brown but the involvement of both with his male double Dion Anthony. He is a man who exists for her pursuer as an idea, absent in the flesh, but very much present in fantasy. And while Hickey had reacted to his wife Evelyn's deathly fidelity with his iceman joke and promiscuity, Slade had rejected Rosa's unfaithfulness by withdrawing to the company of uncritical males. But in every case cuckold finds in cuckolder, as frustrated child sees in all-powerful father, both a betraying enemy and an object of veneration. Jimmy Tomorrow says of his unfaithful wife in *Iceman*, "At least I can say Marjorie chose an officer and a gentlemen," suggesting that one typically creates of his betrayer a narcissistic image of his idealized self. Sometimes, the third member of the *ménage à trois* is not a woman, drink, or shared delusions, but the kind of animal or fetish which often appears in dreams as an incest symbol. Old Cabot rejects Abbie's frigidity for his cows, Con Melody lavishes affection on his aristocratic mare, and Erie Smith claims in *Hughie* that "I'd rather sleep with Man O'War than make the whole follies."

At the tragic end of his quest the O'Neillian hero either denies the loss of his pointless and frustrated life by shifting to a spiritual world his view of life as wonderful and unpredictable. Or he may detach himself from the lost object by undervaluing it, or both, a defensive split Freud discovered in adjustments to mourning. At his most transcendent he envisions some final escape by boat such as the one Jones hopes will take him to Martinique, by plane or even within the body of a bird, mythic symbols of the soul in transmigration. Gordon Evans flies off in an airplane near the end of *Strange Interlude*, a motif which is inverted by Parritt's suicide leap in *Iceman*. Con Melody's British major's uniform, the lost Shakespearean roles James Tyrone once played against Booth, and the numerous masks of the middle period all invoke the mythic device of the magic body fulfilling one's wish for a self-replenishing immortality. Viewing life as an endless separation from original unity, Edmund Tyrone says, "It was a great mistake my being born as a man. I would have been much more successful as a seagull or fish."

At the entrance to the grave, terminal counterparts to O'Neill's threshold guards appear as conductors signaling the way to the Underworld. Invariably, a doctor or his agent functions as bringer-in of death. He announces the death of Curtis Jayson's wife by childbirth in *The First Man*, confirms the imminence of Eileen Brennan's death from tuberculosis in *The Straw*, and appears in the guise of witch doctor just before Jones's last, magical bullet is fired in *The Emperor Jones*. Associated with blackness, hell, and betrayal as a Faustian Devil, Mary Tyrone attacks the doctor figure as willing to "sell their souls! What's worse, they'll sell yours!" His female equivalent corresponds to the mute third sister or

Atropos of folklore, usually associated with spurting blood, accusing eyes, poison, and an orgasmic swoon. The whole sequence appears at the climax of *Bound East for Cardiff* when the dying Yank visualizes the blood spurting from a vanquished rival, feels God's eyes on him, asks his friend Driscoll to buy candy for a barmaid, sees "a pretty lady dressed in black," and stiffens in death. Like Christine's faint after poisoning Ezra Mannon, which is both a denial of an appalling reality and orgasmic, Jamie Tyrone sinks into Josie Hogan's arms in *Moon*, Reuben Light fatally embraces the dynamo after shooting Ada Fife, Eben condemns himself to hang in *Desire*, and Hickey both falls into slumber and condemns himself to ultimate electrocution. Death inevitably rivals O'Neill's heroes, enjoying their loved ones at last. And like most suicides, their deaths manifest a surge of self-justifying aggression against others.

Once O'Neill's hero has initiated a quest for lost innocence, fraternal companionship, and peace, his journey is usually circular, taking him out and away from his origins, through trial by ordeal, and back to his lost harbor. Although many of his plays are based directly or obliquely on classical or Biblical myth, he is at his most effective, it seems, when he creates or parallels not myth but an individual fantasy expressing a symbolic action, equivalent and related to the myth's expression of a public rite. Although his vision of unity between irreconcilable forces may elude his seekers at least in this life, O'Neill may compensate for his and his audience's loss of faith and certainty by creating at his best an order in artistic design and coherence.

3:4 (Winter 1969–70)

REFERENCES

Campbell, Joseph. *Hero with a Thousand Faces*. New York: Meridian, 1956.

Laing, R. D. *The Divided Self*. Baltimore: Penguin, 1965.

Nietzsche, Friedrich. *Thus Spoke Zarathustra*, trans. Marianne Cowan, Chicago: Henry Regnery, 1957.

O'Neill, Eugene. "Hughie." New Haven: Yale University Press, 1959.

————— , ————— . *The Lost Plays*. New York: Citadel Press, 1958.

————— , ————— . "Memoranda on Masks." *American Spectator*, I (Nov., 1932), 3.

————— , ————— . *More Stately Mansions*, ed. Donald Gallup. New Haven: Yale University Press, 1964.

————— , ————— . *The Plays of Eugene O'Neill*, 3 vols. New York: Random House, 1955.

————— , —————— . *Thirst and Other One-Act Plays.* Boston: The Gorham Press, 1914.

Raleigh, J. H. *The Plays of Eugene O'Neill.* Carbondale: Southern Illinois University Press, 1965.

Winther, S. K. *Eugene O'Neill: A Critical Study.* New York: Russell and Russell, 1961.

O'Neill and Otto Rank: Doubles, "Death Instincts," and the Trauma of Birth

Stephen Watt

"You were born afraid."
　　　　Mary Tyrone to Edmund

"But he's dead now [Major Melody].
And I ain't tired a bit. I'm fresh
as a man new born."
　　　　Con Melody

"She loves me. I'm not afraid! . . .
She is warmly around me! She is my
skin! She is my armor! Now I am
born — I — the I! — one and indivisible."
　　　　Dion Anthony

I

In one extremely defensive interior monologue in Eugene O'Neill's *Strange Interlude* (1928), Charles Marsden contemplates the widespread influence of Sigmund Freud's thought on the American intelligentsia. In doing so, Marsden also predicts what interpretive tools many readers of O'Neill's plays will employ when digging through characters' psychological strata: "O Oedipus, O my king! The world is adopting you" (I, 34).[1] Blithely dismissing the Freudian emphases on dream interpretation and "sex" as constitutive of an "easy cure-all," Marsden also anticipates O'Neill's own frustration with the unrelenting stream of Freudian, especially Oedipal, readings of his plays.[2] The literary critical "world," insofar as O'Neill is concerned, has indeed adopted "Herr Freud," as Marsden refers to him, and King Oedipus as well. Even in studies only remotely psychoanalytic, Freud and Oedipus often appear as "givens," figures

17

who on the basis of admittedly very persuasive biographical evidence must be acknowledged.3

Perhaps the most valuable addition to current understanding of O'Neill's appropriation from and manipulation of Freudian psychoanalysis is Robert Feldman's recent examination of the "death-instinct" in *Strange Interlude* and *Mourning Becomes Electra* (1931).4 First elaborated by Freud in *Beyond the Pleasure Principle* (1920), the "death-instinct"—an "expression of the *conservative* nature of living substance" to "restore an earlier [inorganic] state of things"5—becomes for O'Neill's Nina Leeds and Orin Mannon not an instinct but a choice. As Feldman argues, correctly I think, these characters consciously *choose* to escape the pain of life by a sterile marriage in Nina's case and suicide in Orin's. And Feldman's point might be amplified to include a host of O'Neill characters who freely select either death—John Brown in the early *Bread and Butter* (1914), Reuben Light in *Dynamo* (1928), and others—or seclusion from the world of "life"—Orin's sister Lavinia, Deborah Harford in *More Stately Mansions* (1938; reconstructed and published in 1962), and of course Mary Tyrone. For a variety of reasons, some of them biographical, this fact overshadows the presence of the Oedipal project in the plays of O'Neill's middle and later periods.6 My purpose here is twofold: to describe the determinative effect of this non-Oedipal problematic in O'Neill's plays—one which concerns desire for a regressive, oral return to the mother and, in several cases, prompts character splitting or "doubling"—and to suggest the interpretive value of Otto Rank's work in undertaking such investigations of O'Neill's drama.

Readers of *Contour in Time* (1972) might recall Travis Bogard's supposition that the "possible implications" of Rank's *The Double* (1914; abstracted in *The Psychoanalytic Review*, 1919) for "an understanding of the complex personality of Eugene O'Neill are many." Fascinated by O'Neill's representations of a man divided into "opposed but clearly bound beings" in plays such as *Mourning Become Electra*, Bogard discovered in Rank's work an especially appealing explanation of "fraternal rivalry toward the hated competitor in love for the mother and ultimately the death-wish of the subject."7 Nevertheless, fraternal rivalry over the love-object and the so-called "death wish of the subject" are two rather different phenomena. Moreover, the fraternal rivalry over the love-object (Mother, Mother surrogate, or not) so prominent in, say, *Bread and Butter, Beyond the Horizon* (1920), *Desire Under the Elms* (1924), and *The Great God Brown* (1925) recedes into the background in O'Neill's later plays. Replacing this rivalry are the internal conflicts of characters such as Con Melody and Simon Harford in the Cycle dramas and the Tyrone brothers in the more autobiographical *Long Day's Journey Into Night* (1941) and *A Moon for the Misbegotten* (1943), conflicts hardly generated by the son's Oedipal desire for the Mother. On the contrary, as the passages with which I began intimate, these conflicts are characterized by a more regressive oral bond to the Mother (one suggestive of psychical wholeness) and paralyzing fears of life and love. In much of O'Neill, paradoxically, one can be born, as Edmund Tyrone was, "afraid" and psychically divided; one can also be "reborn," as Dion Anthony and Con Melody are, unafraid and undivided. I should like to argue here that this paradox informs much of O'Neill's middle and later plays and, again, that Rank's work is potently empowered to illuminate the fears, doubling, and complex relationship of son to Mother in these plays.

II

Feldman's thesis that many of O'Neill's characters seem to chose death rather than to be instinctively drawn to it parallels Rank's dissatisfaction with the concept of a *"death-instinct"* and recalls the latter's subsequent efforts to account for the theoretical and clinical significance of the life/death opposition. Not accidentally, these efforts coincided with the publication of *Beyond the Pleasure Principle* when Freud's "death-instinct" began to occupy a problematic location in psychoanalytic theory. One indication of the concept's troublesome, yet important status—and also of the importance of the death-instinct to a psychoanalytic revaluation of O'Neill's plays—surfaces in Jean Laplanche's *Life and Death in Psychoanalysis* (1970). At one moment Laplanche contends that the death-instinct does not effect any break or rupture in Freud's thought; in another instance, Laplanche registers surprise that "suddenly" in 1920 the death-instinct emerged "at the center of the psychoanalytic system" as one of the two "fundamental forces" in the "heart of the psyche."[8] Laplanche invests the death-instinct—*not* Oedipal desire—with power by calling it the "very soul of conflict" (p. 5) and by intimating that its source might be uncovered in Rank's "birth trauma" (a term to be defined at greater length below):

It should also be recalled what degree of interest was later pro-
voked on the part of Freud and other psychoanalysts by a notion
such as Rank's "birth trauma.". . . Who can say whether we do not
find there the point of real continuity, "in the beginning," the locus
of internal communication between what will become, respectively,
physical trauma and psychical trauma? (p. 131)

Thus, the death-instinct forms a locus or intersection in psychoanalytic thought of related theories in which Rank and, I
believe, O'Neill were especially interested. And while a number
of these might be delineated, the "trauma of birth" and its
resultant fears are for Rank crucially tied to the "death instinct"
and primarily responsible for doubling in O'Neill.

One further qualification: it is not my intention here to
establish Rank as a *direct* source of O'Neill's drama, but merely
to urge that the former's best-known works—*The Double, The
Trauma of Birth* (1923, English translation 1929), and *Will
Therapy* (1936)—constitute a means by which we might explore O'Neill's split or identical characters.9 It seems quite
probable that O'Neill had heard of Rank, perhaps from Gilbert
V. Hamilton who cites him in *A Research in Marriage* (1929).
O'Neill also owned a copy of Freud's *The Problem of Anxiety*
(1936)—at present part of the O'Neill collection at Long
Island University's C. W. Post campus library—in which Rank's
former mentor delivers an extended critique of the "trauma of
birth."10 Certainly the best-informed American psychoanalysts
had heard of Freud's diminutive student-colleague as early as
1914, the year in which the American Psychoanalytic Association began publication of *The Psychoanalytic Review*. The
youngest member of Freud's select "Committee" or "Inner Ring"
from 1906 to his painful departure from the group in 1926,
Rank was invited as a distinguished guest to the 1924 convention
of the American Psychoanalytic Association, which he addressed
on the trauma of birth.11 His work is abstracted at length,
translated, or reviewed in nearly every volume of the *Review*
from its inaugural issue in 1914 through 1934; between 1924
and 1929—that crucial period in which Rank's formulation of
the birth trauma contributed substantially to his eventual defec-
tion from Freud's committee and also motivated three noteworthy
trips to America—four of Rank's articles appeared in the *Review*, three of them as lead articles in the issues in which they

were featured.12 These publications, along with his lectures in
New York and numerous sessions with patients (many of them
leading analysts themselves) in the late 1920's would seem to
justify E. James Lieberman's claim in his new biography of
Rank that his "initial impact on New York was phenomenal."13

The relationship between the trauma of birth and the death-
instinct remained on both Freud's and Rank's minds long after
the demise of their friendship. In 1936, three years before his
death, Rank returned to issues he had raised earlier; ironically,
as I have already mentioned, in the same year Freud reviewed
the trauma of birth in *The Problem of Anxiety*, firmly dismissing its validity as a psychoanalytic concept. (In a 1937 essay
"Analysis Terminable and Interminable" Freud resumed his
attack on his former pupil, this time aiming at Rank's attempts
to accelerate the analytical process, attempts motivated by his
discovery that for many patients analysis replicated the trauma
of birth. Successful treatment, Rank found out, often concluded
with the patient expressing his newly-achieved selfhood as a
"rebirth."14) Rank's restatement of the "death problem"—he
refused to reify it by calling it an "instinct"—seems especially
relevant to an analysis of O'Neill's most fragmented characters:

> Freud has approached the problem of therapy from the forces of
> life (the libido) and has finally arrived at the death instinct; that
> is, at the death problem, for it hardly concerns an "instinct." As
> I have already pointed out in *The Trauma of Birth*, it seems to
> me essential for the understanding of the neurotic to go at the
> human problem from *the side of fear, not from the side of instinct*;
> that is, to consider the individual not therapeutically as an instinc-
> tive animal but psychologically as a suffering being. (*Will Ther-
> apy*, p. 121; my emphasis)

To be sure, Rank's movement away from his former mentor on
this point is considerable; instead of regarding the neurotic in
terms of drive or instinct, Rank posits an *a priori* fear that super-
sedes them. One especially noteworthy aspect of this theoretical
"move" is Rank's emphasis that the provenience of such fear,
unlike that of the much discussed castration fear in Freud, is
internal, *not* external:

> The inner fear, which the child experiences in the birth process
> (or perhaps even brings with it?) has in it already both elements,
> fear of life and fear of death. . . . (*Will Therapy*, p. 122)

This explanation anticipates Mary Tyrone's analysis of Edmund's
fear: we bring it with us at birth. Further, Rank maintains that

"the stronger emphasis on one or the other of these two fear components" seems "to contain the empirical meaning of the birth trauma for the later fate of the individual" (*Will Therapy*, p. 122).

What is this "empirical meaning" and how does Rank define the fears of life and death? How are these made manifest in adult life, and, more important, how do such fears underlie the process of doubling in O'Neill? Rank constructs binary oppositions to represent these fears, the most descriptive of which are whole/part, totality/individuality, and moving forward/moving backward. In Rank's schema, the human subject's internal conflict between generation and individuation is expressive of an "ambivalent primal fear" consisting of the fears of life and death. These comprise the "trauma of birth":

> If there is a symbol for the condition of wholeness, of totality, it is doubtless the embryonic state, in which the individual feels himself an indivisible whole and yet is bound up inseparably with a greater whole. With birth, not only is oneness with the mother violently dissolved but the child experiences a second trauma, which works just as seriously and much more lastingly, that is, the partialization to which it is forced through adaptation to the outer world. (*Will Therapy*, pp. 134-35)

For Rank, life constantly demands "partial reactions" which neurotics, who cling to a powerful tendency toward totalization, cannot satisfy:

> The unconscious *never* gives up this claim [maintenance of the pre-natal state], which the Ego has to set aside in favor of social adjustment, and the unconscious, in its predominating states . . . is ready every time to come forward with this regressive tendency. (*Trauma*, p. 18)

And when this demand collides head-on with a powerful, opposing tendency, internal division or splitting results. "Life fear," then, is the fear of partialization, of moving forward into relationships; death fear is the fear of losing a hard-fought-for individuality and going backward through death into an embryonic totality.

O'Neill's characters know these fears all too well, because for many of them fears either of life or of death mark the origin of their internal conflicts. Dion Anthony in *The Great God Brown* resorts to hiding behind a mask because of a paralyzing fear of life, a fear so potent that he is only able to enunciate it after removing his disguise:

> Why am I afraid to live, I who love life and the beauty of flesh
> and the living colors of earth and sky and sea? Why am I afraid
> of love, I who love love? . . . Why was I born without a skin,
> O God, that I must wear armor in order to touch or to be touched?
> (III, 264)

Alternatively, the fear of death emerges near the conclusion of
Days Without End (1932) to inform the John/Loving split,
one of the most explicit cases of doubling in an O'Neill canon
replete with such representations. Quite significantly, this fear is
linked to subjectivity in *Days Without End*, deflating the ideal-
ization of a pure, completed subject presumed in much criticism
of O'Neill and many studies of doubling in literature:15

> Father Baird: No. I know you couldn't blaspheme at such a time—
> not your true self.
>
> Loving: It is my true self—my only self! And I see through your
> stupid trick—to use the fear of death to. . . . (III, 559)

To what? Loving never completes the sentence to Father Baird.
However, moments later he taunts his counterpart John with
the fear of death and couches his bullying in decidedly Rankian
terms:

> Surely you cannot be afraid of death. Death is not the dying.
> Dying is life, its last revenge upon itself. But death is what the
> dead know, the warm dark womb of Nothingness—the Dream in
> which you and Elsa may sleep as one forever, beyond fear of
> separation. (III, 562)

As this passage implies, doubling in *Days Without End* is produced both by an intense fear of death (loss of individuality)
and, it would seem, by the fear of separation from the love-
object (loss of totality). The presence of the love-object Elsa
in the maternal womb of death suggests a vaguely Oedipal,
somewhat confused collapsing of the life/death opposition, an
idealized solution of the conflict caused by partialization/total-
ization. Nevertheless, the language of such psychical schisms
is a largely Rankian one. Similarly, in *The Great God Brown*
when Dion Anthony discovers Margaret's love, he is not merely
unafraid—he is reborn into an "indivisible," totalizing "I."
The process of internal fragmentation is halted; Margaret is
"warmly," maternally "around" him in a love resonant of pre-
embryonic security. The fears Rank delineates are vanquished,
and with them, albeit momentarily, so is painful internal conflict.

Like the "trauma of birth," the term "double" requires
brief definition. It is something of a historical-critical myopia

that while scholarly interest in the double in fiction has for a long time been keen, very little attention has been paid to O'Neill's doubles.16 Most studies of the double concern what Rank labelled the "double-projection": the first self's projection outward of a second self which presents a threat or challenge both to his self-love and to his efforts to unite with the love-object. As Thomas F. Walsh explains, Rank derives from Freud the notion that narcissism plays a crucial part in the doubling process; the double, from this perspective, represents the first self's "attempt to rid himself of something he does not wish to recognize in himself."17 This attempt, though, is always unsuccessful because these projected contents are reconstituted in a new form outside the self which returns to confront the first self, a confrontation which often leads to suicide. Hence, "doubles" are separate characters who are at the same time interrelated and interdependent and, as Robert Rogers clarifies, "portraying" or "indirectly generated by" psychological conflict.18

Rogers observes that while most commentary on the double has been confined to overt or "manifest" doubles—the two Golyadkins in Dostoevsky's *The Double* or the two William Wilsons in Edgar Allan Poe's short story—we might also recognize more implicit or "latent" doubles in novels like *The Brothers Karamazov* or, I might add, the splitting ("queer fits," as Phil Hogan calls them) in *A Moon for the Misbegotten, A Touch of the Poet,* and *More Stately Mansions.* Arguing that fuzzy nomenclature is chiefly responsible for misunderstandings about doubling, C. F. Keppler prefers the term "second self," an "intruder from the shadows," distinguishing it from a "first self": "one who tends to be in the foreground of the reader's attention, usually the one whose viewpoint the reader shares."19 Keppler's emphasis of the second self's relative obscurity and what Freud called "uncanny" knowledge of his victim-twin might enhance our readings of John and Loving in *Days Without End* and of the masked selves of Brown and Anthony in *The Great God Brown.* Still, the distinction first self/second self upon which this conception rests is extremely difficult to make in O'Neill's later plays. Who are the first selves in *Mourning Becomes Electra*? Who is the first self in *A Touch of the Poet,* Con or Major Melody? And even in cases of less explicit splitting in O'Neill—the two sides of Jamie Tyrone in *A Moon for the Misbegotten,* for instance—Keppler's rubric is equally difficult to apply. As a result, the motivations of both halves or selves are shrouded in "comparative obscurity." Rank's "trauma of birth" provides one means of lifting this shroud both from plays of more or less explicit doubling such as *Mourning Becomes Electra*, to which I now turn, and from plays such as *A Touch of the Poet* and *More Stately Mansions* in which more implicit doubling or splitting predominates.

III

Like most narratives in which doubles figure prominently, *Mourning Becomes Electra* is centered around characters who resemble each other as closely as identical twins. According to the stage directions, Orin Mannon, the son who returns home from the Civil War in the first act of "The Hunted," bears a "startling family resemblance" both to his father Ezra and to his mother's lover, Adam Brant; as the play progresses, Orin's sister Lavinia grows to form the mirror-image of their mother, Christine. Indeed, the similarity between daughter and mother is so striking that Orin tells his sister she fails to recognize how "like Mother" she has become. As is the case with the doubles Rank and others have described, conflict in the play is located in the struggles between pairs of characters who represent the incompatible drives (or, more properly, fears) of one self: in this case, Orin/Adam and Lavinia/Christine. To the extent that Christine is physically very similar to Brant's mother Marie Brantôme, his desires might be regarded as Oedipal. However, throughout *Mourning Becomes Electra* the most charged psychological conflict is waged between the need to find a satisfactory love-object (object-libido) and the desire to return to that pre-natal peace disrupted by birth (ego-libido). A more Rankian explanation might be articulated slightly differently: tension grows from the fear of life (of the partialization required by relationships) and the opposing fear of death (of being reabsorbed into a pre-embryonic whole after fighting so hard for individuation). Lavinia's retreat to the Mannon home at the end of the play after refusing Peter's offer of love marks the trail O'Neill characters often tread and underscores the terms of psychological division in O'Neill's later dramas.

This conflict splits the most carefully developed pair of male characters in the play: Orin and Adam Brant. Brant's ambitions seem fairly easily understood: he has fallen in love with Christine and plans to run off with her, abandoning his plan to take revenge against Ezra Mannon for sins committed against his (Brant's) mother and father. Orin returns home, discovers his mother's infidelity, and together with Lavinia pursues Brant and kills him. But Orin's motivations for pursuing Brant transcend the motivations typically put forth in analyses of doubling (rivalry over a genital-sexual love-object) and are not nearly so transparent as his counterpart's. Appropriately, Orin's dream narratives contain the most helpful material for making this evaluation, the most revealing of which he relates to his mother in "The Hunted":

> Those Islands came to mean everything that wasn't war, everything that was peace and warmth and security. I used to dream I was there. . . . There was no one there but you and me. And yet I never saw you, that's the funny part. I only felt you all around me. The breaking of the waves was your voice. The sky was the same color as your eyes. The warm sand was like your skin. The whole island was you. (II, 90)

While the island serves as an important symbol for all the major characters in *Mourning Becomes Electra*, Orin's island is vastly different from the islands the other characters discuss or seek. For Adam, the islands are places of uninhibited genital-sexual love with exotic natives or Christine; Ezra believes the islands will be the panacea for his sterile relationship with his wife; later in the play, Lavinia's island will allow her to "forget death" through an awakening of her dormant sexuality. She tells Peter that "there was something there mysterious and beautiful—a good spirit of love—coming out of the land and sea" (II, 147). For all of the main characters, then, the South Sea Islands represent life and genital sexuality, a denial of death.

But not for Orin. For him, the island symbolizes the self in union with the Mother, certainly not genital-sexual union. He expresses his aversion to this variety of love when he complains to Peter that the islands made him "sick"—and the naked women there "disgusted" him. Orin's dream of a maternal island reveals his desire for a long awaited totality, for an almost oral reunion with the mother (and, by extension, the universe). For Rank, this desire is linked to the "problem" of death:

> And so with the thought of death is connected from the beginning a strong unconscious sense of pleasure associated with the return to the mother's womb. (*Trauma*, p. 24)

Like Dion Anthony's characterization of Margaret's love, Loving's description of death as "the dark womb of Nothingness," and Reuben Light's suicidal leap onto the Mother-dynamo,

Orin's dream enforces the connection between the rejection of life and genital sexuality and a return through death to a more primordial totality. Thus, whereas the islands in *Mourning Becomes Electra* generally celebrate a victory over death—as Lavinia puts it, a "forgetting" of death through the individuation expressed in sexuality—for Orin they recall intrauterine or narcissistic oneness with the Mother and betray his profound fear of life.

In re-telling his dream, Orin stresses that the island "came to mean everything that wasn't war" (in part, something that presents no danger and therefore generates no fear). Further, for Orin war is inextricably linked to pursuing the self in his repetitive dream of killing Confederate soldiers, a dream he relates to his sister in "The Hunted":

> I had a queer feeling that war meant murdering the same man over and over, and that in the end I would discover the man was myself. Their faces [those of the soldiers Orin killed] keep coming back in dreams and they change to father's face—or to mine. (II, 95)

Later, after he shoots Brant in the stateroom of the *Flying Trades*, Orin scrutinizes Brant's face and alludes to his dream: "This is like my dream. I've killed him before—over and over" (II, 115). Given the Oedipal theme that permeates the play, one might view the murder of the father-figure (Ezra and Adam) as the slaying of the castrating Law-bearer who has uncovered the designs of his son. On the other hand, if one regards Orin's conflicts as produced instead by his inability to separate himself from a past era of dependence on his mother, then he is eliminating the incestuous self—Adam, who would possess Christine sexually—in his dreams and on board Brant's ship. Orin himself leads us to this reading when in the same scene he compares his position with Brant's:

> If I had been he I would have done what he did! I would have loved her as he loved her—and killed Father too—for her sake! (II, 115-16)

But Orin, I think, is able to recognize that he *isn't* in Adam's place, that he cannot love Christine as Brant loved her, and this is what the war dream portrays. The question remains, of course, as to how Orin reaches this recognition—and why he commits suicide.

While a more instinctual analysis of Orin's behavior might explain his shooting of Brant—the slaying of the rival, we might recall, being an almost conventional moment in narratives in which doubling occurs—it contributes little to an understanding of Orin's suicide. And merely attributing the island dream to the trauma of birth can account only for the part fear plays in this death. How might one assess the complex nature of Orin's guilt, which also motivates his suicide? Here, again, Rank's work seems singularly relevant to a reading of O'Neill's, particularly the former's study in *Will Therapy* and *Beyond Psychology* (1939; published posthumously in 1941) of the relationship between ethical dilemmas and neurosis. The most obvious reason for Orin's suicide emanates from his feelings of guilt over Christine's death; indeed, his painful confessions to Lavinia dominate the play's last scenes. But it is indicative of O'Neill's sophisticated, deeply considered view of human psychology that Orin's suicide expresses a more fundamental psychical reality, one Rank explores in revealing ways: namely, the manner in which guilt accompanies and frustrates the individual's every step toward individuality. That is, as Rank maintains, all steps "on the way to self dependence," most notably the development of the will, are "conceived always as continuous separations." Instead of "overcoming the past through the present," the neurotic becomes, aware "that he dare not, cannot, loose himself because he is bound by guilt" (*Will Therapy*, pp. 72-74). This guilt, Rank avers, "arises from the ego development of the individual and with each new attempt at release is always fastened to that past from which the individual is unable to free himself" (*Will Therapy*, p. 72). In a less technical description of a similar predicament, Mary Tyrone in *Long Day's Journey Into Night* admonishes Edmund for his harsh indictments of his brother:

> It's wrong to blame your brother. He can't help being what the past has made him. Any more than your father can. Or you. Or I.
> (p. 64)

Mary's point evolves into something more than a rationalization when one recognizes, as Rank has, the determinative role played by guilt in the neurotic's inability to escape from the past.

For Rank and many of O'Neill's characters, sharp feelings of guilt inevitably attend willful projects of separation, and the stronger power of guilt haunts Orin throughout *Mourning Becomes Electra*. It is especially important that we discriminate between Orin's guilt over his mother's death and his guilt of the sort Rank describes as associated with projects of individuation. To be sure, Orin's painful admissions of guilt increase sharply after Christine's death; nevertheless, many of these betray a more historical guilt and, just as meaningfully, Orin harbors tremendous guilt long before the play's last moments. Earlier in "The Hunted," for instance, Orin enters in Act Three "ashamed and guilty," feeling like a "rotten swine" even for considering Lavinia's insinuations about their mother's crimes. Later, his rhetorical flights begin to reveal the deeper equation in the play between guilt and both separation and the denial of life. Orin tells his sister that he hates "daylight," because it's like "an accusing eye"; "perpetual night—darkness of death in life"—is, according to Orin, a more "fitting habitat for guilt" (II, 150). And, near the conclusion of "The Haunted," Orin seems amazed that Lavinia could ever contemplate leaving him to marry Peter and, in a lurid, incestuous suggestion, hopes to make her feel "as guilty then as I do." Then, she "would never dare leave" him (II, 165). It is partly out of guilt that, in the play's final scene, Lavinia retreats into the Mannon house, a symbol of Puritan repression and consequent guilt from which she cannot extricate herself.

Thus, while the Eros/Thanatos, pleasure principle (life-instinct)/death-instinct oppositions help clarify one aspect of psychic division in *Mourning Becomes Electra,* so too do Rank's emphasis of life fear/death fear and his adumbration of the relationship between attempts at separation (independence) and guilt. Associated with these issues in O'Neill, as I have mentioned, is perhaps a more fundamental one which especially informs his later work: namely, the persistent questioning in his plays of the concept of a "true self," what Keppler might regard as a "first" self. The inherently idealistic postulation of a true self underlies most conceptions of doubling, yet as O'Neill's characters often lament, a pure or essential human subject is extremely difficult to locate. This problem exists in much of O'Neill and is tied to the Rankian explanations delineated above of neurotics' fears and their inabilities to exist independently. Orin Mannon implies as much when he informs Lavinia that the Orin she loved was killed in the war; all that remains is a living, rotting ghost. Or, as Deborah Harford puts it at the beginning of *More Stately Mansions,* the detritus of life accorded O'Neill's most long-suffering characters is little more than an "interminable dialogue with the self." This dialogue rages throughout O'Neill's last plays.

IV

Simon Harford in a sense speaks for his predecessors—Con Melody, John Loving, Orin Mannon, Dion Anthony, and others—when near the conclusion of *More Stately Mansions* he can no longer manage the opposing pressures which have transformed his mind into a battlefield. Earlier he had admitted to his brother Joel that he lacked the "power" to keep himself "united," and by the play's last scene this diminished capacity becomes apparent:

> I wish to be free, Mother!—free of one of my two selves, of one of the enemies within my mind, before their duel for possession destroys it. I have no longer any choice but to choose. (p. 182)

Freedom is thus attained through a desperate act of will, a neutralizing of the formidable resistance to making just such a decision. In this way, O'Neill's characters resemble Rank's patients insofar as the latter's "will therapy" involves leading the patient to break down resistances—the clingings to a past psychic formation characterized by some minimal sense of security—so that he or she might be "reborn," much as Con Melody is in *A Touch of the Poet*. Significantly, Harford's duality originates in another kind of separation, not one which he inaugurated and labored over, but a painful abandonment akin to the trauma of birth. And it is scarcely astonishing that this trauma is associated both with his mother and a symbolic space of amniotic security, in this case Deborah Harford's protective garden. Orin's island in *Mourning Becomes Electra*, fog in *Long Day's Journey Into Night*, the Mother-generator in *Dynamo*, and the stable where the Major's mare (*mere?*) is kept in *A Touch of the Poet* might all qualify as analogues to the Harford garden. Simon explains his trauma which began one day in the garden when his mother told him a story:

> I have never forgotten the anguished sense of being suddenly betrayed, of being wounded and deserted and left alone in a life in which there was no security or faith or love but only danger. . . . (p. 184)

As Laplanche's meditation on the etymology of "trauma" suggests—the term connotes a wounding or piercing, a violent shock which breaks into the organism "entailing the rupture or opening of a protective envelope" (p. 129)—Simon's betrayal is, to echo his own metaphor, a traumatic wounding or literal separation. Connected to the trauma of birth, this betrayal triggers Simon's desire to go with his mother "beyond separation" where he and Deborah may "be one again."

Throughout *More Stately Mansions,* Simon's aspirations as
a corporative executive—aspirations identical to his father's for
which Deborah Harford feels a "superior disdain"—serve as a
familiar figure in O'Neill for the project of individuation, an
often frantic enterprise to attain freedom. (The opposition
artist/businessman or politician persists in O'Neill from John
Brown/Edward Brown of *Bread and Butter* and Robert Mayo/
Andrew Mayo in *Beyond the Horizon* to Simon Harford in *A
Touch of the Poet*/Simon Harford in *More Stately Mansions.*
It reflects the clash between Edmund Tyrone and his father as
well.) As a corporate magnate, Simon stands courageously, he
boasts, fearing "no God" or no man—only himself. He brags
to his mother that nothing will stand between him and his goal,
yet in this boast Simon betrays the extent to which his own
desire for individuation has been displaced, projected on to his
company:

> Simon: It [the Company] must attain the all-embracing security
> of complete self-possession—the might which is the sole right not
> to be a slave! Do you see?
>
> Deborah: I see, Dear—that you have gone very far away from
> me—and become lost in yourself and very lonely.
>
> Simon: Lost? Oh no, don't imagine I have lost. . . . I can lead the
> Company to a glorious, final triumph—complete independence
> and freedom within itself. (p. 101)

Moments later, though, Simon recalls the "safe haven" of his
mother's garden and longs to return to it. Here he might evade
the fragmenting terror of his quest for independence; in the
garden he might "escape, forget, rest in peace" after having
become "so weary of what they call life beyond the walls" (p.
103). In this case, then, Simon's motive for reunion with his
Mother is clearly *not* genital-sexual, nor is the source of his fear
external—the avenging father. The fear is more regressive, and
his reunion with Sara at the end of the play seems hardly one of
Oedipal dimension.

A similar psychological problematic is foregrounded in the
only play of the planned "Cycle" O'Neill had completed (and
revised to his satisfaction) by the time of his death in 1953:
A Touch of the Poet. Major Cornelius Melody represents man's
tendency to cling to his past, a major concern throughout the

O'Neill canon and especially in the later plays. As the Major attired in his best dragoon finery admires himself in the mirror, he recites lines from Byron that strike a resounding note of his fear of life and resultant desire to live alone in the security of his past:

> I have not loved the World, nor the World me;
> I have not flattered its rank breath, nor bowed
> To its idolatries a patient knee. . . . I stood
> Among them, but not of them . . .
>
>   (p. 43)

However, the life fear/death fear opposition which informs *A Touch of the Poet* is collapsed, hence successfully resolved, in an ending diametrically opposite those of *Mourning Becomes Electra* and *More Stately Mansions*, to name but two. Returning home humiliated after his unsuccessful attempt at serving honor by engaging Simon's father in a duel, Major Melody retreats to his world away from the "rank breath" of the crowd: the stable and his beloved mare. His shooting of the mare, ending the play as most narratives of the double conclude by symbolically murdering his counterpart, represents also the destruction of a psychical formation which opposes life. In this respect, as I have suggested before, the mare and stable are analogous to fog, gardens, generators, the Mannon house, Nina Leeds' Mother-god, and other figures of life-fear in O'Neill. By contrast, earlier in the play, Deborah Harford informs Sara Melody that it will be a great "relief" for her (Deborah) to return to her garden and "listen indifferently while the footsteps of life pass by," never to "venture forth" again (p. 86). Like Charles Marsden and Nina Leeds—and her son in *More Stately Mansions*—Deborah is "weary of life" and has "passed beyond desire." But near the end of *A Touch of the Poet* the killing of the Major brings with it Con Melody's desire to pass *into* life.

The signs of this renewed desire, this defeat of the fear of life, are both numerous and visible at the conclusion of *A Touch of the Poet*. When Con comes in from the stable, he "spakes" in the pronounced brogue the Major loathed and feels invigorated: "I ain't tired a bit. I'm fresh as a man new born" (p. 175). The slaying of the latent double serves to trigger Con's renewed taste for life, for association with the others whom the Major once reviled. In an especially exuberant pronouncement near the end of the play, Con tells Sara of his therapeutic victory by alluding mockingly to the Major's beloved Byron:

> Be God, *I'm* alive and in the crowd they *can* deem me one av
> such! I'll be among thim and av thim, too—and make up for the
> lonely dog's life the Major led me. (p. 177)

The peace of death, the final escape from what Jamie Tyrone
in *A Moon for the Misbegotten* cynically labels the "bum racket"
of life, carries no appeal for the reborn Con Melody. Unlike so
many O'Neill characters—male and female, sons and Mothers—
Con regains his thirst for life at the end of the play.

Nevertheless, Melody's daughter Sara regards her father's
affirmation of life as psychically costly. She pleads with him,
"Won't you be yourself again" (p. 176), threatening that he
will be dead "to yourself." But if he is, he is also "free" to kiss
his wife again—and Sara realizes that—for the Major her father
was incapable of such affection. This self, the substance of Con
Melody, opposes the dead Major's "self," one inhabiting the
past who feared the interaction of life. And where is the "true
self" in O'Neill's later plays, the "absolute subject" which Lacan
has insisted is "unthinkable"?[20] As Mary Tyrone implies, the
"true self" in O'Neill is at least partly fictional, symptomatic of
what Lacan describes as the internal "discordance" within one's
"own reality" which, successfully resolved or not, constitutes
the "I":

> None of us can help the things life has done to us. They're done
> before you realize it . . . until at last everything comes between
> you and what you'd like to be, and you've lost your true self
> forever. (p. 61)

In *More Stately Mansions* Simon asks Sara to be her "old true
self again," and in *A Moon for the Misbegotten* Jamie Tyrone's
"queer fits" reveal the discordances that define his selfhood:
"part" of him, he tells Josie Hogan, always knows when he's
pretending to be "soused" to make sexual advances toward a
sympathetic or willing woman. With special clarity, O'Neill's
late dramas—much like contemporary psychoanalysis which has
launched a searing critique of idealistic conceptions of an absolute subject—probe the difficulty of identifying a "true self."
Instead, in *A Touch of the Poet, Long Day's Journey Into Night,
A Moon for the Misbegotten,* and *More Stately Mansions* the
true self is often difficult to locate, lurking somewhere between
the idealized self (the mirror fiction) and another, often de-
spised self. In more specifically O'Neillian terms, this self resembles Jamie of *A Moon for the Misbegotten,* haunting the club
car between a prostitute's embrace and the casket of his dead

mother and—in the process—continually deconstructing any comfortable virgule between first self/second self.

Hence, when Louis Sheaffer several years ago in *O'Neill: Son and Artist* perceptively discussed the ways in which *More Stately Mansions* foreshadowed *Long Day's Journey Into Night*—stressing the analogy between Mother-son relationships—he was in effect anticipating the psychoanalytic reading attempted here.[21] That is, the structural correspondence or homology between these characters—the mothers and sons of the Cycle and those of the more "autobiographical" dramas—reveals much about internal division in the O'Neill canon. More specifically, a Rankian reading of these plays opens, I believe, another useful line of inquiry into O'Neill's plays. And more work remains. Rank's later thought, which explores the relationship between religious devotion, guilt, and Agape (love for God) and neurosis, seems especially well suited to illuminate psychological conflict in O'Neill. In addition, contemporary psychoanalytic discussion of human subjectivity contains much of interest to students of O'Neill's drama. At any rate, Rank's "trauma of birth" and its accompanying psychic fragmentation and fears explain much about O'Neill and, at the same time, raise questions about O'Neill's understanding of his own inner turmoil. We might recall that in his now famous diagram of psychological development reprinted at the end of Sheaffer's *O'Neill: Son and Playwright*, O'Neill shows the son's binding to his mother as terminating during adolescence; only fantasy, hatred of the Father, and "Reality" remain for the adult.[22] His later plays tell an entirely different story, one more regressive, less Oedipal, than most readers of O'Neill (and this may include O'Neill himself) have yet recognized.

20:3 (Fall 1986)

NOTES

1 All quotations from this and other plays by Eugene O'Neill will be cited in the text and are from the following editions: *The Plays of Eugene O'Neill*, 3 vols. (New York: Random House, 1955); *A Moon for the Misbegotten* (New York: Random House, 1952); *More Stately Mansions* (New Haven: Yale Univ. Press, 1964); *A Touch of the Poet* (New Haven: Yale Univ. Press, 1957); and *Long Day's Journey Into Night* (New Haven: Yale Univ. Press, 1955).

This essay is an expanded version of a paper delivered to the Eugene O'Neill Society at the Modern Language Association's annual convention, Chicago, December 28, 1985. The author wishes to express his gratitude to Paul Voelker, organizer of the O'Neill Society meeting, James Hurt, and Katherine Burkman for their helpful commentary on earlier drafts of this essay.

2 See, for example, Travis Bogard, *Contour in Time* (New York: Oxford Univ. Press, 1972), pp. 334-56. Here Bogard emphasizes the Oedipal content of *Mourning Becomes Electra*. See also John Chioles, "Aeschylus and O'Neill: A Phenomenological View," *Comparative Drama*, 14 (Summer 1980), 159-87. Chioles remarks that in the same play an "Elektra-complex is joined by an Oedipus-complex to wreak destruction" (p. 168). Michael Manheim in *Eugene O'Neill's New Language of Kinship* (Syracuse: Syracuse Univ. Press, 1982) maintains that in *Strange Interlude* O'Neill "turned away from Nietzsche and toward that kind of self-revelation he associated with the writings of Sigmund Freud" (p. 59).

3 For information about O'Neill's reading of psychoanalytic theory, see Arthur H. Nethercot's two-part "The Psychoanalyzing of Eugene O'Neill," *Modern Drama*, 3 (1960), 242-56; 4 (1961), 357-72; see also Nethercot's "The Psychoanalyzing of Eugene O'Neill: Postscript," *Modern Drama*, 8 (1965), 150-55, and "The Psychoanalyzing of Eugene O'Neill: P.P.S.," *Modern Drama*, 16 (1973), 35-48.

4 See Robert Feldman, "The Longing for Death in O'Neill's *Strange Interlude* and *Mourning Becomes Electra*," *Literature and Psychology*, 31 (1981), 39-48.·

5 Sigmund Freud, "Beyond the Pleasure Principle" (1920), in *The Standard Edition of the Complete Psychological Works of Sigmund Freud*, trans. James Strachey (London: Hogarth Press, 1955), XVIII, 36. All further references to this edition, hereafter abbreviated *SE*, will be followed by volume and page numbers.

6 Though Manheim announces that his "fundamental purpose" in *Eugene O'Neill's New Language of Kinship* is to "write a study of O'Neill's plays and not his life" (p. 42), he nevertheless views the deaths of O'Neill's mother in 1922 and his brother Jamie in 1923 as upsetting the heretofore optimistic "rhythm" of kinship in earlier plays. As a consequence, during the 1920's O'Neill "developed feelings of suicidal self-hatred greater than he had ever known" (p. 44). But while Manheim adds that at this time O'Neill felt both "deep and intense fear and guilt," he explains only the sources of O'Neill's guilt—his failure to meet the train carrying his dead mother, his conviction that his brother's talents were superior to his own so that Jamie deserved success more than he, and so on. I share Manheim's opinion about the darker nature of the middle plays and rely on Rank, in part, to explain more fully the nature of O'Neill's fears.

7 Bogard, pp. 442-43.

8 Jean Laplanche, *Life and Death in Psychoanalysis*, trans. Jeffrey Mehlman (Baltimore: Johns Hopkins Univ. Press, 1970), p. 5.

9 All quotations from the works of Otto Rank will be followed in the text by shortened titles and page numbers. These come from the following editions: *The Double*, trans. Harry Tucker, Jr. (Chapel Hill: Univ. of North Carolina Press, 1971); *The Trauma of Birth* (New York: Robert Brunner, 1952); *Will Therapy* and *Truth and Reality* (New York: Alfred Knopf, 1950).

10 I wish to express my gratitude here to Mr. Conrad Schoeffling, Special Collections Librarian at Long Island University-C. W. Post Campus, for providing me with information about O'Neill's books at LIU.

11 Accounts of the causes of the Rank-Freud split vary widely, from Ernest Jones's somewhat mean-spirited accusation that Rank suffered from a nervous breakdown to E. James Lieberman's defense of Rank's intellectual growth which inevitably led to the two disagreeing and finally parting. For discussion of this, see Esther Menaker, *Otto Rank: A Rediscovered Legacy* (New York: Columbia Univ. Press, 1982), pp. 11-28; Lieberman's *Acts of Will: The Life and Work of Otto Rank* (New York: Free Press, 1985), especially pp. 227-61; and Jones's *The Life and Work of Sigmund Freud* (New York: Basic Books, 1957), III, 44-77.

12 The most relevant of these to the concerns of this essay are "The Trauma of Birth in Its Importance for Psychoanalytic Therapy," *The Psychoanalytic Review*, 11 (1924), 241-45; and "Psychoanalytic Problems," *The Psychoanalytic Review*, 14 (1927), 1-19.

13 Lieberman, p. 256. Rank's impact on psychoanalysis in America is still being felt. Perhaps the finest product of this impact is Ernest Becker's *The Denial of Death* (New York: Free Press, 1973), especially pp. 159-207. Here Becker contemplates Rank's study of the relationship between neurosis and ethical/religious issues.

14 See "Analysis Terminable and Interminable," *SE*, XXIII, 209-53. In this essay Freud criticizes Rank's efforts to shorten the time of a patient's analysis, labelling the attempt a "child of its time . . . designed to suit the rush of American life." In Freud's view, the "theory and practice of Rank's experiment are now things of the past" (pp. 216-17). See also Freud's critiqué of Rank's "trauma of birth" in "Inhibitions, Symptoms, and Anxiety" (1926), *SE*, XX, 135-36 and 150-53. Here he disparages Rank's "formula" as "highly disputable from a theoretical point of view." As mentioned above, in *The Problem of Anxiety*, trans. Henry Alden Bunker (New York: Norton, 1936), pp. 93-101, Freud resumes a critique of Rank's birth trauma.

15 Throughout his career O'Neill interrogated the concept of a "true self" (absolute or "essential" subject?) with the effect that his questioning tended to grow increasingly cynical of such a possibility. For example, in *Beyond the Horizon* Ruth Mayo implies that her husband Robert possesses a true self by telling him that if she "could have seen how you were in your true self" (III, 127), she would never have married him. Later in his career, as I attempt to show above, O'Neill seems to grow suspicious of such idealism.

16 See *The Double*, pp. 8-33. See also Claire Rosenfeld, "The Shadow Within: The Conscious and Unconscious Use of the Double," *Daedalus*, 92 (1963), 326-44; Robert Rogers, *A Psychoanalytic Study of the Double in Literature* (Detroit: Wayne State Univ. Press, 1970); C. F. Keppler, *Literature of the Second Self* (Tucson: Univ. of Arizona Press, 1972). One relevant study of character division in O'Neill is Albert Wertheim, "Eugene O'Neill's *Days Without End* and the Tradition of the Split Character in Modern American and British Drama," *The Eugene O'Neill Newsletter*, 6 (1982), 5-9.

17 Thomas F. Walsh, "More on the Double: A Review," *Journal of the Otto Rank Association*, 8 (June 1973), 69.

18 Rogers, p. 4.

19 Keppler, p. 3.

20 Jacques Lacan, *Écrits*, trans. Alan Sheridan (London: Tavistock Publications, 1977), p. 5.

21 See Louis Sheaffer, *O'Neill: Son and Artist* (Boston: Little, Brown, 1973), pp. 482-84.

22 Louis Sheaffer, *O'Neill: Son and Playwright* (Boston: Little, Brown, 1968), p. 506.

Eugene O'Neill and the Cruelty of Theater

Joseph J. Moleski

> The division between signifying written language and in-
> toxicating spoken language opens up a gulf in the solid
> massif of verbal meaning and forces the gaze into the
> depths of language.
>
> Walter Benjamin
> *The Origin of German Tragic Drama*[1]

I

O'Neill's influence, as hypnotic as the rhythm of decompo-
sition that marks one of his plays in the form of a drumbeat
(The Emperor Jones), has abated little in the years since his
death. The negativity of his judgments on human life and
possibility, seemingly the very insignia of courage and sincerity,
easily reconcile themselves in the mind of theater-goer and
critic alike with an intoxicatingly rich "theatrical experience."
Possessor of an almost violent stylistic fecundity, a fecundity
whose origin in the positing of a noumenal "reality" which can
only be death itself as one of his late plays tells us,[2] a fecundity
we simply enjoy without questioning the price we are expected
to pay on its behalf: O'Neill and his heirs continue to hold sway
over the American stage. Ruthless critics though they are pro-
claimed, their popularity seems hardly to have suffered for it.

Yet behind the sumptuousness, the profusion of forms and
techniques (the term "technique" here summarizing the whole
of a tradition that reduces art to the status of a mere *supplement*
to *physis*), stood, according to O'Neill, a simple self-conception
and modest intention: he was to be thought of as having been
"a bit of a poet, who has labored with the spoken word to
evolve original rhythms of beauty, where beauty apparently
isn't. . . ." The innocuousness, the innocence, even the humanism
of that project—as much a program in public perception as an
aesthetic manifesto—are assumed to be obvious, especially

37

when we read in the phrase immediately following that this "beauty" is associated with discovering "the transfiguring nobility of tragedy, in as near the Greek sense as one can grasp it, in seemingly the most ignoble, debased lives."3 It is a familiar schema, "Nietzschean" in its hypostatization of the tragic and its belief in the aesthetic justification of suffering.4

As a statement, these words of O'Neill define the level and degree of his complicity with the culture whose critical son he was to have been, taking us as they do to the constitutive center of Western theater and beyond, to the cardinal postulate of the logocentrism that inspires Western culture in its most fundamental project. The privilege of speech; the unity of voice and meaning in the spoken word; the human voice as origin of difference (thus turning difference into rhythm which is traditionally the realm of patterned recurrence); speech as *archon* of a system of differences from which it is itself exempt, which it sustains without participating in: all these point out the parallelism of O'Neill's dramatic program with the most tenaciously pursued project of our culture.5 Influence, the spell of the other proposing and imposing itself as self-subsistent presence outside the play of difference, is produced by this elevation of the voice. My intention here is not to trace O'Neill's work in its contours back to the project he defined for us, a course that would serve his purposes as well as another, but to situate it, inscribe it in a system of differences it cannot command but whose occlusion is decisive.

II

The most incisive of Antonin Artaud's objections to classical representational theater was its domination by,. its orientation to speech.6 In that phenomenon, really a radical historical intention, he saw the very name of all that the "Theater of Cruelty," that site not necessarily of bloodshed and carnage but rather of "the affirmation/ of a terrible/ and, moreover, implacable necessity,"7 was to raise itself up against. Artaud's denunciation of the inherently theological word was not, however, undertaken as an act of simple metaphysical or aesthetic terrorism, but as a preliminary to achieving a form of writing, a "veritable theatrical passigraphy reaching beyond empirical languages,"8 as distinct as can be—because it includes it, localizes it—from the phonetic writing, writing subject to speech, of the West. Rigor, necessity, the responsibility of theater could only be achieved, Artaud knew, by deposing the voice, liberating writing as the play of difference from its thralldom to the voice. Against the phonocentric theater, against its psychology and metaphysics, he brandished the limit at which the *possibility* of a pure theater (one from which all representation had been purged, that would be *life itself in total non-differentiation*) joins with its *impossibility*.

If I now turn to the case of Arnold Schoenberg, it is not to produce an *analogy* in musical history to the demand Artaud made of the theater. I do so because music, a certain kind of music, a certain *perception* of music, is critical to the situation of O'Neill's work, as the quotation from which we began indicates. Starting from the voice as the source of music (to O'Neill pure, rhythmical, vocalic sonority) in the askesis of meaning, O'Neill condemns himself to the dream of a music that possesses all the self-subsistent presence, the nature and necessity, that the "meaningful voice" alone lacks, *precisely because of* the sacrifice of meaning that was performed to achieve the musicality of speech. This fact is sufficiently indicated in the musical form that is found throughout his plays, the folk song.9 His entire work can be read as the surrender of dramatic reality to the putative substantiality of a certain kind of music.

The whole of Schoenberg's revision of music, like Artaud's revaluation of drama, turns on the issue of the relationship between speech and writing. It can, in fact, be read as the derivation of music from writing (but can we still speak of derivation, a term that implies an ontological primacy it is the very function of writing to contest?). As Theodor Adorno describes the liberation of music, always still to be accomplished, sought by Schoenberg and his followers (though, like Artaud, Schoenberg made imitation precisely *infidelity*), the sense of his act consisted in this: "All organic music proceeded out of the *stile recitativo*. From the very beginning this was patterned after speech. The emancipation of music today is tantamount to its emancipation from verbal language."10 The resituation of speech is one in Schoenberg with the abandonment of musical representationalism, with the critical revision of the organicist heritage in music. One could trace in Schoenberg's articulation, first, of free atonality—itself an impossible limit—and later the necessarily arbitrary institutionalization of free atonality in the

twelve-tone system as motivated by the same intention that
compelled Artaud first to criticize the (phonetic, logocentric)
writing of the theater and then to demand, to dream a totally
different form of writing that would organize the *totality* of
theatrical "elements."

If we now resume our reading of O'Neill *in terms of Stravinsky*, the extremity of whose work from Schoenberg's is studied
in Adorno's *Philosophy of Modern Music*, it is not in the spirit
of a rampant analogism. Nor is it the mere tracing of a circle
which would lead us through a certain controlled detour to our
starting point in O'Neill. Rather, the point is to achieve a certain
squaring of our study according to four positions, nodes, opaque
points, which will give us a quasi-theatrical space or page on
which to play off music and drama against one another, not in
the direction of a totalizing interpretation, but toward a certain
opening of the work of O'Neill. In other words, the argument
of this essay lies in its structure. Very few of the possibilities
this admittedly violent or artificial resituation of O'Neill's work
in a structure neither he nor we can command can be more
than adumbrated here, not for accidental but for essential reasons. But perhaps, in a small way, this essay itself, in its tactics
and their implications, will form a gloss, when we come to read
it, of O'Neill's *Long Day's Journey into Night*, itself a play
constituted by a ternary structure, though one giving itself out
as a *natural* one, i.e., as a family.

III

> The Peyote dance is inside a grater, in its time-tempered wood,
> endowed with the occult salts of the earth. It is in the taut and
> involuted fibres of this wand that the healing virtues of the rite
> dwell, and it is so complex, so withdrawn, it must be hunted and
> tracked down like some beast in the forest.
>
> Antonin Artaud, "Concerning a Journey
> to the Land of the Tarahumaras"11

The Emperor Jones is a Stravinskyan ballet of dissolution.
It exposes the subject to a rhythm, a pulsation, that is split off
from content, fetishized, in much the same way as it is in
Petrouchka and *Le Sacre du Printemps*. As a play, *The Emperor
Jones* can be read as the burlesque of individuation, a fascistic
denunciation of fascism; as constructed upon a wholly non-
dialectical interpretation of the self's claim to difference, to not

being fully accounted for by its position in the collective. The subject's conception of difference is presumed, by the way Jones is characterized and by the very fact that he is uncontrasted in the play, to be a totalitarian act, self-aggrandizement, opportunism. The very idea of a difference that would be neither romantic negativity, the Hegelian "beautiful soul," nor inherently a claim of superiority, is alien to O'Neill, as the play *Diff'rent* attests.12 Adorno's description of the role of rhythm in Stravinsky's early ballets is apposite:

> Rhythmic structure is, to be sure, blatantly prominent, but this is achieved at the expense of all other aspects of rhythmic organization. Not only is any subjectively expressive flexibility of the beat absent . . . but furthermore all rhythmic relations associated with the construction and the internal compositional organization —the 'rhythm of the whole'—are absent as well. Rhythm is underscored, but split off from musical content. This results not in more, but rather in less rhythm than in compositions in which there is no fetish made of rhythm; in other words, there are only fluctuations of something always constant and totally static—a stepping aside—in which the irregularity of recurrence replaces the new.13

The hypostasization of rhythm in O'Neill, the rendering-virulent of rhythm by means of its enthronement (for rhythm is Jones's double), has the effect of drying up the source of rhythm, of delivering up duration to the quasi-spatial tableau. Devoid of the rhythm *of* or at the source, hence of duration and the subjectively expressive, O'Neill writes plays which juxtapose "blocks of time" in the manner of *Diff'rent* and *All God's Chillun.* O'Neill's and Stravinsky's positions in their respective arts are near-doubles of each other.

Rhythm, in its tradition and in O'Neill's work, is, first of all, the rhythm of respiration: ingathering, expulsion; dilation, contraction. This rhythm, because it is "involuntary" perhaps, gives itself out as being natural, which even allows it to be confused with spontaneity and freedom. It dominates in O'Neill's theater, not simply in the sense of the rhythm of the speaking voice— the chant of *Lazarus Laughed,* for example—but as the virtual subject of the plays. Psychological explanations of this phenomenon, as much a factor in Stravinsky's music as in O'Neill's drama, are of no avail; as an extreme reaction to or repression of the limits of logocentrism, it is perhaps explicable.

O'Neill's theater respires; his drama traces the simple alternation of inversely related movements representing itself as nature, objectivity. This inverse parallelism, this respiration, is the signature of the phonocentric work. In comparison with rhythm itself (but is such a thing possible?), "content" is unimportant in this sense: the more extreme the dualities, the more reassuring their inscription in the anthropomorphic movement that proffers and withdraws them. Even dualities like God the Mother and God the Father *(Strange Interlude)* or hope and despair *(The Iceman Cometh)* are primarily significant insofar as they provide this rhythm with substance on which to act, with a "medium." The presence of rhythm, as the movement of an inverse parallelism, may be interpreted as the signature of the human in non-human or transpersonal phenomena like history or "nature." Its "perception" there can produce a fundamentally reassuring, because "familiar," non-alien, effect. "Rhythm" is, thus, one of the resources of anthropocentric reassurance, the reassurance of anthropomorphism, even when this rhythm's "matter" is inherently destructive. The entire point becomes clear when we see Artaud ultimately attempt to create what is a writing of the breath itself (see, for example, his "An Affective Athleticism").

At the nadir of Jones's disintegration in *The Emperor Jones,* then, lies a trance-like state that brings us, I think, to one of the points of greatest difference between O'Neill's and Artaud's response to the historical repression of writing, a repression which, because it served the purpose of his desire for status as a classicist, O'Neill was never to seek to undo, but which he was therefore condemned to repeat endlessly *as if in a dream.* At the limit of his attempted escape from the collective his pretentions have incited to homocidal fury—the escape presided over by the pulsation of the drum, the tympanum, the *ear* against which O'Neill delivers his blows—Jones finds himself confronted with a *"Congo Witch Doctor"* who brandishes *"a charm stick with a bunch of white cockatoo feathers tied to the end."*14 Jones is *"paralyzed with awed fascination. . . ."* The Witch Doctor's voice *"rises and falls in a weird, monotonous croon, without articulate word divisions."* But, though he cannot speak, the Witch Doctor can nevertheless make himself understood: he *"points with his wand to the sacred tree, to the river beyond, to the altar, and finally to* Jones *with a ferocious command.*

Jones *seems to sense the meaning of this. It is he who must offer himself for sacrifice"* (p. 201).

The "wand" wielded by the Witch Doctor points out the elements of a pre-constituted space, an apparently primordial theater, and this action is experienced as a commandment of self-destruction. Originary malice on the part of the Other combined with fear on the part of the Self, a quasi-Hegelian opening to a dialectic of Master and Slave? Certainly it is this, but other elements of the scene are more decisive for our purposes here. As we have already noted, the dominant note of this crooning voice that O'Neill hears at the origin is this: it is "without articulate word divisions"; an originary voice which writing, the principle of articulation, has not yet divided, not yet subjected to meaning. Inviolate, it stands at the origin with all its presence intact, all cruelty already delegated to the "wand"—or writing instrument—that must thereafter carry the full burden of the gesture of authority as of cruelty. As speaker, at least as speaker intent on reactivating the purely musical origin of speech, I am innocent, the *innocent* master. Insofar as I write, in any *active* sense, *affirming* writing, I am inculpated, doomed to the dialectical movement of history. O'Neill dreams a virginal speech exorcised of the spirit of domination as a sanctuary from evil, cruelty, writing.

For O'Neill as for the baroque writers studied by Benjamin, "sound is and remains something purely sensuous; meaning has its home in written language. And the spoken word is only afflicted by meaning, so to speak, as if by an inescapable disease; it breaks off in the middle of the process of resounding, and the damming up of the feeling, which was ready to pour forth, provokes mourning. Here meaning is encountered . . . as the reason for mournfulness."[15] We are not far from O'Neill's *Mourning Becomes Electra:* as Orin says to Lavinia, "I hate the daylight. It's like an accusing eye! No, we've renounced the day, in which normal people live—or rather it has renounced us. Perpetual night—darkness of death in life—that's the fitting habitat for guilt!"[16] And the mask-like quality of the human face, the face insofar as it functions as a sign within a system of similarities and differences, committing the presence of the true face to meaning, is experienced as well as a doom. The other side of the situation is *Lazarus Laughed;* there joy can express itself in a chanting of the triumphant "liberation" of

voice from the necessity of meaning—in a burning which finds
its absolute contrary in Artaud's vision of an utter expenditure:
"And if there is still one hellish, truly accursed thing in our
time, it is our artistic dallying with forms, instead of being like
victims burnt at the stake, *signaling* through the flames" (my
italics).17

O'Neill's dream of a (lost) spontaneously arising plentitude
played out within/as language, within/as the *affliction* of writing
as incision/mark/*stigme/techne,* has these consequences for
his work: the repeated eruption of fantasies of "primitive" cultures—the crews of the old sailing ships, island natives18—as
innocent as they are distant in time or space; the recourse, when
it is a question of representing his own culture, to the virtual
apotheosization of a principle that operates with the automatic
functioning of a machine (a "return of the repressed" automatic
functioning, or death, within speech) as in *Dynamo* or, as we
have seen, in *The Emperor Jones,* where the drumbeat that rules
the action finally becomes a "baffled but revengeful power";
and, finally, the "internalization" of this *still unassimilated*
mechanical principle as the repetition-compulsion that characterizes the mother of *Long Day's Journey into Night* as well as
the society of *The Iceman Cometh.* In other words, a dramatic
opus that is the endless tale of possessed self-dispossessors; because—unlike O'Neill and like Artaud—we confess now to
never really having believed that the discovery of the wand
already in the possession of another was a situation before which
we are powerless, must destroy ourselves. The wand, as Artaud's
journey to the Land of the Tarahumara shows, can be—if not
stolen, an act that would confirm the proprietary right—earned.

IV

If Artaud, too, in his way dreamt the eve of history-as-the-
time-of-dispossession, of all those doublings and repetitions that
(under the names of God, Being, and a certain dialectics) come
to rob the self and its theater of presence, he will thus be seen
to have been very close to O'Neill. The difference, consumate
because it derives from the greatest similarity, lies in the
difference between two kinds of reaction to the loss of originary
presence. Faced with the "same" insight, Artaud and O'Neill
do "act" differently and that difference can reveal, in a limited

way, the difference between a theater that would erase repetition from the "standpoint" of the origin (Artaud's) and a theater that seeks to ceaselessly reactivate the origin of repetition (O'Neill's). The line, taken rigorously, is imperceptible, a threshold, the difference between a before and an after, between a cruel generosity and a generous cruelty.

In a passage cited by Derrida, Artaud writes: ". . . as for my forces,/ they are only the supplement,/ the supplement of an actual state,/ it is that there has never been an origin."[19] In O'Neill's *Strange Interlude,* we read: ". . . the only living life is in the past and future . . . the present is an interlude in which we call on past and future to bear witness we are living."[20] Contrasting the recognition of the absent ground, basis of a whole metaphysics and its theater, to the situation of the un-divided voice *within* that absence of the present, these quotations show us the difference between Artaud and O'Neill at its most acute.

Strange Interlude expresses much, if not all, of O'Neill's response to the dissipation of force and disruption of presence so unremittingly denounced by Artaud. It is a drama of the loss of presence, *of the origin insofar as it is representable* within language, a certain language; O'Neill is rigorous in his exclusion of presence in this drama in which virtually every scene is prospective or retrospective, deferral of consumation until its possibility has become merely the memory of what was apparently possible, allusion to an elsewhere. It is a drama purged almost completely of all but speech. Its law of operation is that of the "compensating substitute" (p. 166), as one of the characters calls it, simply repeating the irrationality of the con-cept of mimetic representation. For if the "substitute" merely doubles, "stands in for," a presence or present that could appear in its own right, for what does it "compensate," com-pensation requiring a previous defect, partiality, absence?[21] Nevertheless, the description, delivered by one of the characters a propos a particular situation within the play, cannot be localized in its significance because it exposes the law of the working of language itself: language as the mimesis of the object forever announces itself as the "compensating substitute" for a thing, a self, that can always be recovered, whose absence is not fundamental but accidental, temporary, conditional. The present can always be restored, even if it is only the articulation of the loss of the present, a "call" upon the past and the future to affirm existence.

In the figure—more accurately, in the voice—of Nina, the "central" character, we find dramatized precisely the thirst for presence amidst a succession of unsatisfactory substitutes, displacements, deferrals that beset that thirst. The events that set this chain of "compensating substitutes" in motion, that account for the lack that inaugurates these series, that beget desire and memory, as in the whole of the tradition that interprets language metaphysically, are made to appear as catastrophes coming from the outside: the incursion of war, the genetic accident, etc. Had war not destroyed Gordon Shaw, for example, eternalizing the desire for consumation in an endless succession of surrogates to atone for an initial deferral; had not a hereditary defect arisen to drive Nina to further substitutions, substitutions for substitutions; fulfillment, it seems, the negation of past and future in the living present, could have been achieved. Everywhere and always, *Strange Interlude* accounts for the absences that some form of surrogation must come to cover, redeem, as the result of empirical, accidental, catastrophic events that come to contaminate, to disrupt.22

As in the relation between Self and Other, so, too, in language: the Professor's library, within which the Greek and Latin that death has *historically* befallen are entombed, provides a context for some of the play's most passionate utterances about the emptiness of words and the prerogatives of life and its speech. In that library, itself a metaphor and projection of the self that withdraws from the call of the present, the distance between the self and the present is explained by recourse to psychology: it is the effect of a cowardice and allows for the play of a variety of other emotions. In the library, "secure with the culture of the past at his back, a fugitive from reality can view the present safely from a distance, as a superior with condescending disdain, pity, and even amusement," as the stage directions tell us. In other words, with a certain cruelty that is the *effect* of an unnecessary non-participation, the result of fear or the desire for superiority.

Thus far, we have seen a pattern of valoration take shape that is highly traditional in all its elements. Psychology, history, genetics, and a variety of other disciplines are called upon to so shape the play as to account for the loss of presence and the present; to make absence, distance, death *derivative*, equipped as we are with explanatory events and states that make them seem inessential, non-originary, above all non-linguistic. Characters who refuse the call of the present like the Professor are condemned; those like Nina who accept it are praised.

But how are we to explain the very profusion of explanation of the differences that divide the self from itself, the present from itself, if not as the hysterical reaction to, or repression of, absence, distance, death in all its forms? The very profusion of explanation *registers in reverse* the recognition against which the speaking self must defend itself, that absence is not "accidental," the acute suspicion that loss is not loss at all but original difference, division at and of the origin . . . and that it inhabits even the calling voice itself.

If the whole of *Strange Interlude* can be read as a defense of the possibility of presence and the present against radical absence, such an interpretation must take account of the play's most obviously innovative "technical" achievement, the presentation of internal monologue in alternation with mundane speech. On the one hand, this technique brings a strong deconstructive force to bear on what could be called the "Romantic" view of subjectivity: "thought" or the internal monologue, traditionally taken to be situated in some inner reserve of absolute self-proximity within which no interruptive distance that would turn this interior into a theater need neccessarily arise, is directly staged, with no apparent denaturing of that "thought." In fact, much of the play's interest derives from the characters' reactions to this "thought" with which they can have a specular relation. Marsden, for example, is said to "stare idly at his drifting thoughts" (p. 4). From this point of view, *Strange Interlude* delivers a liberating blow against the illusion of a privileged, pure interiority lying beyond/above language and the world.

At the level of spectacle, however, the case is different: this abrogation of the difference between thought and speech, interiority and exteriority, representation and presence, is an act performed by and for the theatrical spectacle. The interiority that the characters *will* themselves, mark off, refuse to put in circulation, is simply negated, *sacrificed* to the collected spectators and the authority of the spectacle. The act is simultaneously a castigation of the impulse to withdraw/preserve *and* an implicit claim that this withholding is only illusory. The spectator is allowed to watch this dispossession of interiority, *survive his own death,* secure in his distance and putative difference from the figures on the stage. And it is this that turns *Strange Interlude* into a Mass, a ritual of human sacrifice, one precisely *to* the God that Artaud struggled with—the interloper or thief who always already has dispossessed me of my speech, divided me from myself. The ritual of the author/god who steals from the self its own self-proximity is celebrated in *Strange Interlude,* renewing the acceptance of that original theft in the assembled spectators. The proximity here between these two men of the theater is so great that, if we were to image it, we would say that Artaud himself—whose cardinal demand was for a total exposure, an absolute self-expenditure without reserve *in reality and not in theatrical illusion*—is the victim of O'Neill's sacrificial theater. We touch, perhaps, the uttermost difference within a nearly complete similarity when we juxtapose these two voices that cry out as if to one another across the threshold of history-as-dispossession:

> My three men! . . . I feel their desires converge in me! . . . to form one complete beautiful male desire . . . which I absorb . . . and am whole . . . they dissolve in me, their life is my life . . . I am pregnant with the three! . . . husband! . . . lover! . . . father! . . . and the fourth man! . . . little man! . . . little Gordon! . . . he is mine too! . . . that makes it perfect! . . .
>
> *Strange Interlude,* p. 135.

> I, Antonin Artaud, am my son,
> my father, my mother,
> my self . . .
> "Here Lies"23

V

As O'Neill's early plays stage the sacrifice of thought to poetry, the late works, like those of Stravinsky's neoclassical phase, perform the sacrifice of poetry to thought. Adorno's description of the later works of Stravinsky could stand as an interpretation of plays like *Long Day's Journey Into Night* and *The Iceman Cometh:* "Out of the disintegration of the subject it [objectivistic music] designs for itself the aesthetic integration of the world. It recoins in counterfeit the destructive law of society itself—of absolute power, that is—as the constructive law of authenticity. The farewell trick of Stravinsky—who other-

wise, in an elegant gesture, renounced everything astonishing—
is the enthroning of the self-forgotten negative as the self-con-
scious positive."24

Long Day's Journey Into Night: a play written "with deep
pity and understanding and forgiveness for *all* the four haunted
Tyrones."25 In the play, "understanding," the word itself already
including forgiveness and pity (the emotion Nietzsche dreaded
most and Artaud labored against in the Theater of Cruelty), is
the acceptance of the self and other as products, as the necessary
effects, of the past to which all generative power and substantiality is relegated. Tyrone says: "Mary! For God's sake, forget
the past!" And Mary, with a *"strange objective calm"* replies:
"Why? How can I? The past is the present, isn't it? It's the
future, too. We all try to lie out of that but life won't let us"
(p. 87). Understanding here is the capitulation to the past, not
in a recognition of its role in the construction of the present,
but in its co-extension with the present and future. Thus, understanding is always already the understanding of fate and itself
a fatality. Fate, pure objectivity, is the obverse of the doctrine of
presence.

This theater of understanding, of understanding *understood*
as a fundamentally passive relation to a priority that has assumed
complete authority, can only endlessly stage one thing: the gift
of the mother's bridal gown to the father. At the play's conclusion, Mary, now deep in a narcotic state, re-enters: *"Over one
arm, carried neglectfully, trailing on the floor, as if she had
forgotten she held it, is an old-fashioned white satin wedding
gown . . ."* (p. 170). To the father's question, "What's that she's
carrying, Edmund?" the son replies, "Her wedding gown, I
suppose." Then Tyrone *"gets to his feet and stands directly in
her path—in anguish.* Mary! Isn't it bad enough—? *(controlling
himself—gently persuasive.)* Here, let me take it, dear. You'll
only step on it and tear it and get it dirty dragging it on the
floor. Then you'd be sorry afterwards. *(She lets him take it,
regarding him from somewhere far away within herself, without
recognition, without either affection or animosity")* (pp. 171-
72). Mutely, the sons watch the act, the consummation of the
play *Long Day's Journey* and of every other theater of memory
and understanding as objectivity: the repossession by the
father of the bridal gown, sign of virginity, virgin sign, the pure
present. Like Jones before the wand of the sorcerer, the sons

watch, never even tentatively raising a hand to intervene, never questioning, their sonship confirmed/reconstituted in the act. To be a son is to be condemned to watch endlessly this reconfirmation of the father's proprietary right, the celebration of the power of sheer anteriority; is to understand.

Long Day's Journey Into Night stages the impossibility of any dialectical confrontation with the past: on the one hand, there is an immutable, inviolable past that simply is, right or wrong; on the other, is its product that only through willful ignorance, through a deluded sense of "originality" or "authenticity," can assert its own inaugural power, can possesses itself at all. Within this framework of *filiation, given* this *familialization* of the relationship between self and other within history, no non-violent solution is possible. The best that can occur is to travel the interval between a past from which we were absent and its repetition; to inhabit for a while that numbed passage of time when, for a moment, there is an apparent uncertainty about the ultimate recipient of the wedding gown, before the circle closes upon itself. Under the given conditions, O'Neill's, however, we were never really ever in doubt about the gown's destination.

The wand of the magician, the bridal gown of the mother: between these two reflected dispossessions we have tried to show something of O'Neill's addiction to a certain form of cruelty, the cruelty to which one perhaps must yield if one respects the limits of the possible, respects the factuality of the subjugation of writing to speech, of difference to identity.

But, to this possibility, we can reply with the Manifestos of the Theater of Cruelty and the music Schoenberg finally came to write. Both are thoroughly proleptic; both total in their demand; both essentially articulating what is impossible and therefore most worthy of hope. The one premeditates an invisible theater, the other an inaudible music.26

NOTES

1 Walter Benjamin, *The Origin of German Tragic Drama*, trans. John Osborne (London: NLB, 1977), p. 201.

2 "All things are the same meaningless joke to me, for they grin at me from the one skull of death" (*The Iceman Cometh*, in *The Plays of Eugene O'Neill* [New York: Random House, 1954], p. 649). A single, inanimate, unchanging "reality" beyond phenomena is the prerequisite of a "stylist" like O'Neill who draws his freedom, animation, richness from the fact that all these styles *as styles* are equally distant from an origin.

3 From a letter to Arthur Hobson Quinn, in *O'Neill and His Plays*, ed. Oscar Cargill, N. Bryllion Fagin, William J. Fisher (New York: New York Univ. Press, 1964), p. 125.

4 The reference, of course, is to Nietzsche's *Birth of Tragedy* and the claim of an aesthetic justification of suffering. For a rhetorical reading of this text and an interpretation of that claim that is completely the reverse of O'Neill's, see Paul de Man, *Allegories of Reading: Figural Language in Rousseau, Nietzsche, Rilke, and Proust* (New Haven: Yale Univ. Press, 1979) where he shows that Nietzsche's statement "should not be taken too serenely, for it is an indictment of existence rather than a panegyric of art" (p. 93).

5 On the ensnarement of Western language in the onto-theological constitution of Western metaphysics, a fact manifested in the historical project of phonetic writing, see all the works of Jacques Derrida, especially *Speech and Phenomena and Other Essays on Husserl's Theory of Signs*, trans. David B. Allison (Evanston: Northwestern Univ. Press, 1973); *Of Grammatology*, trans. Gayatri Chakravorty Spivak (Baltimore: Johns Hopkins Univ. Press, 1976); and "La Pharmacie de Platon," in *La Dissémination* (Paris: Éditions du Seuil, 1972), pp. 69-197.

6 My remarks throughout this essay and especially those on Artaud draw on Derrida's reading of Artaud's argument with the *single, coherent* system of Western metaphysics and theater. Though Derrida refers throughout his published works to Artaud, he discusses him directly in "La Parole Soufflée" and "The Theater of Cruelty and the Closure of Representation," *Writing and Difference*, trans. Alan Bass (Chicago: Univ. of Chicago Press, 1978), pp. 169-96 and pp. 232-51.

7 The description is quoted by Derrida, "The Theater of Cruelty and the Closure of Representation," p. 232.

8 "La Parole Soufflée," p. 191.

9 Nietzsche's description of the folk song, read *without* the vigilance de Man calls for, accurately reflects O'Neill's sense of it and defines the kind of function folk song plays in O'Neill's works: "But what is the folk song in contrast to the wholly Apollonian epos? What else but the *perpetuum vestigium* of a union of the Apollonian and Dionysian?"—F. Nietzsche, *Birth of Tragedy*, trans. Walter Kaufmann (New York: Vintage Books, 1967), p. 53. O'Neill implicitly interprets the folk song in this manner, ignoring the adjective *"perpetuum,"* i.e., he implicitly ignores the fact that the folk song is the *trace (vestigium)* of a present, a unity, that *never was (a) present*. Music can have, for O'Neill, the wholeness, the self-subsisting being, that drama cannot possess; but, by another interpretation, music is the wholeness drama does not *wish* to possess, i.e., is relieved of attempting to achieve, as Artaud seeks to achieve it.

10 *Philosophy of Modern Music*, trans. Anne G. Mitchell and Wesley V. Blomster (New York: Seabury Press, 1980), p. 128.

11 *Antonin Artaud Anthology*, 2nd. ed., trans. Jack Hirschman (San Francisco: City Lights Books, 1965), pp. 79-80. The whole of Artaud's journey should be read

as tracing the rebirth of the artist *as writer*, he who "draws and quarters the Elements."

12 *Diff'rent*, in *The Plays of Eugene O'Neill* (New York: Random House, 1955), pp. 493ff.

13 *Philosophy of Modern Music*, p. 154-55.

14 *The Emperor Jones*, in *The Plays of Eugene O'Neill* (New York: Random House, 1954), p. 200. All further references are to this edition.

15 Benjamin, p. 209.

16 *The Haunted*, in *The Plays of Eugene O'Neill* (New York: Random House, 1955), p. 150.

17 *The Theater and Its Double*, trans. Mary Caroline Richards (New York: Grove Press, 1958), p. 13.

18 See Paddy's reminiscences in *The Hairy Ape*, in *The Plays of Eugene O'Neill* (New York: Random House, 1954), pp. 213-14.

19 "The Theater of Cruelty and the Closure of Representation," p. 232.

20 *Strange Interlude*, in *The Plays of Eugene O'Neill* (New York: Random House, 1955), p. 166. Further references are to this edition.

21 The "compensating substitute," in O'Neill's play, functions as the concept of the "supplement" does in the work of Rousseau. See *Of Grammatology*, pp. 141-65.

22 On the *necessity* of this kind of recourse to "supplementary" incidents, conditions, etc., that appear as catastrophes, cf. *Of Grammatology*, pp. 152ff.

23 *Antonin Artaud Anthology*, p. 238.

24 *Philosophy of Modern Music*, p. 205.

25 Dedication to the play. (New Haven: Yale Univ, Press, 1956). All further references are to this edition.

26 In "Arnold Schoenberg, 1874-1951," *Prisms*, trans. Samuel and Shierry Weber (London: Neville Spearman, 1967), Adorno describes Schoenberg's late works as "paradigms of a possible music" (p. 171). Similarly, Derrida describes Artaud's theater of cruelty as a theater delivered from appearance: "The Theater of Cruelty and the Closure of Representation," p. 249.

Aeschylus and O'Neill:
A Phenomenological View

John Chioles

I

The Deuteragonist Offers a Dialectic.

> The theatre
> is the state
> the place
> the point
> Where we can get hold of man's anatomy and
> through it heal and dominate life. . . .[1]

The theatre's double are those events in a communal life that make up man's domain, his individual story. For Artaud, the purging of the dark forces of that story was an obsession, a priestly function of the theatre artist, the duty and the right of the spectator. Man's story in tribal-communal life is a kind of theatre (that sometime art form), no more than a swift turn of the same coin to capture and explode flagrant violence, plague, and the psychic disasters that man needs to bring against himself. And by defusing these, we prevent the double, the theatre of life in society, from making its degrading use of them. If Artaud yearns for the kind of unity that comes from the gaping mouth in the posture of a scream, spanning language, gesture, and the violation of space, Aeschylus demands a dissolution in the mode of healing after the "plague" and the rift. Essentially, the one theatre is no different from the other: Artaud mistrusts cognitive language, while Aeschylus transcends language's cognitive use; Artaud surrenders to a visual language with anguishing sound, as Aeschylus forges an edifice to found *through language* a complex landscape ranging from the psychic to the physical, from the mystical to the immediate.

These mark the one variable in their theatre. And that

53

variable is only a cultural difference in their conception of language. Artaud's theatre endures through the necessity of misapprehending his indeterminate language; Aeschylus' theatre endures through our need to make his language fixed and cognitive, while rendering his resolution banal, robbing it of the "cruelty" that marks the path to dissolution and knowledge. The theatre of both endures through basic misapplication, a very telling departure from the danger of their central proposition.

Artaud is the perfect actor to play Cassandra in Aeschylus. He can rage against language itself, against its inadequacy to express true horror in forethought; he can struggle and collapse into massive disorder of mind while trying to convey vast visions from the god's primitive past to his bloody future—all passing in a fleeting moment:

> . . . see the horror here—
>
> .   .   .
>
> Apollo Apollo
> Lord of journeys, my ruin. . . . (1076, 1080-81)2

Aeschylus is the dramatist with the intellective force and sociopolitical structure to make perfect sense of Artaud's manifesto for healing, the rite of passage toward a proper apprehension of the world: a searing vision shared by both as theatre.

With O'Neill the issue is compounded, for he struggles to bring "real life" to the surface and expose it as "cruel"; while Artaud by poetic force compels that life and theatre be one (or perhaps co-extensive, belonging in the same, phenomenologically), O'Neill persists in unearthing a moral evil in the basic natural cruelty of real life. In his trilogy *Mourning Becomes Electra,* O'Neill identifies life with the intensified morbidity of the world he has constructed, a world without healing and without redemption, lest psychoanalysis itself be thought redemptive. The point of convergence in Aeschylus, O'Neill, and Artaud is ideological; and it is best stated in Artaud's words:

> Like the plague the theatre is the time of evil, the triumph of somber forces that are nourished by an even deeper force until their extinction. (IV, 37)3

However, where these authors *do not* converge is crucial and instructive. Their dramaturgy, in all its important differences, lies on the same latitudinal line, so to speak, and belongs to the same impetus. Yet the differences are vital. The conception of crisis has a different rhythm in each. And God is nowhere in O'Neill, at once unknowable and on an earthly plane in Aeschylus; and in Artaud he is everywhere visible, an expanding Hegelian infinite, an evil metaphysic.

O'Neill rallies the somber forces to a triumph that is unique —a triumph of evil within modern consciousness that is closer to a mythic past than to cause-and-effect psychological realism. Its uniqueness belies historical man, forcing him into a mask, a face with many layers, where he is for the most part unable to tell the proximity to real life. Artaud's "god" would not allow such a state, because "cruelty" is a catharsis, clean and simple, intended like a whirlwind to drop us at the center of real life— where there are no masks. The characters in O'Neill's trilogy wear the mask of their mythic past, while at the same time they make a super-human effort to take part in a historical flow of the world they move in by mere accident. The immendiate Mannon family—Ezra, Christine, Brant, Orin, and Lavinia— must wear the masks of their "unevolved" state as part of their anatomy. The theatre's accommodation of contradiction may give particular strength to the arch rhythms of psychological-clinical language on the one hand and to the mythic fixity of a mask in single-minded repose on the other. The dialectic created by the contradiction reveals a "rift" at the core of "real life" and shows O'Neill as a far greater dramatic genius than his critics would allow. The rift is Artaud's disorder of mind (his universe in chaos); and it is Aeschylus' imponderable, his hard center of pessimism, the impasse that provides the massive need to found the trilogic structure with which to heal socio-aesthetically the wounds of a received world.

All three—Aeschylus, Artaud, O'Neill—have charted a way of approaching experience that is basically phenomenological, in the sense that it places man at the center of his world. From these authors a deep mistrust emerges concerning the subjective-objective dichotomy: Man is his world, and he is thrown-into-it. He affects a creative impulse on the world through relatedness and dimension; he goes through a multiplicity of phases and keeps altering and shifting perspectives on fixity. The theatre, as the perfect forum of phenomenology, provides the conclusive "living metaphor" of man in action, affecting a creative vision, in his dimension as being-in-the-world, in his relation to objects and other actions, in the "living world" as consciousness stemming from his own creativity. The man-in-action world of *The Eumenides* is such a living world. Likewise, O'Neill's "mask in repose" that holds his trilogy ideologically together; and Artaud's insistence that man—actor and spectator alike—be at the center of experience. To understand the intimate relationship of theatre to phenomenology[4] we have but to look at trilogic structure to see how man constructs a "living world."

II

The Trilogic Issue.

> The sun will not overstep his measure;
> if he were to do so, the Erinyes,
> handmaids of Justice, would seek him out.[5]

As with Phaethon's sun-chariot, *The Oresteia* reveals an unimpeded pace of misfortune, a fateful inevitability, gathering to such momentum that it threatens to break through the form: there the son, the human transgressor, will be sought out having overstepped his measure. Indeed, the cumulative tension of the tragic generates greater internal terror than the aesthetic construct we call tragedy can actually hold. As in Herakleitos, the "handmaids of justice," a developing avenging force—the Erinyes of the third play—will seek out the transgressor; and, as Phaethon is punished for his tangential veering off course with the steeds of the sun, so the human (and divine) agents in Aeschylus' trilogy are brought to account for breaking down the boundaries of justice, for breaking through the frame of tragic events. The time and the place where man shall answer for such a collapse of the race will necessitate social and psychological reconstitution of the forces of order under communal *dike,* under an Athens to be shaped through human mind and necessity.

Artistic expression, taking on the necessity of theatre, knows nothing of illusion here. In the nascent state of the art, the thought contained becomes transitive and immediate. It is not thinking about something, which naturally ushers in illusion; rather, the thing itself turns to thought, leaving illusion as a "future relic," alien to the needs of present expression. As with Phaethon and the chariot of the sun—and here lies the crux of Herakleitos' pertinence to the trilogy—the events of *The Oresteia* function as direct healing of the state of innocence, altering it to a state of knowing. *Didaskalia,* then, harsh and painful but a necessary prerogative *and not illusion,* stands at center of the trilogic art, not unlike the pre-Socratic Thinker's force of idea, inseparable from his metaphor. Artaud authored the notion of the double to take the place of the theatre's original sin: didacticism at an immediate level, not through illusion as palliative.

The ordering structure of the trilogy suggests a deliberate artifice strained at every turn through human pain, until a resolution emerges from outside its perimeters, from another region of the communal sphere, in order to teach and to heal. Structuring, de-structuring, and piecing together of a world comprise the sum-total processes of the trilogic form; a developing Being, human and divine, shapes itself in the space of the dramatic construct, in its tragic overreach and healing resolution. The trilogy is a formal unit that functions to contain tragic thought. But the unyielding nature of the tragic seems invulnerable to this kind of containment, defying both order and rational experience which prevents a work from becoming mere "social realism" and thus localizing its solution. So with *The Oresteia:* the tragic, irrational like Phaethon's team leaves behind a blazing trail in the mind; it will not be harnessed, except through an aesthetic leap, through the didacticism of experience and the paideia-function of art. Only in this way may the tragic be contained, made to stop short, as a didactic, comprehensible unit and made to answer "paideia-logically" to mind, *dike,* and the experience in dramatic convention in the open space of a theatre. For that reason "the handmaids of Justice would seek him out"—would seek out the sun, his chariot, Zeus, and Orestes in his turn.

Aeschylus' aim stands within this sweeping view of the trilogy, which is to make containment of misfortune as much a part of the nature of the tragic (and the form of tragedy proper) as is its inevitability, the unimpeded pace. These two functions oppose each other: containment on the formal level, and an unleashed rhythm of those desperate events, belonging to a primordial nature. The framing of misfortune, the harnessing of tragic thought, embodies in its underpinnings a mechanism of perpetual strife, and so demands a formal solution astonishing in its didactic simplicity. Such a transvaluational vision welding together the dimensions of repose and of revolt involves the uneasy piecing of parts, the healing and celebration of a world, one that belongs to Aeschylus alone of the dramatists; hence the subtle political remedy of peaceful co-existence in the herd, grafted in a true pre-Socratic thinker's mode.

Herington's notion that the trilogy is "a new and very transitory art form" characterizes precisely the difference between Aeschylus and Attic tragedy of the later Periclean age: "When we can next pick up the story of attic tragedy the earlier plays of Sophocles, that art form has vanished—and vanished forever from the tragic contests of the Dionysia."6 The form of Aeschylus' trilogy, as much as his content, gives us a strong poetic insight to the time before Socratic thought. His rough-hewn structure, his harsh metaphors, wild antinomies, and movements of seismic proportions, involving nothing less than a total concept of the race, enable us to see in Aeschylus not some limited equivocal idea of religious ritual in primitive man, but rather a cosmogony where knowledge is of a dramatic nature, where communication has a poetic structure, and understanding is achieved through subtle personifying. The philosophic conceptualization of reality which marks the pre-Socratics is embodied in Aeschylus' dramatic metaphors in which the idea cannot be isolated from the metaphor. Healing and celebration in the resolution of the trilogy become necessary parts of an intelligible structure; they authenticate the "tragedic form" where story and frame of story become one, and action is fundamentally tragic action, a victim of time and perishing.

In *The Oresteia* the outer reaches of the story—the muted past and the implied future—constitute the frame of the tragedy. The continuation of Atreus' line, the elopement of Paris and Helen, the sacrifice of Iphigeneia, the burning of Troy, the sheltering of Orestes at Phokis, Apollo's kinship argument, Athena's building of her polis—these provide the dimensions of a formally structured world. They are the events which function as the *ostensible* perimeters of the work, where the form is simple, yet ostensive, technically defined, unified and above all complete. Yet the real perimeters, the inexorable form, lurk in danger in the very breakthrough that threatens these provisional events. The sense of completeness here also embodies implicit, purposive restrictions. The importance of these restrictions becomes clear when the misfortune is virtually loosed upon the race beyond the confines of the tragedy.

Then, it follows that this completeness needs to be arbitrary, an imposed function of provisional form. This form holds within its confines not an individual in his substance, not a Klytemnestra as subject, as is often supposed in theatre aesthetics following Artistotle, but rather a giant shadow cast to threaten, in utter cruelty, the mind of the race. And such a Klytemnestra is an essence of Being.

In the fifth century, essence was not generally conceived as substance (or subject), as has been the case in the "model of a mobile order" of Western thought since Aristotle. The question of Being was explored through an essence of things in the world, rather than through the substance of particular as subject. Form for the Greek mind was mainly an ordering principle, internal and external, which made things manageable, simply understood, and may be seen by us as having pictorial and spatial qualitites. It functioned as a kind of personification aimed at concrete knowing. For Aeschylus specifically, form's most important function is the philosophical one: to see essence in a sweeping vision, the *thea* of *theatron,* and form as a means of comprehension. Whatever may be seen as tension between the thing contained and the containing form in *The Oresteia,* it needs to be understood as the cosmic force which grates against the experience of existence. To understand *The Oresteia* as evoking a model of illusion through particulars is to see it from the viewpoint of individuals in action, thus robbing it of its communal character and its serious threat. Since this viewpoint clearly limits the overall vision, we are riveted to essence, to archetypal force, rather than individual character as the major concern in the work. Character is an "efficient cause," a particular; essence is the total vision and might be understood as the "formal cause" in Aristotle's terms. Specific action, individual character, in the trilogy is a distillation of essence chosen for its "universal mythopoiesis" context. Klytemnestra as character acquires monumental significance as the Mother with a community of Kindly Ones turned Furies in the deepest recesses of her private history.

The relationship of form to essence, then, is the attempt to make the vision comprehensible, while at the same time this relationship raises "the question of Being" where tragic thought is imminent. But essence in the question of Being is not, as in Aristotle, understood through definable substance. In other words, the broad question of the race is on every level visible, and essence is only provisionally measured through the materiality of individual existence; rather, essence as vision becomes the larger formative aspect of a developing world: the piecing-together of a New Man. This kind of distinction seems necessary, for, as with the history of thought, we are living under the spectre of an "Aristotelian West" where our inherited notions on tragedy not only place us in disagreement on the superficial aesthetic level with Aeschylus, but together with Aristotle, we find ourselves opposed to the trilogic form for the very reasons that Artaud would find exulting:

> The question, then, for the theatre, is to create a metaphysics of speech, gesture, and expression, in order to rescue it from its servitude to psychology and "human interest." But all this can be of no use unless behind such an effort there is some kind of real metaphysical inclination, an appeal to certain unhabitual ideas. . . . These ideas which touch on Creation, Becoming, and Chaos, are all of a cosmic order and furnish a primary notion of a domain. . . . They are able to create a kind of passionate equation between Man, Society, Nature, and Objects.[7]

The Oresteia needs to be seen as an open, irrevocable *orama*; a three-fold *thea,* a vast and multi-dimensional picture, whose landscape touches the outermost parameters of the human and the divine world; as a work of art it stands, a point of convergence for a breadth of parallel causes which shape human and divine reality, where the spectrums of good and evil, the mystic and the rational, divine *Ate* and human *Dike,* are all brought to consciousness in an inescapable shock. It is all in all an uprooting experience. The complete work must be seen all at once as a triptych which opens into a panorama, or a tablet with three leaves or *ptychoi* unfolding in ceremonial expectancy. The first leaf of the triptych is *The Agamennon,* where the world sways with grief in its blood-guilt structuring through the use of cause-and-effect, the perception of criminal act and nemesis; the second, *The Libation Bearers,* where the entire earth is destructured and left in ruins; and the third, *The Eumenides,* where the world is pieced together and healed anew. The continuity of action is not what links the *ptychoi* together. Selective action, not of individual character, but of archetypal images on a seemingly static panoramic canvas provides both the point of linkage and the special characteristic of each *ptychos,* or formal composition, within the profound disorder of the larger reality implicit in the world of the trilogy.

The larger reality in O'Neill's trilogy is everywhere visible, the result of direct probing and constant unearthing of the psychic forces. The profound disorder within a collective fate that befalls the House of the Mannons unravels itself near the surface of the dramatic action. The structure of the trilogy becomes convincing when the cause-and-effect action is left behind by the inexorable mask that compels movement and uses, ever so elementally, psychological motivation as a mere excuse for the inevitable, born of, not a metaphysic, but a senseless *ananke.* And here lies at once the weakness and the ultimate pessimism of O'Neill's world. When Lavinia turns around to enter the house as the shutters bang closed at the end, O'Neill will salvage nothing of that world; he will romantically insist that life will have no more to do with such bloody dreams of pain. They will eradicate themselves with their built-in destruction, and Peter and Hazel will emerge uncontaminated.

Conditional to understanding *Mourning Becomes Electra* in this manner becomes the leaving behind of its psychologically motivated action-line; the rendering of that action-line to a deflective role—to be sure, an all-important function—one that occupies attitudinal space for the purpose of preparing the ground upon which to launch the larger horror that befalls the race unimpeded. To achieve such a purpose aesthetically, it becomes necessary to take O'Neill literally[8] in his insistence of the Mannon mask:

> One is struck at once by the strange impression it gives in repose of being not living flesh but a wonderfully lifelike pale mask, in which only the deep set eyes, of a dark violet blue, are alive.[9]

This of Christine's face; of the others, a similar description occurs. Consider, for example, the following. Ezra: "a mask-like look of his face in repose . . ." (263). Lavinia: "the same strange, life-like mask impression . . ." (231). Brant: "a life-like mask rather than living flesh" (240). Orin: "There is the same lifelike mask quality of his face in repose . . ." (286).

O'Neill's intent in these descriptions seems enlightening. It may be more purposeful to deal with concrete masks (whether of make-up or removable) in performance in *Mourning Becomes Electra* than it would in *The Oresteia.* Whereas Aeschylus has constructed an edifice distilled from the experience of myth through complex thought, O'Neill has gone inward to look at a single phase of the human soul and explore how that phase suffuses the particular edifice of the myth. Where Aeschylus has erected a number of masks (subjective and objective) to cover the multiple phases that he built into the verbal and the visual matrix, O'Neill reveals a single (subjective and naked) raw moment, sustained through pain and cruelty. It is, therefore, possible for our age to eliminate the much-argued convention of masks in Aeschylus without loss of power in his work; but it is questionable whether the same can be said of O'Neill.

Consider the dynamic contrast that can be created by verbal revelations, as if to a psychoanalyst-spectator, made by an imposing mask, as if from a distant past: psychic immediacy superimposed on mythic repose, the particular emerging from utter fixity, a world seen as evil. Such a contrast shows O'Neill the intuitive artist covering the gaping spaces of his dramaturgy left by O'Neill the thematic artist, who constructs a conscious psychoanalytic edifice single-mindedly. The mask, then, and its resonating force in contrast, reinstates in O'Neill's trilogy the multiple phases of the myth, taking it beyond a "mechanistic" view of the psyche. An Elektra-complex is joined by an Oedipus-complex to wreak destruction.

The trilogy acquires through the mask a connective and a cumulative significance beyond its story-pattern, without losing in modernity or elemental power. If we were to ask what constitutes trilogic structure in O'Neill, the answer would have to center around the mask as the "great mover" of events that necessitates the ideological follow-up of the unimpeded pace of misfortune. The adventure-melodrama in its subjective phase alone cannot force necessity. O'Neill himself in his Work Diary on the trilogy observed, "Mannon drama takes place on a plane where outer reality is mask of true fated reality—unreal realism."10 And even though he had some doubts about the mask while at work on the trilogy, Bogard, commenting on the Work Diary, shows the spirit with which O'Neill went into the final draft:

> The concept of the mask he decided to keep, but now he saw that make-up could achieve the effect he wanted—that of a death-mask "suddenly being torn open by passion."11

He sustained his dramatic effect throughout the trilogy, giving the individual a base from which to spring and partake of the world; his individual characters acquire dimension within the ground of the myth—and do so very much through the mask. In 1934 O'Neill wrote, "I should like to see *Mourning Becomes Electra* done entirely with masks, now that I can view it solely as a psychological play."[12] With his expressed desire the dramatist authenticates the force of the contrast and gives proper significance to the trilogic structure.

III

The Chorus as Attitudinal Stance. The communal order that underlies the trilogy manifests itself by the progressive function of the Chorus as a means of containment. The Elders are both the consciousness in which mythmaking visions occur and the internal audience for whom archetypal stories are played out. Unlike individual characters who find themselves victims on the road to society's state of knowledge, the Chorus endures through their cumulative understanding of mythmaking, through the unforced didacticism of an archetypal story. They contain the story and nurture it, but they are not specifically its victims; they take upon themselves the burden—for better or for worse— of its teachings, for theirs is an objective participation, in the main, as it spans the whole world of the trilogy. They partake subjectively where stance and reaction to an event is as crucial as the *logos* used to convey it, however subtly different that stance may be in meaning from the actual words. Thus, their participation has a double edge: on the one hand, they are the ghosts of Mycenae, the Argive world; and on the other, they are the willing spectators, fifth-century Athens, whose understanding of their world is immediately affected by myth and who must themselves partake in mythmaking to accommodate the expansion of their own *paideia* (i.e., the socio-political, spiritual, and the psycho-physical spheres of their education).

Of course, each of the three Choruses varies, but their world is constant and their function even more so—including the Chorus of Furies who are also a "community" out of the dark and mystical, out of the ageless earth. The living mass, that attitudinal, pulsating world that coalesces and informs the myth, then, becomes the real "throughline" of the trilogy—a connective with the angle of perception of an imposing necessity to go on, much like the simple syllogistic will that brings about completion. Hence, from the agile, reflective old men of the first *ptychos,* the maids-turned-accomplices of the second, to the purely active-emotive furies of the third, the Choruses form the most intelligible link of the three *ptychoi.* The effects of action remain theirs to bear, and the vast movement toward Justice is compelled on their behalf. Figures on the landscape of action are prototypes, selfless victims for the communal vision where even the gods alongside men must be given their ordered place. Their collective force acquires a further dimension when in addition they are seen as a triple mass in some cosmic, sub-real landscape of struggle for the race, apart from individual men and gods.

In a very real way, the strength and· force of the Chorus serve the function of a powerful sense of ambiguity. The peculiar "authority of ambiguity" in *The Oresteia* is so carefully entrenched that it functions as a delimiting factor on the cognitive understanding of cause and effect. It extends from the simplest aspects of structure to the more complex modes of personificational and dramatic thinking to the "ring-structures" and prolepses of imagery. Moreover, the Chorus itself by its transmutational attitude at times thrusts intuitive understanding toward more than one direction of meaning. The Chorus as embodied ambiguity, indicating in part mass-participation and reaction to human and cosmic events, is the "audience-within" in subtle control. However, it should be understood that the ambiguous construct as such reveals poetic intention and this intention works toward ambivalence as well as the sense of confusion gained by the shifting perceptions that the community of Chorus is prone to act from—or, more often, not act at all. There is always a sense of incomplete perception of the details of events involved here; thus, the Chorus assesses its position through the veil of sense perceptions, understanding only the impact of sweeping brushstrokes on the overall canvas. From the dramatist's point of view, the shifting perceptions of the Chorus are a vehicle through which he penetrates and reveals the complexity and depth of the events.

The parodos of *The Agamemnon* presents perplexity as a dramatic quality: here the Chorus is at a loss; their minds are traveling in many directions at once. They are given to a sense of free association, their perceptions traveling back and forth in time. It is not until the presence of Klytemnestra that they are jolted into confronting the present moment. They refer to their old age as "veins of leafage withering," as "aimless dreams in broad daylight" (79, 82). Clearly, Aeschylus has designed the kind of imagistic texture that will strengthen the authority of his cumulative structures of the ambiguous. Thus far in the first parodos we have seminal suggestions of eagles, of nests, of perishing young, and of transgressors. These suggestions are no more than subliminal flashes until, in a cumulative fashion, they are given body and concrete association. Their rooting becomes apparent as the story unfolds and the Chorus reveals in multiple perceptivity how these suggestive symbolic elements are woven into major significance. But the perplexity, in a multiplicity of attitudes and meanings, still remains.

Likewise in *The Choephoroi:*

> Struck in awe none may resist, none may struggle,
>   none war against of old;
> For it resounded in all men's ears,
> In all men's hearts—such respect
> exists no more. . . .   (55-58)

Here they attend to generalized perception and onomatopoeic ambiguity (in the original sounds), connected loosely through allusion to the overall thrust of the first ode. The striking intention is to reveal concrete landscape and oppressive atmosphere: the women of the Chorus strengthen their dramatic sense of responsibility through a pictorial language of allusion. They put aside for the moment their discomfort, their being awakened in the middle of the night by Klytemnestra ("She sent me here, the godless woman . . . ," 45), and encompass a larger picture; thus their scope is the human predicament which is in turn related to the specific situation of Orestes and the Argive community through allusion, veiled association, and the strength and authority of the ambiguous construct, lacking in casual sense but rich in possibility.

It is true, however, that the Chorus in *The Choephoroi* is less ambivalent and less perplexed than that of *The Agamemnon* or *The Eumenides*. Their function is virtually revolutionary. They are oppressed Elektras in their perception of the world. It is no accident that the figure Elektra springs from their midst and is left behind along with them when the oppressors are eliminated. But for all that, the Chorus are still those possessed of communal wisdom, partaking of a general vision, thus offering a link with the nonhistorical flow and ebb of the world. In *The Eumenides,* on the other hand, the Chorus are in their last throes of nightmare where shifting perceptions become a landscape of past dreams stained with blood, struggling to retain their authenticity. The allusive construct commands enormous authority within their landscape: the more they try to explain themselves the more inexplicable they remain.

> Over the victim placed on the altar
> This is our song: gash deep into reason
> Terror with frenzy, blow on the brain,
> Son of the Furies
>
> . . .
>
> At birth we drew these lots for ourselves,
> the immortals must leave hands off. . . .
> (341-44, 347-50)

Their position is understood through an intuitive grasp of myth and archetype; their essential nature is impenetrable and ambiguous in the way of anachronisms. Nevertheless, in their *antidikos* position of perverse legality they present a powerful link in the rounding out of the underlying order of the world. That underlying order, although lacking the significance of history, becomes the communal myth fraught with psychic tension. The old men of the first *ptychos* understand the ebb and flow of their world against a spatial metaphor, a landscape of indeterminate shape whose edges wander off into a sea of unknowables. It may be tempting to think of such a landscape in the shape of the orchestra of the *theatron,* but we would not be able to account for the "eternal return" principle, the circularity of time, in Aeschylus' thought. Rather, it is more fruitful to adduce and look for significance in the landscape as a pictorial vision, where perishing leaves a profound sadness and time is fundamentally moral and egressive, that is, transitory. So with the community of *The Agamemnon:* time reveals itself through patches of light as from an eclipse; it becomes transvaluational, thus strengthening the mythic context as partaking fundamentally of space. The old men travel the gamut of the landscape from Aulis to Troy and back again, ignoring the "wound" of history, its objectivity and ultimate impenetrable metaphysic. Instead, they cling to personification to reveal (mystically to themselves) the Zeus-first-Principle; likewise, they need the transvaluation principle for understanding the moral perishing in time.

Space, on the other hand, is a constant and functions as an authoritative sea of ambiguity. It is penetrated through myth and archetypal sensation. Dramatic form relates by way of complement to the overall spatial metaphor of the work. In the second leaf of the triptych, the link of underlying order emerges in the very hues of oppression. The women suffer that coloration of blight. Nothing is in order, even the color of the world is off within the communal revelation. The Chorus itself must partake in its own cleansing and subsequent terror. They help move the world a step back to the black dream of the Furies before the decisive leap into Justice and the objective world of historical apprehension.

These ideas, which emerge through a theatrical understanding of the Chorus-function, are in themselves dramatic. Personification, pictorialization, and coloration are raw dramatic qualities. Because Aeschylus uses them to reveal a grand design, a colossal leap out of myth and repose and into history, he does not mean for us to ignore the essentially dramatic content of thought. Through abstraction he is revealing the astonishing drama of culture in his century: there is no difference between thought and the theatre since all expression is dramatic. But it is fair to reiterate that these notions become clear only when we take the protagonist of *The Oresteia* to be the communal vision of the world, the Chorus themselves.

What is meant by the Chorus as protagonist is that it stands as ground upon (and through) which a moral structure is built. This unit becomes the relationship of general ground to particular character with oscillatory movement. The Chorus are possessed with communal wisdom, but understand little of the individuation; they, as Chorus, seem only to accept the necessity for individual consciousness, together with its attendant tragic overtones. Their response to individual action is austere; their apprehension of individual consciousness is of a tragic chord in their own world. Individuation is either an Agamemnon crossing a sea of blood or an Orestes plunged into the frenzied nightmare of matricide. It is either a Klytemnestra unable to decipher and cope with the lust of her house or it is Kassandra dying in full lust for her Apollo—or at best it may be the culmination of the oppressed in the twisted wretchedness of an Elektra. In any case, the wisdom of the herd is to be preferred as refuge. Individualism is again a *thymele* for the distillation of communal knowledge. The oscillation from Chorus to individual character and back again is on the one hand a way for communal wisdom to perfect itself, and on the other a means to reach, and cope with, the tragic chord in their moral world. Take, for example, Agamemnon's return: there the Chorus display the mood of premonition, not unlike that of the Watchman in the prologue, for they are unable to articulate any clear edge of knowledge. Likewise with their relationship to Kassandra before she enters the palace. However, this principle is momentarily reversed in *The Choephoroi* as Kilissa carries the burden of general knowledge during the striking dramatic twist of turning the women into accomplices; in this instance it is clear that they are acting more in the person of "Electras" than in their formal Chorus-function. Again, in the last play the principle of the movement from ground to affective particular obtains, especially with the Furies' relation to Orestes, or for that matter to Apollo or Athena.

The implied psychoanalyst-spectator built deep into the "confessional" scheme of O'Neill's trilogy serves the function of Chorus as a means of containment. In his concern to parallel "the old stories," O'Neill naturally offers the peripheral characters, the various gossips, as Chorus. But in fact they are no more than conventions of realism, probably to offset the dramatist's deeper intuition, so that he can work unhindered with his five characters toward that swift and bold excitement of the dialogue, riveted to a morbid fascination of transmitting self-knowledge in often painful terms. The ground that "receives" this self-knowledge is the Aeschylean Chorus translated into psychoanalyst *cum* spectator. The story of the Mannons (like that of Atreus' clan) nurtures the psychoanalyst-spectator-Chorus as a "partaker" in the myth of a special kind of reality. This provides the morbid fascination to *stay with* the Mannons, to hear them out, for we are a part in the making of their myth. Ours may be an objective participation, but our stance beyond the meaning of words is fundamentally dramatic and subjective—even should one take the stance of utter rejection of the Elektra and Oedipal upheavals of Lavinia and Orin. We as psychoanalyst-spectator-Chorus take a silent role in providing a dimension and a relation of self in an agonizing form of *gnothiseauton* in the world.

O'Neill's characters speak in constant agony; and, like that of Aeschylus, it is a distilled speech, not incidental and realistic, but true and real without the usual conventions of conversation. That in itself provides the clue that these characters are mythic constructs of our own modern consciousness, and we provide for them a ground. We have placed ourselves clinically in an open scientific domain from whence O'Neill's characters will appropriate their authenticity. Here the modern dramatist has read his classical theatre with unsurpassing insight; for, what is different between Aeschylus and his audience-Chorus and O'Neill and his "triumvirate"? *Mythopoiesis* is the protensive outcome of both, through a kind of discomfort, cruelty, embarrassment in Artaud's theatre. *Mythopoiesis* is only possible with an "intervention" from without the aesthetic construct. O'Neill achieves it through the imperceptible diction which is unreal enough and painful enough to engage the spectator through the deepest recesses of self and authenticate the psychic forces in his character.

The odd connection of choric song in O'Neill begins on the surface with the chanties "Shenandoah" or "Hanging Johnny" to set an atmosphere which will lead toward a pervading lyricism evoked in us through lilacs, cannon blasts, neo-classical porticos, and foreboding silences—not unlike the odes of *The Agamemnon,* or the moments before the murder of Klytemnestra and Aegisthos in *The Choephoroi.* The various soliloquies, too, no matter how carefully they blend into the realistic frame, serve as reflective moments for the "psychoanalyst" and reveal a different relation of character to "Chorus" while in contemplation from the driven relation while in action.

The choric ode is dramatic not only because it tells a story of conflict, but also because of the relationship of the Chorus to the story and that of the audience to the story. The story of Paris in itself is of limited significance. But the *attitude* of teller and spectator towards Paris' exploits, the lyricism and the response, invests the story with powerful feelings of ambivalence. It is, then, the "how" and the "why" of story within an ode and not so much the story in and of itself.

For a total view of the work, for a full understanding, the answer lies in performance, for only there can the how and the why be authenticated and worked into the fabric. Attitude holds the key to meaning. Understanding attitude in choric passages reveals the reason for parabolic language and allusive choices in story-telling. In performance language, attitude involves the identification impulse of the spectator, thus making him a part of the communal vision while witnessing his archetypal world in the process of mythmaking. As we wonder what it is that jolts us into the performance proper when watching *The Oresteia* unfold, the Chorus is always there to authenticate our wonderment through their attitudinal sifting and multiplicity of perspectives. They, too, wonder, and do so through dramatic expression. Before long, then, we begin to grasp, albeit ambiguously, that what is going on before us concerns us archetypally in precisely the same way that it concerns the Chorus. That feeling is inescapable.

The relationship between communal vision and individual action functions as nature does to a life form, where the individual "feeds" provisionally from the vision. That vision leads itself only conditionally to whatever is tragic in individual action. The proviso is the individual's awareness toward a common perfectibility as the commune's price for partaking in the tragic. The Chorus *cum* spectator can apprehend their own relationship to action provisionally as containment, as the ground from which such action springs. The communal vision of the Chorus in *The Agamemnon* harbors the individual and lends a base, a universal referent ground, for action and suffering. That action turns back on itself and comes to haunt the community through the Chorus, whence it received its real ground. Again, it is important to characterize the Chorus in this role in order to understand the tragic overtones which spring from the relationship between the individual stage-figure and the Chorus as his world, the ground of his suffering.

An irrevocable sense of disorder stands as the constant threat to that relationship. Understanding of the tragic involves an intimate grasp of choric song, its resolve into a "beacon speech," and back again to choric plaintive evaluation through parabolic attitudes. The relationship is simple; it is hardly determined by anything other than an ethic of individualism and perishing. Individualism becomes the trap of perfectibility; and, in relation to a communal vision of the world, individualism is fatal. It stirs irrevocable disorder in the person of Agamemnon, of Klytemnestra, even of Orestes. In O'Neill, Lavinia

and Orin suffer the blight of individualism in their fatal attempt
to perfect what is cruelly imperfect. But there is no "blame"
attached to attempts at individuation; to the Greek world it is
the *pathei-mathos* principle, which is supposed to bring about
the condition of calm after the storm. Even so, "understanding
through suffering" is particularly terrifying, because communal
understanding is different from individual anguish: the Chorus
know little of Kassandra's *pathei-mathos;* and even less, in
another mythmaking ritual, of Oedipus at the end of the
Coloneus. The relationship, then, that *reductio* concept, between
the herd and the individual is fraught with danger and points
rather decidedly toward a tragic end—but not, for all that, in a
pre-determined fashion.

Again, it is this relationship which is involved in the resolution. Not only in the resolution as regards the human dilemma,
but as it concerns the divine paradox as well. If Apollo or the
earth spirits are blood-thirsty, they must find a means to resolve
their godhood dilemma in relation to the divine community. Of
course, the human resolution goes a long ways toward disarming
the divine paradox, but not I think all the way. Order and calm
are an artifice with a relationship to chaos which, again, is
fraught with danger; in a proper sense this artifice is the mean,
the precarious and sought-after balance, between inertia and
excess. It is precisely what Athena's aim is for her polis in the
third play.

The difficulty with grasping the elemental thrust of the
resolution in *The Eumenides* rests with the over-simplified
paradox of the deities, and hence of the universe. Perhaps more
importantly, the difficulty rests with the virtual irony implied
in the simplistic bickering amongst the personified forces of the
world within a very human landscape. But maybe that difficulty
really lies with the modern consciousness. In Wellek's view,
"The Greeks differ from us in their feeling for landscape and
nature: they do not know the mechanistic view of the universe;
they see nature animated and lived in. . . . The Greeks are
objective, unselfconscious, and direct in their ethical relations."13 Hence it is fashionable to assume the "unselfconscious"
healing and celebration at the end as something foreign to us.

And yet, inasmuch as the idea remains dramatic, it is not
a foreign idea. The fact that the Greeks see nature as animated
and lived in and have no inkling of a mechanistic universe sheds

light on the offhand manner of characterizing the gods in *The Eumenides*. Human life is open; it is public: the Gods must be given a clear and simple place in the "animated and lived in" nature. The order which they, in collusion with humans, help to bring about is a social order embodying diversity. The divine agents, along with the human agents—the voting citizens of Athens at the end—have made a firm commitment toward altering the communal vision of calm. Instead of trying to find such calm in the House and its lustful interrelationships, instead of trying to find it in the release from oppression through vengeance, such order and calm can be achieved through a sharp break, through a cultural leap, from the House to the Polis as focal understanding of the world.

Thus in the third *ptychos* the expansive vision of the priestess—unlike that of Apollo's Kassandra of violence and lustful disorder—is far reaching in its adherence to order and calm. It gives a clue to humanized religion and unassuming virtue; and it carves a delicate balance *(meson)* out of animal instincts and tradition, egress and pro-gress, discord and harmony. This Apollo representative has already conformed to Athena's lightning-energized world of social justice and humble existence with the modest olive branch as its symbol. The remarkable sense of quiet, warm light approaching as of a time when things die and new things are born, a world of infinite possibilities settling all around Delphi—these moments give the spectator supreme confidence and profound calm. Somehow the community of mythmaking spectators will now rest easy only to observe the appropriately light-hearted "tragedy" of the Furies, the deities which must no longer reign. The Priestess at Delphi conveys the mood for the pious, religious-like *transubstantiation* from Furies to Erinyes; a change which involves the very order of the world: a dissolution of the *ousia* of a blood-avenging order, and a realignment—a transubstantiation—of that *ousia* to another landscape, that of social order and communal justice.

IV

Containing Myth, Gods, and Men. An important idea virtually overlooked in the trilogy, that of transubstantiation, resonates much like the beacon trail. Social reason, a rather concrete concept for the Greeks, is transubstantiated into the plane of godhood where man in pictorial actuality possesses the fruit of such reason, and tangentially has a hand in the making of social justice. Social justice is a *teleios*-type of ground where accord and perfectibility are the norm. Life on such a landscape is public; it entails a break with the subjective order, and demands a rejection of the cabalistic view of the unknowable. Understanding the view of life as public goes a long way to justify the existence of the Chorus at the center of Greek Tragedy. Concrete elements are often manifestations of spirit-concepts, a dissolution on the one hand and a subsequent re-alignment into a concrete spatial reality on another plane. Transubstantiation, then, is fundamentally dramatic, and insofar as it is also pictorial, it can best be understood through theatrical realization.

Aeschylus in his theatre is deeply concerned with turning communal vision—a kind of intellectual archetype—into theatrical substance which operates by way of cumulative pictorial expanse. This is a parallel idea to the fact that the trilogic dramatist was concerned with time as process. Time in *The Oresteia*, in part, unlocks the riddle of the Chthonic and Olympic elements. Past events must be forever considered on the stage of present time where aetiological history is not yet a question. As time becomes suspended and turns into a vision, historical consciousness is nowhere apparent. In Kassandra's moments the time-vision is manifested in a set of pictures, where past (*Ag.* 1197ff.) and future (*Ag.* 1280ff.) are exploded by the immediate vision of the present: what is now happening inside the palace.

But perhaps the most significant understanding of transubstantiation involves the total story with all its unfolding parallels and proleptic process:14 the myth is Mycenean. The sophistication of the story belongs to the fifth century. No doubt the status of the myth has shifted somewhat, and perhaps its meaning is now pointing in a different direction, to a more subtle form of communication. The difference, of course, is the re-alignment of the fragmented forces of meaning from the past toward a new realization through dramatic process. True, the archetypal lines of the myth did not originate with the fifth century (nor for that matter with Homer or Hesiod), and in that sense Aeschylus' age was not mytho-poeic; but it cannot be disputed that the myths were really *made* anew, remolded in a "dramatico-poeic" fashion. It is inevitable that this should be the case since religion for the Greeks was not doctrinaire, and transvaluation of religion was constant through cults and acts of one kind or another, remolding even the received stories of their gods in order to accommodate new insights and perspectives. The myths as religion in Aeschylus' time presented the most important means for sensing and managing the world as reality. This manner of thinking is the simplest of all, for it involves transubstantiation at every level, often out of the concrete and into a concept—as it must surely be the case in the attempt to grasp Zeus in the famous ode of *The Agamamnon.* It is simple in the sense that it does not appear to be weighted down with paradox and mysticism. Something is either knowable or it is not; if it is not, some aspect of personification is attributed to it and a forged penetration becomes possible ("Zeus. . . . if to be called by this name pleases him").

We have here a preliminary form of understanding something about the unknowable. The communal relationship to the gods in the darker vision of the world remains mythic. Agamemnon relates to Zeus through an omen; Orestes relates to Apollo before the deed through a command; but the tangibility—or dramatic actuality in Orestes' action and response—of Apollo and Athena in the third *ptychos* signifies as transubstantiation in contrast to the less tangible, merely schematic relationship between men and gods in the Klytemnestra-Agamemnon events. The overall movement in processional time is clear. What is less clear, however, is how this movement relates to space. It is a simple operation, yet it must be apprehended complexly as regards its rather profound implications. No scientific view can help in this respect, as it will involve the mechanistic aspects of the universe, and that is altogether inappropriate. Consider: the suggestion that Zeus "occupies" a certain space runs through every instance where the Olympian hierarchy is mentioned. To the point is the second stanza of the hymn (*Ag.* 167-75) which is so suggestive of the plight of Orestes in *The Choephoroi* that it might be thought that the dramatist is creating a "spatial parallel" between Zeus and Orestes as they both struggle to free themselves from the catapulting dark visions of dethronement and perishing on the one hand and blood-guilt on the other.

Consider also that the spatial proximity of the gods is greater as the trilogy moves to its methodic conclusion; until at the last stand, they occupy virtual space, and in fact are to be found at a specific hillside. Finley believes that "Space to

Aeschylus is time's concomitant." The idea here is that space herds itself into contraction to keep its constant bond with past time, which is singular and continuing present. And further, "If space is conceived as the mind's free dimension and place as the actual setting where, since we are not gods, our limited lives must be worked out, then freedom seems for Aeschylus some sort of merging of space with place."15 True, but it is also the sort of freedom which seeks to merge place with "vast time."16 In *The Oresteia* this is achieved through the principle of transubstantiation as it obtains from the earlier proleptic elements through to the more theatrical developments in concrete dramatic terms. The re-alignment of the gods is perhaps the most powerful of several paradigmatic parallels. Here is a certain freedom attained, which is both artistic and cultural in the concomitant relationship between space and time.

The gods change in exact proportion to the changing concept of justice. The community of men change under the impact of justice, and so the gods which men transubstantiate are molded to their vision of the just in life. The non-doctrinaire aspect of cult religion allows for a good deal of shifting, re-evaluating, and re-forming of god-hero legends. These legends are shaped by communal men in action, not historically but spatio-culturally, i.e., the legend of Helen is spread across different regions. In one case it is intimately connected with Aphrodite; in another, it is irrationally thought that Helen went instead to Egypt rather than to Troy. That she is "responsible" for the great war is a cultural possibility, as are the other variations. The god-hero mythology is not static. Religion has no fixity. It is a kind of mythopoiesis and that is a function of consciousness all too human: ritual and dream being the throes of vision, conscious and unconscious, intensified for the process of mythmaking.

Mythopoiesis is here understood as the artistic description of mythmaking or reformulation of cult legend. Ostensibly, it is not the same as mythopoiesis in limbo for the bare essentials of communication; but in Aeschylus it may well be for the bare essentials of the intellect. Thought in its nascent form in Aeschylus is to be found in that union of ritual-dream. The running proleptic explorations of dreams and omens through *The Oresteia* reveal sparingly the "pre-logical" and "pre-verbal" necessity for action, as in the case of Kassandra's maddened vision or Orestes' thrust of the sword in his mother's womb. Likewise, it is a "social expression" of ritual and dream which "mythopoiesizes" with the tools of the god-hero legends toward a communal religious end—and, for Aeschylus' ancillary purpose, toward an artistic end as well. Conclusively, *mythos* and *dianoia* in *The Oresteia* are the proponents both of mythopoiesis toward justice in gods and men, and of creativity therefrom toward an artistic end.

The gods in Aeschylus function as developing paradigms within human consciousness, and the source of divine evolution is *to a significant degree,* though not exclusively, the human mind. If this point has thus far been understood as no more than an allusive suggestion, it is because we must first locate some sort of satisfactory if provisional answer to the following question: Does Aeschylus, in fact, see the divine as an actual force, and the change in human consciousness as a reconciliation of the human and the divine reality—or does he see the divine as created by the human imagination?

There is more than one answer to this type of question, and whatever we posit can only serve as a theorem. First, it is eminently clear that Aeschylus is concerned with the *possibility* of the divine beyond the reach of the human mind. This is his point of pessimism. However, as a dramatist perhaps ought, he wavers much in the fashion of Heracleitos. The pessimism lasts as long as the Hymn to Zeus; it lasts as long as Eteocles' powerful howl against the unknowable just before he assigns himself to fight against his brother at the seventh gate; and perhaps as long as Io is in fact on stage. It is the terrifying factor of his metaphysics. Heracleitos in Fragment 119 frames the dilemma appropriately: "Wisdom is one and unique; it is unwilling and yet willing to be called by the name of Zeus."17 The "unwillingness" for Aeschylus is no more than the dark spots in the bright sun of the human mind. And, when the human imagination finds Zeus is unwilling, things have no shape, there is little drama; his unwillingness becomes conceptual philosophy. The world becomes properly dramatic when we find him *willing to be called names.*

The second and more theatrical answer is the diametrical opposite of the first. We are confronted in Aeschylus with an overriding concern with process, a kind of development in the divine. It is easy to underrate this development as a mere theatrical convention; yet we know that convention with the Greeks is tied to communicative reality, commanding greater authority than similar conventions might have in the modern theatre. Further, it is safe to suppose that Aeschylus' use of "devices" has a many layered function carefully thought out. We cannot, therefore, assume because he represents gods as stage-figures that he does not mean they undergo a change in an immediate dramatic sense, in the same way that the communal structure undergoes change. We must not assume this for the drama, the artistic unit as such. But we can modify our rejections of such an assumption *to a degree* when we remember Zeus and the *terror of the unknowable*. The real burden lies with the just understanding of the divine alongside the human, and the role the imagination plays in the human formulation of the divine. Pylades is not imagined, yet Apollo *is* during the second part of the trilogy. The proleptic emblem of Pylades-Apollo becomes *shaped* into the actual Apollo as the necessity of the human mind demands. In a sense it is artistic necessity— or at least it is cloaked in that guise—at first. But it loses no time to fire the imagination toward "this *may* be the whole truth"—though the power of the human mind, through the commanding vision of the poet, does not allow for such total complacency by using the tantalizing position of the inner dark forces beneath the rock, the bulwark which houses communal justice that ranges from the divine to the human.

Now that we have partially understood the basic question of the gods in *The Oresteia* we should make an attempt to locate individual man, if "individual" is not a contradiction in the terms we have thus far been using. In fact, the use of "communal theatre" as an operative term does not exclude the individual; it merely places him in a proper perspective in regard to the communal vision. The good life for an individual in the trilogy is marked by victory which entails lust and bloodshed; the non-moral life, its relative opposite, is marked by victimization which also entails lust and bloodshed. Lust and violence comprise the common factor apparent in the two types of individual existence in *The Oresteia*. The solution to the dilemma is inevitably a moral one—under which metaphysics, culture, politics are subsumed. It is not surprising that the Greeks understood the workings of the world to be fundamenally ethical, and, by the time of Plato's Academy, philosopher and artist were both in search of "the good life."

Agamemnon, Klytemnestra, Kassandra, Elektra, Orestes—all these, whatever societal forces they may be carriers of, are marked by individual lust and violence. They belong to a House (Kassandra to a different but equally complex one) which cannot contain their lust. The House has a built-in fire of eros which cannot be accommodated under simple family jurisdiction. Individuals in the House seek to abandon the cloak of tactile intimacy within their own hearth and search for their solution outside the family where history may absolve and define them. The distinctive energy of human lust is thus contained within communal recognition, and violence is now understood as the incontinent act—an action which does not partake of Athena's rock with its communal recognition of opposites as balance and continence. Victory is no longer—during the healing and celebration—to be understood as an individual solution. Orestes disappears and is forgotten when instead of victory conditional existence becomes the New Man.

Nature and reason, chaos (accident) and cosmic reality (justice, the good life) are dichotomies in whose unity is found not only harmony but also the locus of disintegration. The unsettling mood at the end of the trilogy is the unity between Athena and the Furies. That very harmony is also the tragic muse. Such harmony redeems; it exonerates. But it fails to transform; it merely tames, and leaves a profound unhappiness beneath the exaltation. Individualism in our modern sense, as we've come to understand it, say through Ibsen, is not to be found here. When *The Oresteia* is over, we are numb from the pain. But we are also historically conscious and for the moment consoled in the exaltation of history. And we know that the tragic muse will always be at hand lest we forget the ground of conflict. But historical man presents no consolation. In fact to the Greek mind historical man may have remained a condition, something to be mistrusted, to be in awe of. At least Aeschylus, in the extant works, has not dealt conclusively with the individuality of historical man. He abandons the individual at the outskirts of history, still within the visionary structure of the world. He deals with history, unquestionably; but not without the vision, and not with individual man within history. He stops just short of an Orestes in the midst of Athenian democracy.

This is not unlike the profoundly mythic testament of Genet's modernism in the theatre. His statement may just as well be that of Aeschylus:

> One goal of the theatre is to help us escape so-called 'historical' time, which is really theological time. From the very start of the theatrical event, the time-flow belongs to no calibrated calendar. . . . Even if 'historical' time (I mean time marked from a mythical and controversial event, called Advent) does not entirely vanish from the spectators' consciousness, another time, with neither a beginning nor an end, unfolds, in which the spectator lives fully: it destroys the historical conventions necessitated by social life and in so doing also destroys social conventions—not in order to create just any kind of disorder, but rather to pave the way for liberation. The dramatic event now suspended—on its own time, outside of recorded time— has led to a vertiginous liberation.[18]

Of course Genet does not speak of healing and celebration as formal artistic completion; he is content with the sophisticated "vertiginous liberation." The difference, if any, is small. The modern theatre in more recent years has been returning to its roots toward mythic individuation and the world of vision, rather than face slow death within the oversaturation of psychological individualism. Aeschylus faced the same problem in reverse: historical man as a necessity authenticated his tragic muse; he became the barbaric possibility that would reach the inaccessible and heal the wounds, lessen the fires of lust, and resolve in a human way the divine force. The dramatist is ambivalent, mistrustful of the solution; he walks a tightrope and the tragic is everywhere imminent—even beyond the solution itself.

If we remember that Aeschylus is dealing on two very powerful levels with this mistrust, the dilemma becomes even more dramatic for the race. On the one hand he is taking up a received myth with all its glorious implications for the race, then he is remaking it for his own century, and between the "received" and the "remaking" of the myth lies the critical dimension which conveys a sad mistrust of history. On the second layer, this mistrust is delivered subtly in the progression of the work unaided by prior communication between myth and spectator. The individual himself is the carrier of this mistrust. If we take the second level to be the work itself conceived in historical time, in the fifth century (relying and not-relying on prior myth-communication), then we see Agamemnon as failing to achieve anything through victory; we see Klytemnestra as a victim of process; we see Kassandra lost to a lustful misapprehension of the divine; and finally, Elektra (presumably) and Orestes (surely) absolved by and lost in the ultimate communal vision of Athenian history. That is the second layer of communication within the trilogy, which, naturally, is not possible without—nor separable from—the first.

The end of the trilogy with its transmutation of primeval discord into social harmony relies on an exaltation of communal man; it rests its case on the matrix of social forces. This is a collective character which men create for themselves: the polis. But the artifice of transmutation is everywhere visible. It is in fact a spectacle carved in pictorial expanse: the tragic muse itself, its affirmation. In the final vision of profound unhappiness, through the cry of pain in the dark and the cry for joy in the light, the poet authenticates his art. The polis (man creating his own history) has the tragic muse to remind it of its dark forces, of how it contains its own disintegration. Likewise, the tragic muse has the polis which authenticates the vision. Unquestionably, this is not a way of explaining the phenomenon of Greek tragedy. But it is one way of understanding that culture's massive need for it—the reasons it flourished so close to the center of the sociopolicial sphere.

14:2 (Summer 1980)

NOTES

1 Antonin Artaud, *Aliéner l'Acteur*, 12 May 1947, as quoted by Martin Esslin, *Artaud* (London: John Calder, 1976), p. 76.

2 Stanford Drama, *Aischylos' The Oresteia Trilogy*, dir. and trans. John Chioles, Stanford, Calif., 24 February 1976. References are given in the text parenthetically from this translation-production.

3 Antonin Artaud, *Oeuvres Complètes* (Paris: Gallimard, 1956-57), IV, 37, as quoted by Naomi Greene, *Antonin Artaud: Poet Without Words* (New York: Simon and Schuster, 1970), p. 115.

4 I have dealt with this issue elsewhere; see John Chioles, "A Phenomenological Inquiry into Some of the Literary/Dramatic Aspects of Beckett, Shakespeare, and Sophocles," *Annual Scholarly Publications, The School of Philosophy, University of Athens*—ΕΕΦΣΠΑ—(Athens: Athens Univ. Press, 1979), Ksʹ, 430-91).

5 Philip Wheelwright, *Heraclitus* (Princeton: Princeton Univ. Press, 1959), p. 102.

6 C. J. Herington, *The Author of the Prometheus Bound* (Austin: Univ. of Texas Press, 1970), p. 87.

7 Antonin Artaud, *The Theatre and its Double*, trans. Mary Caroline Richards (New York: Grove Press, 1958), p. 90.

8 Two productions of the '70's which opted out for a surface realism, ignoring O'Neill's directions on masks, ended up with unconvincing performances, making even the writing appear embarrassing: American Shakespeare Festival, *Mourning Becomes Electra*, dir. Michael Kahn, Stratford, Conn., Summer 1971; and Circle in the Square, dir. Theodore Mann, New York, Winter 1973.

9 Eugene O'Neill, *Three Plays of Eugene O'Neill* (New York: Vintage Books, 1959), p. 230. Future references are to this edition by pagination in the text.

10 Eugene O'Neill, *Work Diary* (unpublished), as quoted by Travis Bogard, *Contour in Time: The Plays of Eugene O'Neill* (New York: Oxford Univ. Press, 1972), p. 339.

11 Ibid., p. 338.

12 Eugene O'Neill, *Work Diary* (unpublished), as quoted in Leonard Chabrowe, *Ritual and Pathos—The Theatre of O'Neill* (Lewisburg: Bucknell Univ. Press, 1976), p. 212.

13 Rene Wellek, *A History of Modern Criticism: 1750-1950* (New Haven: Yale Univ. Press, 1955), I, 238.

14 Anne Lebeck, *The Oresteia: A Study in Language and Structure* (Washington: Center for Hellenic Studies, distrib. Harvard Univ. Press, 1971), p. 1: "The form which repetition or recurrence takes in the *Oresteia* is that of proleptic introduction and gradual development. The word 'prolepsis' here denotes a brief initial statement of several major themes *en bloc*. The full development toward which each repetition builds may not occur for several hundred lines." While Lebeck uses the term to denote image patterns, I take it to be applicable to the total scheme as well.

15 John H. Finley, Jr., *Four Stages of Greek Thought* (Stanford: Stanford Univ. Press), p. 37.

16 *chronos . . . makros* in Sophocles' *Oedipus Coloneus*, vv. 7-8, is a case in point.

17 Philip Wheelwright, *Heraclitus* (Princeton: Princeton Univ. Press, 1959), p. 102.

18 Kelley Morris, compiler, *Genet/Ionesco: The Theatre of the Double; A Critical Anthology* (New York: Bantam Books, 1969), p. 108-09.

Correcting Some Errors
in Annals of O'Neill

Louis Sheaffer

"It is extraordinarily moving to find the inmost track of a man's life and to decipher the signs he has left us." Saul Bellow, *The New York Review of Books*, Feb. 17, 1983.

Eugene O'Neill was generally critical of what was written about him. When his first biographer, Barrett H. Clark, sent him a sketch based on a number of sources—on interviews and articles in newspapers and magazines, on material drawn from questioning O'Neill's friends and associates—the playwright wrote back that the sketch "is legend. It isn't really true. It isn't I" (*Clark*, p. 7).

Decades later he sounded a similar note while reminiscing about his life to Hamilton Basso, who was writing a "Profile" of him for *The New Yorker*. (This was the last time he ever was interviewed for public print.) After his wife Carlotta Monterey had interjected, in one of his sessions with Basso, that "nearly everything" that had been written about him was "all wrong," O'Neill added: "What Carlotta just said is true. Nearly

83

everything that has been said about me *is* all wrong" (*Basso*, 3/13/48).

Since he felt this way, you would imagine that he must have made some efforts to correct the record; yet, on the whole, the opposite appears true. According to Barrett Clark, Miss Monterey once told him that she had "discussed with her husband the anecdotes I had picked up from time to time. She had had 'quite a talk about these things, and I begged him to take the time some day and go over them with you, straightening out the anecdotes, putting "truth" in them! He said, "Nonsense, what do I care what they say—the further from the truth they have it, the more privacy I have! It's like a mask!" ' " (*Clark*, p. 8)

O'Neill did more than take comfort from his "mask"; he helped to create it. From years of researching his life to write a comprehensive biography, I found a good many errors in print, chiefly about the years before he became famous, and it turned out that some of them could be traced to O'Neill himself. He gave misleading impressions or accounts, for instance, of his seagoing career, of his suicide attempt at Jimmy the Priest's (the waterfront dive that would give him material for both *Anna Christie* and *The Iceman Cometh*) and of his brief fling at acting with his father in vaudeville. By and large, however, others were responsible for the errors that I have noted and corrected here. (For the sources identified by a catchword in the text, see the list of works cited at the end of the article.)

*   *   *

Forebears. "I know little about my father's parents," Eugene replied to a writer who was working on a monograph of James O'Neill. "Or about his brothers and sisters. He had two older brothers, I think. I remember him saying one brother served in the Civil War . . . was wounded, never fully recovered and died right after the war. He had three sisters, all dead now [in 1940], whom he never saw except when a theatrical tour brought him to the Middle West where they lived" *(San Francisco)*.

In one respect, regarding the sisters, O'Neill's account is inaccurate. According to Mary Keenan, a cousin of the playwright, James O'Neill had five sisters, not three, while yet another relative, Manley W. Mallett, who has done extensive genealogical research on the O'Neills, discovered that there were six. The following family history is partly based on Mr.

Mallett's summary of his findings. (Letter from MWM to LS, 11/12/74; for previous accounts of James O'Neill's parents and siblings, see: *Bowen*, pp. 23-24; *Alexander*, pp. 29-30; *Gelb*, pp. 20-22; and *Sheaffer I*, pp. 27-28.)

James O'Neill's parents were third or fourth cousins, with Mary, the mother, hailing from the "Black Nialls" and the father, Edward, who was about twenty years older than his wife, from the "Red Nialls." Fleeing from the potato famine in Ireland, they sailed about 1850 with their eight children on the *Great India* to Quebec, a voyage of six weeks, and settled in Buffalo, where their ninth and final child was born. Richard, the oldest one, died relatively young, while the family still lived in Buffalo. The other children, in the order of birth, were Josephine, Anna, Edward, the Civil War veteran; James, Mary, Delia, Anastasia (Mr. Mallett's grandmother), and Margaret.

After the family had lived in Buffalo a few years, the father, leaving his family to shift for themselves, returned to Ireland, where he died soon afterward from poisoning. One of Mr. Mallett's sources of information, his uncle Frank A. Kunckel (a son of Anastasia), told him that the elder O'Neill was "poisoned by saleratus bisquits baked by his favorite niece. She had mistaken a can of strychnine for baking soda."

Eugene O'Neill, who had heard about the poisoning from his father, mentions it in a secret document he wrote, intended solely and strictly for his own eyes, in which he summarized his parents' family backgrounds and their early years together. The paper was an attempt on O'Neill's part to organize his thoughts about the forces that had shaped his elders and, in turn, himself. The paper reads, in part:

"M [his mother]—Lonely life—spoiled before marriage . . . fashionable convent girl—religious & naive . . . ostracism after marriage due to husband's profession—lonely life after marriage . . . husband man's man—heavy drinker—out with men until small hours every night . . . stingy about money due to his childhood experience with grinding poverty after his father deserted large family to return to Ireland to spend last days (He died of poison taken by mistake although there is suspicion of suicide here in a fit of insane depression—guilty conscience for desertion (?) (In later days of his life husband periodically talks when depressed of doing as his father did, deserting family, going back to Ireland to die . . ." (*Sheaffer II*, pp. 509-12).

In *Long Day's Journey Into Night* the playwright-son again referred to his grandfather's abrupt death when he has James Tyrone (read James O'Neill) say: "When I was ten my father deserted my mother and went back to Ireland to die. Which he did soon enough, and deserved to, and I hope he's roasting in hell. He mistook rat poison for flour, or sugar, or something. There was gossip it wasn't by mistake but that's a lie. No one in my family ever—"

By 1860, after nearly ten years in Buffalo, Mary O'Neill was living in Cincinnati with her younger children, including James; the older ones, while still quite young, had left their hard-pressed mother to strike out on their own. "The eldest daughter Josephine," Mr. Mallett writes, "was said to have been married at the age of 13 to a prosperous saloon keeper from Covington, Ky. In any event, she apparently was well established in the Cincinnati area before her father died and no doubt was instrumental in moving the family from Buffalo."

Mr. Mallett next alludes to a published interview with James O'Neill in which he said that when aged about fourteen he went to work for a brother-in-law who dealt in military uniforms in Norfolk, Virginia, during the Civil War. "He was a man of liberal tastes," said James, "and, liking the theater, took me with him twice a week. It was then that I formed my taste for the theater. When the war was over my brother-in-law sold out his business and moved back to Cincinnati, and I went with him" (*Theater Magazine*, April 1908).

"If James O'Neill's story of living in Norfolk with an older sister is true," Mr. Mallett continues, "only Josephine could meet the description. As I knew her at age 80, she was . . . tall, erect, energetic, well-read and cultured. She seemed to have always lived well, but never had any children, and might well have taken an interest in this young brother." Apparently overlooking that he knew this great aunt and his grandmother only in their final years, Mr. Mallett adds, "Neither Josephine nor Stasia spoke with the Irish brogue which James struggled to overcome [as an actor]."

Since James' contacts with his sisters and their families appear to have been minimal after he had turned actor, it seems likely that his relatives tended at once to admire and resent him, an assumption that is verified by Frank Kunckel. In a letter to his nephew, Mr. Mallett, in 1937, he said: "I can still see him strutting across the stage and hear him call out, 'The world is mine!' He married a Cleveland Society Girl who was close to a Millionairess, and that [was] the reason we never saw or became intimately acquainted with him, and as far as [his being our] uncle, us poor kids might just as well not had an uncle."

"My uncle [James O'Neill] hardly knew his sister Stacia's married name." Rather cryptically, he added, "But if my father, your Granddad, had been a little reasonable, things might have been better."

Turning his thoughts to another side of the family of whom he was critical, Mr. Kunckel wrote: "The Platzes—that's Aunt Maggie's family—always wanted to be High Society and always lived in the Silkstocking Neighborhoods. But they never really crashed up there."

Aunt Maggie—more formally, Margaret Platz—became a footnote in James O'Neill's history when, all in black, she suddenly appeared, unexpected, uninvited, at his funeral in New London, Connecticut, in 1920. Arriving in midservice at the church, still carrying her suitcase, she looked around with an irate expression before joining the deceased's immediate family. Much to the annoyance of Ella O'Neill and her two sons, Mrs. Platz wanted a final look at her renowned brother; in the end, the coffin was opened briefly for her sake at the cemetery. That same day, after Mrs. O'Neill had retired to her hotel suite, Mrs. Platz called on her to ask about her brother's will; on learning that he had left everything to his widow, she lost no time in returning home.

A few years later her daughter, Alma O'Neill Platz, who had literary ambitions, published a newspaper article that was widely reprinted in which she reminisced, under the name of "Alma O'Neill," about the celebrated playwright as her "mother's favorite nephew" (New York *Post*, 12/19/25).

How O'Neill felt about the Platz family can easily be imagined. In reply to the writer of the James O'Neill monograph, who had asked about these relatives, the playwright said, "I have no information about Mrs. Platt [the writer had her name wrong] except that she lived in St. Louis, not in Cincinnati" (in the monograph and *Gelb*, p. 432). This was untrue, for Mrs. Platz had lived—and died—in the Ohio city. Evidently O'Neill hoped to prevent the writer from locating, and interviewing, any of his aunt's children, particularly "Alma O'Neill."

* * *

Home Base. The nearest thing to a home the James O'Neill family ever had, the Monte Cristo Cottage in New London, Connecticut, which inspired the settings of both *Ah, Wilderness!* and *Long Day's Journey Into Night*, was scarcely the showplace some accounts suggest. From *Bowen* (p. 32) we learn that "some reports said it cost $50,000," while *Alexander* (p. 12) says the report of a Boston paper that "the house had cost $40,000—a fortune in 1883—could not have been far off," an estimate repeated by *Carpenter* (p. 21) and *Raleigh* (p. 90). In reality, the cottage was put together, at a cost of a few thousand, from several structures already on the site—a combination store-and-dwelling and a onetime schoolhouse (*Sheaffer I*, p. 48). The New London *Day* on September 1, 1897, described it as "quaint, picturesque but old-fashioned and plain."

*   *   *

Dead Child. In a serious error, *Bowen* (p. 32) says: "In March of 1885, while on tour with his parents, little Edmund [the O'Neills' second child] contracted measles and died." Actually, had the child been with his parents at the time, his fate would have been different, although it's impossible to guess the course his life might have taken. Following, at any rate, is what really happened:

Yielding to her husband's plea that he was lonely without her, Ella O'Neill left year-and-a-half old Edmund and Jamie, aged six, in her mother's care in New York to join her husband for a time as he toured in the West (*Sheaffer I*, pp. 16-17). During her absence, Jamie caught the measles, and then the baby, after Jamie had ignored orders to keep away from him, fell victim. As soon as the parents in Denver heard about the chidren, Mrs. O'Neill rushed to catch the first train home, but before she could, word came of Edmund's death—a death that would shadow the family members all their lives. Ella, never able to forgive herself for having left the children, also continued over the years to blame her husband for urging her to join him, Jamie for infecting his brother. "I've always believed that Jamie did it on purpose," the mother says in *Long Day's Journey Into Night*. "He was jealous of the baby. He hated him."

The circumstances of Edmund's death, a memory kept alive and exacerbated by Mrs. O'Neill's charges, were a major source of the intense guilt feelings within the family circle.

Had Edmund lived to adulthood, it seems doubtful that

Eugene O'Neill would ever have been born. Against Ella's wishes, at her husband's urging and pleas, she had a third and final child to replace poor Edmund. When Eugene eventually learned that his mother had unwittingly become a morphine addict as a result of his birth, he inherited his full share of O'Neill guilt.

* * *

Mrs. O'Neill's Cancer. At some stage of her life Ella O'Neill had a mastectomy, but her son's biographers differ among themselves as to when this happened. Obviously, it is important to know when, for if she underwent the ordeal while relatively young, it undoubtedly would have had a more drastic effect on her outlook, on her personality, and, through her, on the family climate than if she had had cancer late in life. In 1887 Mr. and Mrs. O'Neill spent several months in Europe—on holiday, the actor told friends— but both *Bowen* (p. 32) and *Alexander* (p. 14) contend that the trip was made so that Ella could be operated on for cancer of the breast. According to the two writers, London and Paris had noted surgeons who specialized in the new operation. (*Alexander* also maintains that it was in this period that Ella became a drug addict, a statement contrary to evidence from various sources which indicated that she became addicted as a result of Eugene's birth a year later.) On the other hand, *Gelb* (p. 109) declares that the second time the O'Neills went abroad, in 1906, was the time Ella suffered from cancer and had the operation. None of the writers, however, documents or cites any sources for his or her account.

As it happens, two doctors' reports are extant (*Sheaffer I*, pp. 440-41) which establish that the surgery took place toward the end of her life. The reports follow in their entirety:

34 West 76 St. [New York City]   April 14, 1919
Dear Mr. O'Neil [sic],
I am enclosing a report of the pathologist in the findings of the specimen sent him. It shows a recurrence of the primary disease. We shall live in hopes that it may not recur again.

                Very truly yours,
                John Aspell (M.D.)

. . .

St. Vincent's Hospital—Dept. of Pathology
Accession No. 2999
March 28, 1919   Dr. Aspell
Patient: Mrs. O'Neil [sic]

Div. Gynecology   Tissue: Cicatrix (breast)
Examine for: Pathology
Chief symptoms: Nodule following breast amputation of about 6
            mo. ago.
Clinical diagnosis: Recurrent carcinoma
Pathological report: Adeno Carcinoma
                                    Alex Fraser
                                    Pathologist

End of doctors' reports. So far as is known, Mrs. O'Neill never suffered a further recurrence of cancer before her death in 1922.

*   *   *

Phantom Railroad. Around the turn of the century James O'Neill employed a press agent known as A. Toxen Worm (full name, Conrad Henrik Aage Toxen Worm, a Dane) who, like many of his fraternity, tended to embroider on fact and even to weave whole cloth from thin air. Seeking to foist on the public the illusion that the actor lived as munificently offstage as in his role as the Count of Monte Cristo, Mr. Worm told the press that Mr. O'Neill "is now having prepared the plans and specifications for a magnificent library which he is to present to New London. The estimated cost of this temple of literature will not be far short of a million dollars." The New London *Telegraph* published the story on January 3, 1900, under the headline: NEWS THAT IS FALSE.

Undeterred, the incorrigible Mr. Worm issued a story that Mr. O'Neill had given his 12-year-old son a junior-size railroad, consisting of an engine and car large enough to carry Eugene and a companion that ran on hundreds of yards of track around the family's summer home in New London. Although the plaything, which would have cost a few thousand dollars (today, over a hundred thousand), was another of the agent's fabrications (*Sheaffer I*, p. 47), the story appeared at length in the New York *Herald* on December 9, 1900, together with a drawing of the alleged railroad.

While the story of the million-dollar "temple of literature," published only in the New London daily, was quickly forgotten, the railroad fable was picked up by other newspapers, and twenty-five years later it again figured widely in print when Alma O'Neill Platz wrote about Eugene as "my best beloved playmate." (In reality, she scarcely ever saw him.)

Her story, which originally appeared in the New York *Post*

on December 19, 1925, reads in part: "His father had a railroad engine, child's size, built for him. A track was laid on the grounds surrounding their cottage. Gene had to be both fireman and engineer to enjoy this toy, but to him it was all play . . . the engine consumed half a ton of coal a day. The miles he traveled in that engine, both actually and in fancy!"

As a result of Miss Platz's reminiscences in the *Post* and other papers, the phantom railroad rolls again in *Alexander* (p. 19) and *Gelb* (pp. 62-63). Offhand, this whole matter may seem unimportant, but the Worm-ridden story serves to contradict O'Neill's portrait of his father in *Long Day's Journey Into Night* as miserly. How could James O'Neill have been tight-fisted if he gave his young son so costly a toy?

* * *

Fall from Innocence. In *Long Day's Journey Into Night* we are told that Edmund Tyrone (read Eugene O'Neill) first learned of his mother's drug addiction when she, out of morphine, dashed from their cottage one night and tried to drown herself in the nearby river. "It was right after that," Edmund recalls, "that Papa and Jamie decided they couldn't hide it from me any more. Jamie told me. I called him a liar! . . . But I knew he wasn't lying. (His voice trembles, his eyes begin to fill with tears.) God, it made everything in life seem rotten!"

Carlotta Monterey, the playwright's widow, gives a different version. According to her, he returned unexpectedly from school one day to the family's New York apartment to find his mother injecting herself with a hypodermic needle, after which his father and brother explained that she was a victim of morphinism, that her addiction had begun innocently with his birth.

Since we know that O'Neill revised reality in some respects, for structural and dramatic purposes, in writing his autobiographical drama, Miss Monterey's story can not be dismissed out of hand. At the same time the writer knows from first-hand experience that his widow, in recalling their life together and various things he had told her, tended to edit fact and not infrequently to indulge in outright invention.

Although *Bowen* (p. 36), *Gelb* (pp. 72-73) and *Carpenter* (p. 28) follow her account, the bulk of circumstantial evidence, including one of her details, suggests that *Long Day's Journey* is closer to what actually happened. On the Sunday following Eugene's disillusionment, as he and his father were descending the stairway at home, bound for Mass, the widow has said, Eugene suddenly declared that he would never again go to church. Mr. O'Neill, her story continues, grabbed his son and tried to take him along by force, but he finally had to desist as his son fought back. The struggle on the stairway could have occurred only at the cottage in New London, not at the New York hotel apartment.

O'Neill learned about his mother, everyone agrees, while in his early teens. In 1903—when he was nearly fifteen—the summer began in New London with a dreary month of rain, fog, and foghorn. Most likely it was during this period that Ella O'Neill, marooned at home for weeks and unable to renew her supply of morphine, ran from the house in her nightdress for the river. The O'Neills had endured other stretches of bad weather in the house by the Thames River, but this time, evidently, the prospect of remaining there all summer became intolerable (*Sheaffer I*, pp. 87-89). Jamie suddenly took a job with a stock company in Massachusetts, while Mr. O'Neill shipped his horses and carriage to New York and, before leaving town, told friends he was taking his wife and younger son to the Adirondacks.

*   *   *

Interviewer Nods. While being interviewed for a series of articles in the New York *News* entitled "The Odyssey of Eugene O'Neill," January 24-30, 1932, the playwright recalled at one point that he had prospected for gold in Spanish Honduras in 1909 and 1910. Mischieviously, apparently to test the alertness of the writer, O'Neill said that he had returned home by way of the Panama Canal. And thus it appeared in the *News*, subsequently in *Gelb* (p. 137), but the Canal, under construction since 1904, was not opened until 1914, a few years after O'Neill had left Honduras.

*   *   *

The Seaman. The smell of salt air is seldom missing from O'Neill's writings; indeed, ships and the sea bulk so prominently in his works that one gets the impression he must have followed the sea for years. "Bound East for Cardiff" and "Thirst," "Fog" and "In the Zone," " 'Ile" and "The Moon of the Caribbees" all take place entirely on the water, while three other one-acters, "The Long Voyage Home," "Warnings," and "Where the Cross Is Made," also have a maritime flavor. Further, shipboard episodes or the lure of the sea figure importantly in many of his long works, from *Beyond the Horizon* and *Diff'rent* to *Gold* and *Anna Christie*, from *The Hairy Ape*, *The Fountain*, and *Marco Millions* to *Strange Interlude, Mourning Becomes Electra*, and *Long Day's Journey Into Night*. In reality, though, the playwright's seagoing career was surprisingly short; he shipped out as a crew member less often than he led us to believe.

Reminiscing years afterward about a voyage he had made in 1910 on a Norwegian windjammer, the *Charles Racine*, from Boston to Buenos Aires (a two-month sailing he always treasured as a high point of his life), O'Neill said: "It happened quite naturally—that voyage—as a consequence of what was really inside of me—what I really wanted, I suppose. I struck up one day by the wharf in Boston with a bunch of sailors, mostly Norwegians and Swedes. I wanted to ship with somebody and they took me that afternoon to the captain. Signed up, and the next thing we were off" (Boston *Post*, 8/29/20).

Taking their cue from his words, a good many articles and quite a few books, including *Bowen* (pp. 45-46), *Alexander* (pp. 138-42) and *Gelb* (pp. 144, 148-52), draw colorful pictures of O'Neill splicing ropes, clambering up among the rigging, and reefing sails while the vessel pitched and swayed. The fact is, though, his presence on the windjammer did not happen as casually as he said, nor was he a regular member of the crew (*Sheaffer I*, pp. 160-70).

While serving as assistant manager for *The White Sister*, in which his father was touring, Eugene, always drawn to the sea, hung around the waterfront when the drama played a fortnight in Boston. He was particularly attracted to the *Charles Racine*, among the last of the old sailing ships, and in talking with some of its hands he learned that while it was not certified to carry passengers, it sometimes unofficially, for a price, took along a man or two who occupied an in-between status. In the end, O'Neill, with his father's approval, paid $75 for his passage to Buenos Aires (no small sum in those days) with the understanding that he was to help in the lighter duties, nothing hazardous, at the captain's discretion. Rather than being squeezed into the fo'c'sle with the crew, O'Neill and a friend of his, who likewise paid for his passage, had a small cabin to themselves (usually, the sick bay) and they took mess with the ship's officers.

In a moment of truth-telling years later, O'Neill said, "I

landed in Buenos Aires a gentleman, so called, and wound up a bum on the docks in fact" (New York *Herald-Tribune,* 8/8/26). But scarcely any of his chroniclers seem to have noticed the first part of his remark.

O'Neill arrived in Buenos Aires at the start of August 1910 and left in latter March of the following year. During the period, he often told interviewers, he made a round-trip between Buenos Aires and Durban "tending mules on a cattle steamer," but he was not allowed to go ashore in South Africa since, as required by local law, he did not have at least a hundred dollars. There is reason, however, for doubting that he ever made such a voyage. His name does not appear among any of the crews on file with Britain's General Register and Record Office of Shipping and Seaman for vessels that made the round-trip during the period in question (he once identified the ship as British). Although the voyage, both ways, would have taken about two months, "tending mules" was all he ever said about it, yet he had a good deal more to say about ships on which he served a much shorter time. When, furthermore, he signed on the British freighter that carried him home from Argentina, he stated that this was his "first" ship, meaning his first berth as a regular deckhand. Since he was a "workaway," anxious to make the trip to New York, he received the nominal pay of one shilling a month, not, as one biography says, $25 a month.

Some ten years after he had quit the sea, he told a reporter that he could not recall the name of the tramp freighter that had brought him back from Buenos Aires—a vessel that became the model for the fictional *S.S. Glencairn* in some of his one-acters. Apparently he wanted to prevent anyone from tracking down and interviewing some of his old shipmates, for years still later he did name the vessel, but whether he or his interviewer was at fault, it appeared in the New York *News* (6/25/32), and subsequently in *Gelb* (pp. 158-61), as the *S.S. Ikalis.* In reality, he returned on the *S.S. Ikala,* a sister ship of the other one (*Sheaffer I,* pp. 185-87).

The remainder of his seafaring consisted of a round-trip to England on passenger ships—shipping out as an ordinary seaman (not, as one biographer says, as an able-bodied seaman) on the *S.S. New York* and returning as an A.B. on the *S.S. Philadelphia.* In summary, excluding the *Charles Racine,* where he had a special status, and the questionable turn-around trip to South Africa, Eugene O'Neill spent a total, on the *Ikala* and the two liners, of only about six weeks as a regular, *bona fide* seaman.

* * *

Jimmy the Priest's. Between ships, O'Neill used to hole up at a waterfront saloon and flophouse in lower Manhattan known as "Jimmy the Priest's" after its proprietor, an enigmatic figure who looked rather clerical and yet, for all his quiet manner, had an intimidating air. His name, though unknown to any who frequented his place at 252 Fulton Street, was James J. Condon; his counterpart would later appear as Johnny the Priest in *Anna Christie*, with the opening scene of the play modeled on his saloon.

"Jimmy the Priest's," in O'Neill's words, "certainly was a hell hole. It was awful. One couldn't go any lower. Gorky's Night Lodging was an ice cream parlor by comparison. The house was almost coming down and the principal housewreckers were vermin" (*New York Times*, 12/21/24, and New York *World*, 11/9/24).

But he dramatized the place, he exaggerated; it was much sturdier than his words suggest. About a hundred years old when he took refuge there in 1911, the building, starting in the early 1920s, was occupied by a ship's chandler that loaded its floors with heavy maritime machinery and supplies until it was razed in 1966, together with other structures of the area, to make way for the World Trade Center (*Sheaffer I*, pp. 189-92).

In the only O'Neill short story ever published, "Tomorrow" (*Seven Arts Magazine*, June, 1917), set in Tommy the Priest's, a place similar to Condon's, the author in writing of his waterfront period took liberties with fact. The story has been accepted, however, by some of his chroniclers as more or less factual (*Bowen*, p. 49; *Alexander*, pp. 149-51, and *Gelb*, pp. 161-63). It is of minor significance that the flophouse accommodations at Condon's were cruder, more basic, than in the story, but it is important that "Tomorrow" helps to give, by implication, a misleading impression of the time O'Neill felt so forlorn and desperate that he tried to kill himself.

Told in the first person, the story ends with the narrator's ineffectual roommate, "Jimmy Tomorrow," who constantly vowed to get a grip on himself and reform tomorrow, committing suicide by jumping from an upper window at Tommy the Priest's. Since a friend and fellow-lodger of O'Neill, one James

Findlater Byth, nicknamed "Jimmy Tomorrow," did end his life
in such a way, the story leaves the impression that Eugene was
living there at the time. Lending weight to the notion, O'Neill
years later disclosed to George Jean Nathan, as the latter reported, that he had attempted suicide through an overdose of
Veronal at Jimmy the Priest's "a month or so after James Beith
(a friend of O'Neill's) took his life" (*Nathan*, pp. 35-36). By
now, since Nathan's account has been followed by *Bowen* (pp.
42-44), *Alexander* (p. 154), *Gelb* (pp. 186-87), and *Carpenter*
(pp. 31-32), it is universally accepted that O'Neill's suicidal
mood was partly induced by depression over his friend's death.
In reality, Byth (not Beith) killed himself more than a year after
O'Neill's skirmish with death and his permanent departure from
the Fulton Street dive" (*Sheaffer I*, pp. 211-14). In fact, Byth
was chiefly responsible for saving Eugene from his suicide
attempt.

The future playwright first met Byth when the latter became
James O'Neill's press agent about 1907. Although Eugene, a
shy, wary soul, was usually slow to make friends, he took an
early liking to the agent, a cheerful bantam with an inordinate
thirst for liquor, a whimsical sense of humor, with himself often
the butt of his stories, and, as he told it, a colorful, adventurous
past. In time Eugene heard about the immense family estate
in Scotland ("heavily mortgaged," the other admitted), an extensive journalistic career, not only in Edinburgh and London
but as a Reuters correspondent in the Boer War, and his decline
in family regard as he became the black sheep of the Byths
(*Alexander*, pp. 115-16).

Although Eugene doubted some parts of the other's history,
his doubts didn't go far enough (*Sheaffer I*, pp. 129-31). The
son of a struggling upholsterer in a coal-mining area of Corn-
wall, Byth never had a privileged upbringing and, while he may
have worked obscurely as a reporter in Britain, he never served
as a Boer War correspondent. His made-up memories of the
war (O'Neill would draw on them in writing *The Iceman
Cometh*) were acquired while working as a publicist for "The
Great Boer Spectacle," a theatrical extravaganza shown at the
St. Louis World's Fair in 1904 and later at New York's Brighton
Beach. Down on his luck a few years afterward, from drinking
himself out of jobs, he joined his good friend, the youngest of
the O'Neills, at Jimmy the Priest's.

By naming Byth as a factor in his suicidal mood, Eugene

showed that the other man was important and dear to him, a fact emphasized by his several attempts to give "Jimmy Tomorrow" literary immortality, first in "Tomorrow," next in "Exorcism," a one-acter based on the author's near-fatal move, and at last definitively in *The Iceman Cometh*. Further, by linking Byth to his own desperate act, O'Neill used him as a coverup of the real reason he had felt suicidal. Shortly before he took the Veronal in the early days of 1912, he had gone to a whorehouse, with several men as witnesses, to provide evidence for his first wife's divorce suit against him. The episode had left him feeling degraded, in the darkest of moods, so disgusted with his past and hopeless about his future that death seemed the only solution.

The suicide of another regular of the Fulton Street saloon, a burly seaman named Driscoll who was one of Eugene's favorite drinking companions, is also mentioned by *Gelb* (pp. 171, 186) and *Carpenter* (p. 31) in connection with O'Neill's attempt. Driscoll, whose image recurs in the *Glencairn* playlets and most importantly as "Yank" in *The Hairy Ape*, was, in O'Neill's words, a "giant of a man, and absurdly strong. He thought a whole lot of himself. . . . It seemed to give him mental poise to be able to dominate the stokehold" (*New York Times*, 12/21/24). Yet, for all his swaggering self-confidence, he jumped overboard in midocean; but here again, as in Byth's case, his suicide had nothing to do with O'Neill's despair, for he vanished into the sea in August 1915, several years after O'Neill's ascent from the lower depths (*Sheaffer I*, p. 335).

Like Driscoll and Byth, Chris Christopherson, an aging seaman reduced to bargeman, was another Fulton Street hanger-on who came to an untimely end, but his was accidental. "He had followed the sea so long," O'Neill said, "that he got sick at the thought of it . . . he spent his time getting drunk and cursing the sea. 'Dat ole davil,' he called it. Finally he got a job as captain of a coal barge. . . ."

"His end in real life was just one of the many tragedies that punctuate the history of Jimmy the Priest's. Everybody got very drunk at Jimmy's one Christmas Eve and Chris was very much in the party . . . [He] tottered away about 2 o'clock in the morning for his barge. The next morning he was found frozen on a cake of ice between the piles and the dock. In trying to board the barge, he stumbled on the plank and fell over."

O'Neill's account, which appeared originally in the New

York *World* (11/9/24) and the *New York Times* (12/21/24), is repeated in *Bowen* (p. 117), *Alexander* (p. 269), and *Gelb* (p. 170). However, whether O'Neill was misinformed or as a born dramatist could not keep from embellishing the story, Chris fell overboard not at Christmastime but in October 1917, and his body was found floating a week later near the Statue of Liberty. In any case, like Byth and Driscoll, he helped to inspire O'Neill's writings; a few years after his death he appeared under his real name, still cursing "dat ole davil," in *Anna Christie* (*Sheaffer I*, pp. 202-03).

*   *   *

Two Poems. Shortly after his last turn at sea, in 1911, O'Neill visited New London, where he had a reunion with friends of his on the two local newspapers, the *Telegraph* and the *Day*. Not long afterward, the *Telegraph* ran a poem entitled "Not Understood" whose author was given as "Unknown." Following is one of the stanzas:

> Not understood. We gather false impressions
> And hug them closer as the years go by,
> Till virtues often seem to us trangressions;
> And thus men rise and fall and live and die—
> Not understood.

For several reasons—chiefly, he had ambitions as a poet and, further, "Not Understood" sounds like him—*Sheaffer I*, (p. 201) surmises that he was the author. In reality, the poem was written by Thomas Bracken, an Irishman who emigrated to Australia in the mid-19th century, and is well known Down Under. It seems likely, though, that Eugene came across the poem while on the beach in Buenos Aires—the international mix there included Australians—and that he brought it to the *Telegraph*'s attention.

In another misattribution, *Sheaffer I* (p. 290) has O'Neill making up some lines that he inscribed for a friend in a copy of *Thirst*, his first volume of plays. Instead, the poem, which begins, "All that I had I brought," was written by Ernest Dowson.

*   *   *

Vaudeville Tour. To believe O'Neill, the weeks he and his brother toured with their father in vaudeville in 1912, in a tabloid version of *Monte Cristo,* were a time of drunken hilarity. "The least said about those acting days," he wrote to a friend, "the better. The alcoholic content was as high as the acting was low. They graduated me from the Orpheum Circuit with a degree of Lousy Cum Laude" (EO to Charles O'Brien Kennedy, 10/29/38). And to another friend: "I am proud to say that I preserved my honor by never drawing a sober breath until the tour terminated. My brother and I had one grand time of it and I look back on it as one of the merriest periods of my life" (EO to Joseph A. McCarthy, 2/18/31).

Eugene's appearance with the troupe, he used to say, happened entirely by chance. His story, substantially, was as follows: While living at Jimmy the Priest's he found five dollars, ran it up to five hundred (a thousand in one version) at a gambling casino, threw a party for everyone at Condon's, where the liquor flowed like water, and he came to his senses a day or two later on a train bound for New Orleans. By coincidence, his story continues, his father was headlining there at the time in vaudeville; since Eugene was now virtually broke and his father refused to pay his return fare, he had no choice but to join the tour.

O'Neill's account of the tour as a farcical high point of his life can be found in *Alexander* (pp. 158-60) and *Gelb* (pp. 173-76, 181-85). One important fact he never mentioned was that his stint in vaudeville followed directly after his suicide attempt; had he linked the two developments together, his friends would rightly have suspected that he was glossing over a painful period of his life. Contrary, however, to most evidence that he underwent his crisis prior to New Orleans, *Gelb* (pp. 186-88) maintains that O'Neill, quitting the tour before its end, returned to Jimmy the Priest's and that it was during this period that he tried to kill himself.

O'Neill's picture of the circumstances under which he joined the vaudeville production and of his behavior—his brother's, too—onstage and off is contradicted on practically all points by Charles Webster, a young actor with the troupe. A summary of his account follows:

In mid-January 1912, while the Dumas piece was playing in Memphis, Tennessee, members of the company noted that Mr. O'Neill appeared agitated, as a rumor spread among them that his younger son had suffered "some kind of misfortune." Soon afterward they heard that he had sent money to Eugene to join him, which he did in New Orleans, the next stop of their itinerary. As for the brothers' conduct, Webster said that if Eugene "gave the impression later on that the two of them pulled all kinds of funny things on stage, well, he was just making up a good story." The actor added that Jamie "practically always smelled of alcohol when he went on, but he was never staggering, it was impossible for the audience to tell he'd been drinking," while Eugene, he continued, "took a drink or two after a performance, but never before." It seemed to him that both brothers were "pretty respectful" toward their father (*Sheaffer I*, pp. 214-21).

*   *   *

Rival Reels. After half a lifetime of playing the Count of Monte Cristo, James O'Neill, in his final appearance, performed the role for the movie cameras in 1912 under the auspices of the Famous Players Film Company, newly organized by Adolph Zukor and Daniel Frohman. Despite publicity that the film would be made at great expense in Bermuda with well-known actors in the supporting cast, it was filmed at a cost of slightly over $13,000 in ten days at sites in and around New York, with James the only name player in a cast that included his elder son. The New London *Telegraph* reported in an interview on August 13, 1912, that as Mr. O'Neill "recounted the way in which the scenes were laid, his voice shook with emotion and his mobile face took on the varied characteristics of his part." According to the report, he was offered $10,000 outright for his interest in the film, but that he expected to make more from his twenty percent share of the profits.

Before long, when a three-reel *Monte Cristo* made by William Fox preceded the five-reel O'Neill film to the screen, the veteran actor realized he had made the wrong choice. It is not true, however, as reported by some movie historians, as well as *Gelb* (p. 220), that Famous Players withdrew their production after a few showings. Instead, the longer film was widely shown for several years, but it was never the money-maker its star had hoped; Mr. O'Neill's share finally totaled close to four thousand (*Sheaffer I*, pp. 223-24).

*   *   *

Cub Reporter. After O'Neill had become famous, some of his friends in New London liked to recall that he was once considered a hopeless aspirant for success as a writer. It appears, in fact, from their reminiscences that his brief career on the local *Telegraph* set a new low in journalistic history. In an article that has been widely quoted, Malcolm Mollan, the *Telegraph* city editor, once recalled that he complimented the cub reporter on the way he had set the scene in a story before he, Mollan, added: "But would you mind finding out the name of the gentleman who carved the lady and whether the dame is his wife or daughter or who? And phone the hospital for a hint as to whether she is dead or discharged or what? Then put the facts into a hundred and fifty words and send this literary batik to the picture framers" (Philadelphia *Public Ledger*, 1/22/22).

Two veteran newspapermen, Arthur McGinley and Robert A. Woodworth, both of whom said that they were on the *Telegraph* at the same time as O'Neill, have added other details. McGinley, whom Eugene used to consider a wit, said that if the other was sent to cover an accident or a fire, he would return with an "Ode to Death." His description is almost complimentary compared with the article Woodworth wrote under the headline, "The World's Worst Reporter" (Providence *Journal*, 12/6/31). After sketching O'Neill as haunched meditatively over his typewriter without writing a word, he adds: "Night after night for a week or more it is the same story. Smoke and dream, smoke and dream!"

" 'Hey, Mal! When is that guy going to get busy and do some work?' one of us asked the city editor. 'He sits in there and smokes, but he never turns in any copy. If he'd do something, some of the rest of us wouldn't have to run our legs off. . . .' "

The article runs on at length in this vein, but at a time when Woodworth and others were said to have run their "legs off" because of the unproductive cub reporter, Woodworth was on the rival newspaper, the New London *Day*. So, for that matter, was Art McGinley.

Apparently corroborating the legend of his incompetence, O'Neill himself cheerfully agreed once that he had been a "bum reporter." But what good writer ever looks back with pride on his fledgling efforts? Actually, the future playwright made a quite creditable start in journalism. Like virtually all novices, he overwrote in his eagerness to make an impression (hence Mollan's allusion to "literary batik"); but a close survey of the *Telegraph* in the few months Eugene was on the staff turns up a good many stories that, from internal evidence, appear to have been his—all this in addition to a score or so of poems, topical, humorous, at times serious, that he contributed to a special column of the paper (*Sheaffer I*, pp. 226-31, 233, 236).

Further, in direct contrast to the recollections of Woodworth *et al*, Frederick P. Latimer, the paper's editor-in-chief, said of Eugene: "The four things about him that impressed me at once were his modesty, his native gentlemanliness, his wonderful eyes and his literary style. It was evident that this was no ordinary boy. . . ." A man of good-will and independent thought, a lover of books, the editor, who was better equipped than Mollan and the others to appraise O'Neill, also said: "From flashes in the quality of the stuff he gave the paper and the poems and play manuscripts he showed me, I was so struck that I told his father Eugene did not have merely talent, but a very high order of genius" (*Clark*, pp. 18-19).

O'Neill in turn said that Latimer was "the first who thought I had something to say, and believed I could say it." In more lasting tribute, the playwright used him as the chief model for the genial father, a newspaper publisher, in *Ah, Wilderness!* Even their names are similar—Latimer, Nat Miller. (For other accounts of O'Neill as a reporter: *Bowen*, pp. 58-59; *Alexander*, pp. 163-66, and *Gelb*, 195-202.)

                              *   *   *

Two Sanatoria. After working for the *Telegraph* several months, O'Neill had to quit late in 1912 when he fell ill with chills and fever, a condition tentatively diagnosed as "pleurisy." But he was stricken with something far more serious, tuberculosis, commonly called at the time "the White Plague" or "the Great Killer," also known as "the Irish disease" because so many Irish succumbed to it in their homeland or the tenements of America.

Some of the bitterest exchanges in *Long Day's Journey Into Night* take place between Edmund Tyrone (read Eugene O'Neill) and his father over the question of the sanatorium he should enter; indeed, this issue is one of the central points of conflict in the play. James Tyrone favors a state-run institution (one, in reality, in Shelton, Connecticut) that costs almost nothing and is chiefly for the poor, while Edmund counters furiously: ". . . to think when it's a question of your son having consumption, you can show yourself up before the whole town as such a stinking old tightwad! Don't you know [Dr.] Hardy will talk and the whole damned town will know. Jesus, Papa, don't you have any pride or shame?"

In the play, as the father relents, the two agree on a sanatorium subsidized by a philanthropic group that has a good reputation and charges only a modest fee (in reality, the Gaylord Farm Sanatorium in Wallingford, Connecticut). In life, however, Eugene did enter the "state farm" in Shelton. Referring to this episode, *Gelb* (pp. 221-23) says, "Apparently his destination was an ugly secret between father and son," since none of Eugene's close friends at the time could later recall that he had gone to the state institution.

Actually, New Londoners did know, for both local papers published the news. The *Telegraph*, for instance, said on December 9 under the headline GOES TO SHELTON TODAY: "Eugene O'Neill of the *Telegraph* staff, who has been seriously ill with pleurisy . . . will leave today for Shelton, where he will take what is called the 'rest cure' for several weeks. The acute attack of pleurisy . . . was a heavy strain on his lungs and, while neither is affected, it was deemed wise by his physicians to give them the benefit of outdoor living and sleeping. . . ."

Where one biography talks of an "ugly secret," the author of another, who evidently didn't know that such a place as Shelton existed, much less that Eugene had ever gone there, assumes that Gaylord was the state-run institution that aroused Eugene's opposition and anger, as expressed through young Tyrone (*Alexander*, pp. 166-73).

It appears, at any rate, that none of Eugene's friends remembered Shelton because they were more or less ignorant about the place; hence the news of his going there made little, if any, impression on them. Indeed, since he did enter Shelton, it appears that he himself knew almost nothing about it; but it was so desolate and forbidding that he left there in two days. Thus, it was *after* he had gone there, not *before*, that he was furious at his father; but in writing *Long Day's Journey* he took liberties with, among other things, chronology (*Sheaffer I*, pp. 236-43).

Shortly after Shelton, he was examined by two nationally-known physicians, specialists in tuberculosis, and was admitted to Gaylord, the scene, he used to say, of his "rebirth." There, for the first time in his life, he had the leisure, quiet, and peace to meditate on his past and think of the future; there, he made the crucial decision to write for the theater.

*   *   *

Film Writer. In 1914, about a year after his discharge from Gaylord Farm, where he had spent five months, O'Neill received a questionnaire from the sanatorium regarding his health, type of employment, and financial situation. Eugene replied that he was working at "the Art of Playwriting—also prostitution of the same by Photo-play composition," that his average weekly earnings were thirty dollars, and he added, "I am speaking in the main of the returns I have received from the Movies" (*Sheaffer I*, pp. 288-89).

On the basis of this statement, *Bowen* (p. 72) reports that "Eugene was earning some money on the side"—apart, that is, from a weekly allowance from his father—while *Gelb* (pp. 253-54) ventures to say, "It is conceivable that O'Neill did try his hand at a photoplay or two." The facts are, he wrote much more than a "photoplay or two" but he never earned a penny from the movies till years later when Hollywood began to buy some of his stage works.

Hoping to make himself less dependent on his father, Eugene began turning out movie scripts—chiefly comedies and tales of derring-do à la *Monte Cristo*—about the same time that he dedicated himself, in 1913, to writing for the theater. Members of the Rippin family of New London, with whom he lived during the winter of 1913-1914, recall that after his film scripts came back, as they did invariably, he tore them up and dashed off another.

Later, after a playwriting course at Harvard, he made a fresh attempt at film writing, and for a time it appeared that he was on the verge of success. He told friends that Edwin Holt, a vaudeville star, had commissioned him to write some scenarios, word that was carried on July 16, 1915, in the New London *Day*. His first script, the paper said, has been "accepted and will soon be produced." The *Day* again, on August 11th: "The Eastern Film Co. of Providence, which has engaged Edwin Holt as one of its leading actors and Eugene Gladstone O'Neill of this city as a writer of scenarios, has purchased the *Morning Star*, a New Bedford whaling bark. The bark will be used to stage a number of moving picture scenes and actors will do all kinds of stirring deeds from the decks while she is anchored in the lower harbor [of New London]." But the *Morning Star* project never materialized.

Although it sounds incredible, since O'Neill was a private person and extremely shy, he at one point, according to the press, considered acting in a movie version of *The Last of the Mohicans*, to be made locally by actor-director Guy Hedlund, a former New London and a childhood acquaintance of

Eugene's. Presumably O'Neill, who was supposed to play Uncas, considered acting before the cameras in hopes of learning something about film-making. Finally, after the collapse of his various efforts and prospects, young O'Neill decided to confine himself to the theater (*Sheaffer I*, pp. 311-12).

* * *

Shooting in Mexico. Despite the autobiographical bent of his talent, O'Neill occasionally got ideas for his plays from articles in the newspapers. *All God's Chillun Got Wings*, for example, was partly inspired by accounts of the suicide of boxing champion Jack Johnson's white wife, *The Iceman Cometh* by the murder case of newspaper editor Charles E. Chapin, who shot his wife, he insisted, from reasons of love. The earliest and, perhaps, clearest instance of a journalistic source in O'Neill's writings can be found in one of his slightest works, "The Movie Man," a comedy about two Americans in Mexico to film a revolutionary army's battles against the government forces. Pancho Gomez, the leader of the rebels, has been paid to cooperate with the film-makers.

Unlikely though the story may seem, it is based on fact; indeed, the reality was more ludicrous than the playwright's fiction. Shortly before he wrote his one-acter in 1914, the American newspapers ran front-page stories about Pancho Villa, the Mexican revolutionary, signing a contract with a New York movie company to wage his war only in daytime and under other circumstances favorable to the photographers. Since the movie men were dissatisfied with his appearance—ragged civilian clothes, a slouch hat—Villa meekly submitted to being outfitted with a smart-looking uniform. Faithful to his contract, he delayed an attack on Ojinaga, besieged by his forces, until the cameramen arrived; not to be outdone, a general on the other side deployed his army for a large scenic shot. (For a full account of the matter: *A Million and One Nights*, by Terry Ramsaye, 1926, pp. 670-73.)

Unaware, apparently, of the Pancho Villa episode, with its close resemblance to O'Neill's playlet, *Gelb* (pp. 262-63) never mentions it but instead declares that "The Movie Man" was "inspired" by the dispatches of John Reed, the dashing young correspondent who first won renown covering the Mexican insurrection for *Metropolitan* magazine. Although Reed rode for a time with Villa's men, he had no connection with the movie negotiations or contract, nor, for that matter, did he ever write about the movie deal. *Gelb* further says that Reed befriended O'Neill shortly before he left for Mexico and wanted the other to accompany him south of the Border. According to the best available evidence, though, the two men first met in Provincetown several years later.

*   *   *

Jamie's Romance. Like the rest of the family, Jamie O'Neill was inclined to self-dramatization, a trait most evident, perhaps, in the story he spread around of his abortive romance with Pauline Frederick, a great beauty of the stage and, later, of the movies. The two had met when they appeared on Broadway in a grandiose production, *Joseph and His Brethren*—she as a principal, Jamie in a minor part. According to Jamie, she loved him but refused to marry him unless he quit drinking, something he was unable to do.

Eugene, who appears to have been half-skeptical about the matter, helped to circulate the story but he also said to his brother: "Pauline is just an image that you fool around with in your sentimental moments. You convince yourself that if she'd marry you, you wouldn't be hanging on to Mama, and letting her secretly hand you out a quarter a day" (*Part of a Long Story*, by Agnes Boulton, 1958, p. 210).

O'Neill seems, nevertheless, to have had his brother and the actress in mind when he wrote in *Ah, Wilderness!* of the pathetic romance between Lily, an old maid, and the bachelor uncle, a likeable alcoholic who repeatedly drinks himself out of a job (he's a nostalgic, softened image of Jamie). Although Lily loves him, she has refused for years to marry him unless he reforms.

By now, from retellings in print, particularly *Bowen* (p. 114), *Gelb* (pp. 239-40, 256) and *Alexander* (pp. 182, 237, 240-41, 288), the legend of Jamie's hapless love is an established part of O'Neill family history. Regardless, though, of how many times it is retold, there is ample reason for doubting that the reputed lovers ever had a close relationship. Judging, first of all, by the recollections of actors Brandon Tynan, Gareth Hughes and Malcolm Morley and of stagehand John Cronin, all of whom were associated with *Joseph and His Brethern*, the alleged romance's only possible basis in fact appears to have been that Jamie was secretly infatuated with the brunette star. Listen to Tynan: "I never heard a word about it, and you know what a

hotbed of gossip the theater is. If there had been anything between them, I'm sure I would have known." To Hughes: "No,
the Pauline Frederick story is just that—a story." To Morley:
"I heard nothing about his attachment to Pauline. I'm certain
there was nothing there." And to Cronin: "Polly was very
democratic, well liked by the company. She had just left a
wealthy husband to return to the stage. I never heard of anything between her and Jimmy, and doubt there's anything to it"
(*Sheaffer I*, pp. 270, 429).

Even without the testimony of Cronin, Tynan and the others,
various circumstances—in fact the entire shape and direction of
Jamie O'Neill's life—strongly suggest that any affection he may
have had for Miss Frederick must have been limited and transitory. For his heart was turned elsewhere: From childhood on-
ward, the great love of his life was his mother. In spite of his
dissolute ways and reputation as a ladies' man, he was, in the
common term, a "mama's boy." Indeed, his drinking and woman-
izing, begun at a relatively early age, indicate that he was sorely
beset. After Ella O'Neill used to take a bath, her bachelor son
liked to paddle his hands in her scented bath water.

Once his father, his life-long enemy, had died and he had
his mother all to himself, Jamie gave up drinking at her request,
all his dissipations, and became her escort, her constant companion. For a long time he didn't touch a bottle, not until her
terminal illness, at which point he resumed drinking more
heavily than ever. In less than two years after her death, he
achieved his own.

* * *

Sad Homecoming. The night *The Hairy Ape* opened, March 9,
1922, loomed to O'Neill as an ordeal, not from concern over
his new play but because that same night his brother, coming
from the West Coast, was to arrive with the coffin of their
mother. She and Jamie had visited California to check on some
property belonging to her when she fell mortally ill. From Jamie's
garbled telegrams and his delay in returning, Eugene realized
that the other, who had been on the wagon almost two years,
was again hitting the bottle.

Since his brother's train was due to arrive at Grand Central
Terminal while *The Hairy Ape* was being performed, Eugene
had his wife Agnes Boulton attend the premiere with his friend
Saxe Commins. According to *Bowen* (p. 148), Agnes went to

the station with her husband, while Commins (in an unpublished account) and *Gelb* (p. 497) report that he went alone. Instead, all three are in error, for O'Neill never met the train (*Sheaffer II*, pp. 85-86). Feeling in need of moral support, he had arranged for one of his parents' oldest friends, William P. Connor, to join him, but when the time came, O'Neill's nerve failed him— he couldn't face a reunion with an emotional, overwrought Jamie—and he would not be budged.

Connor, accompanied by a nephew of his, found his quarry in a drunken stupor, made arrangements about the coffin and, after depositing Jamie at a Times Square hotel, telephoned O'Neill. In the midst of his account Connor, who had loved the elder O'Neills, upbraided Eugene for not joining him at Grand Central, but he reserved his sharpest words for Jamie. When Agnes and Saxe returned from *The Hairy Ape*, O'Neill, relaying some of the things Connor had said, left them with the impression that he had met the train, hence the erroneous account of Commins and Gelb years later.

Jamie subsequently confessed to his brother that he not only had drunk his way across the country but, trying to blank out thoughts of his mother, had taken up with a "blond pig who looked more like a whore than twenty-five whores . . . So every night—for fifty bucks a night . . . [but] I didn't forget even in her arms!"

O'Neill would never forget his brother's torment and self-loathing as he told of his behavior on the train bearing his mother's coffin. Decades later, in *A Moon for the Misbegotten*, the playwright would have Jamie Tyrone (read Jamie O'Neill) retelling the story of his nightmarish journey with such agony that it all seems to have happened only yesterday.

*   *   *

New York Debut. Although several critics saw the initial bill of the Provincetown Players in Greenwich Village in fall of 1916, none of them, according to *Gelb* (p. 318) bothered to write about the event—a seemingly minor event that would prove historic in the American theater. In reality, though, one critic did report on the occasion. Stephen Rathbun of the *Evening Sun* published a long article on November 13, 1916, in which he described the group, told of its birth on Cape Cod, and reviewed its opening bill in the Village, consisting of *The Game* by Louise Bryant, *King Arthur's Socks* by Floyd Dell, and O'Neill's *Bound East for Cardiff*, which marked his bow in a New York theater (*Sheaffer I*, p. 363).

Rathbun dismissed the Bryant piece as "so amateurish that the less said about it the better," called the Dell one-acter "good fun," and saved his chief praise for *Cardiff*. "The play was real, subtly tense," he summed up, "and avoided a dozen pitfalls that might have spoiled it."

* * *

From Hindsight. A few years after the playwright's death, Stark Young published a magazine article titled "Eugene O'Neill: Pages from a Critic's Diary" (*Harper's*, June 1957), an episodic account stringing together his memories and impressions of his subject. Young, whose career had been devoted almost entirely to dramatic criticism and fiction, recalled that he once tried his hand at directing, the occasion being *Welded,* among O'Neill's more autobiographical works. Inspired by the author's marriage to Agnes Boulton, *Welded* out Strindbergs Strindberg in its shrill, almost hysterical account of a couple with clashing personalities who are bound to torment one another and yet who find that they cannot separate; they're welded together.

The 1924 production co-starred Doris Keane, an actress best suited to costume roles (she had starred for years in New York and London in Edward Sheldon's *Romance*), and Jacob Ben-Ami from the Yiddish theater of Second Avenue. As Young tells it, Miss Keane had been "persuaded" by Robert Edmond Jones and Kenneth Macgowan, O'Neill's partners, to undertake a role that soon proved all wrong for her. She had, Young writes, "an almost painful tenderness toward any suffering in human beings, but these two people in *Welded*, with their wrangling violence . . . belonged to another world from hers."

After a week's rehearsal, she reportedly wanted to leave, but again Macgowan and Jones "persuaded" her to remain. "I knew," Young adds "that Gene's personal life in the period that *Welded* came out of had not been all smoothness, not between two such vivid temperaments as he and Agnes, for all the love between them . . . I can see them now at some of the rehearsals, sitting side by side . . . and listening to every speech, good or bad, and taking it all as *bona fide* and their own."

Another time he expressed himself more bluntly: "Those God-awful speeches! Yet Gene and Agnes drank it all in as though it were poetry" (*Sheaffer II*, pp. 131-32).

Since Stark Young was one of the most acute critics of his day, why, if he thought the play so bad (it is, actually, one of the author's worst), did he consent to direct it? Also, since he happened to adore Doris Keane, though only platonically, why didn't he dissuade her from assuming a role so ill-suited to her? The chief answer can be found in a letter he wrote Morgan Farley, an actor friend of his, shortly after the magazine article had appeared: "I'm so glad you liked the Gene O'Neill piece. I had no diary, of course—the form was an experiment. But I covered most of the main points about him, not too obviously, I hope" (*Stark Young/A Life in the Arts*, ed. John Pilkington, 1975; Letter from SY to MF, 9/10/57).

The article, in other words, was written from hindsight years after the fact, rather than being "notes from a critic's diary" written at the time. It is misleading both in things it says and what it omits. Contrary to Young's word to one writer that he assumed the direction at O'Neill's "urgent request" (*Gelb*, p. 543), he was eager for the assignment (perhaps, as a confirmed bachelor, he was drawn to the play by its misogynistic picture of marital life). He won his chance, at any rate, through the influence of Mrs. Willard Straight, a good friend of his and a chief backer of the Macgowan-Jones-O'Neill setup. Further, it was Young himself, not Macgowan and Jones, who talked Miss Keane into assuming the role; not that she needed much persuasion, for several years earlier she had asked O'Neill to write something for her. "I wish I had a play of yours to prepare for," she wrote him on April 12, 1921. "It would be such an incentive."

However his wife Agnes felt about the play, O'Neill, despite Young's account, was dissatisfied with the way the production was shaping up. Although usually adamant against out-of-town tryouts of his works, he was so doubtful about this one that he had it tested for a week in Baltimore. After he caught a performance, he wrote in his diary: "Saw *Welded*—rotten!" (*Eugene O'Neill Work Diary*, Yale University Library, 1981, p. 4).

*   *   *

Drinking Problem. Expressing doubt that liquor had a "serious hold" on O'Neill, in view of his great productivity, *Bowen* (pp. 89-90) says: "His indulgence probably did not often exceed the bounds of social drinking." O'Neill himself knew better. He began drinking, he told a friend, when he was fifteen, and left the impression he meant drinking to excess. (It was shortly before he reached fifteen that he first learned of his mother's drug addiction and that it had begun unwittingly with his birth.)

Bowen is not alone in error. Taking a different tack, *Gelb* (p. 573) says that on January 1, 1925, during O'Neill's first stay in Bermuda, he "swore off" heavy drinking and, in an effort to control his "alcoholism," confined himself to a single glass of ale with dinner. In addition, *Gelb* quotes, without questioning or disputing, a statement by Dr. Louis Bisch, a New York psychoanalyst, who became acquainted with the playwright on the island: "O'Neill never drank in Bermuda." Bisch, actually, was in no position to know, for he visited his wife, a temporary resident of Bermuda, only once briefly throughout this period. The fact is, 1925, the year O'Neill wrote *The Great God Brown*, saw some of his heaviest, most frequent indulgence in years, as though he were under a compulsion to follow the course of Dion Anthony, the protagonist of *Brown*, who drinks himself into precarious health and finally to death (*Sheaffer II*, pp. 162, 175, 177, 179-80, 183, 187).

O'Neill knew himself to be a periodic alcoholic. During one of his short drying-out periods a Bermuda physician lent him an issue of *The Practitioner* (October 1924), a British medical journal, devoted entirely to the subject of alcoholism, which the playwright found "very interesting and applicable to me." His comment was probably inspired by an article by Sir James Purves-Steward on "paroxysmal dipsomania. This is a recurrent psychosis," the article says, "consisting of attacks during which the patient has an irresistable impulse to take alcohol to excess. The dipsomaniac individual sometimes drinks himself into a state of acute alcoholic poisoning."

"Careful inquiry into the history of such patients shows that many of them have a marked neuropathic heredity, and that practically all of them, before they happen to acquire the habit of paroxysmal excessive drinking, have had previous neuropathic symptoms, such as phobiae, obsessions, emotional depression, visceral discomfort, etc. . . . the patient discovers that he can mask his deficient will-power and 'drown his sorrow' by a dose of alcohol, which comforts him for a time. . . . He drinks heavily for a few days until his bout is brought to an end by alcoholic gastritis. . . . His attack then subsides, and he is free from alcoholic craving, and full of good resolutions, perhaps for weeks or months, until his next attack. Sometimes during this interval he even has a positive distaste for alcohol. But his psychosis inevitably recurs."

Since Eugene O'Neill was one of the most autobiographical writers in theater history—images of himself, his parents and his brother recur constantly in various guises in his canon—it was to be expected that a periodic drinker should appear among his protagonists. Usually his self-portraits are easily recognizable, being tall, lean, dark, intense—the newspaperman in *The Straw,* the playwright in *Welded,* the tormented apostate in *Days Without End*—but once, with his counterpart in *The Iceman Cometh,* he did his best to be self-effacing. He did not want anyone to identify him with Theodore ("Hickey") Hickman. Short, plump, with a breezy personality that "makes everyone like him on sight," Hickey eventually reveals himself as a man driven half-mad by guilt feelings, one who periodically goes on binges that end with his resembling, in his own words, "something lying in the gutter that no alley cat would lower itself to drag in—something they threw out of the D. T. ward at Bellevue along with the garbage, something that ought to be dead and isn't!"

Through Hickey, who explains with twisted, diabolic logic that he killed his wife because he loved her (actually because she made him feel so guilty over his binges and whoremongering), O'Neill felt free—Hickey seeming so unlike his author—to voice his agony over his mother, his hostility to her, his deadly resentment over her morphinism. In becoming a drug addict, though innocently with his birth, she bequeathed to her younger son life-long guilt feelings and self-hatred, something he could never forgive. Hence the legion of dead wives and mothers in his plays, a far larger number than is generally realized, as the playwright-son took symbolic revenge again and again on addicted Ella O'Neill. Hence, too, his compulsion from time to time to punish himself by drinking himself ill (*Sheaffer II,* pp. 498-500).

The *Practitioner* article, so far as it applied to O'Neill, was mistaken in one respect. Though it says that the "psychosis inevitably recurs," O'Neill went on the wagon in 1926 and thereafter, except to fall off several times for brief periods, he remained abstinent till his death in 1953. Give up drinking, the doctors had told him, or risk an early death. Since he had an irresistible need to vent his inner torment through the written word, the autobiographical playwright took the pledge.

* * *

Secret "Journey." As *Bowen* (p. 276) tells it, O'Neill on finishing *Long Day's Journey Into Night* in 1941 sent a copy to Saxe Commins, and after he and publisher Bennett Cerf had read it, the play was locked away at Random House with the following notation, as directed by O'Neill: "Not to be opened until twenty-five years after author's death."

This is erroneous. Saxe, one of the few privileged to read *Journey* during O'Neill's lifetime, typed the play while visiting O'Neill in California, but the latter kept all the copies. When he returned to New York several years later, the play was secured with sealing wax, without Cerf being allowed to read it, and stored in the publisher's vault with a note by O'Neill about its ban.

When Carlotta Monterey released *Journey* for publication and staging only several years after her husband's death she was criticized for violating the playwright's trust. In defense, she said that he had imposed the restriction at the urging of his elder son, who felt that it showed his paternal forebears in a severe light; but after Eugene Jr.'s suicide in 1950, O'Neill, according to Carlotta, lifted the ban. Some writers, among them *Bowen* (pp. 347, 361) and *Carpenter* (p. 158), have accepted her story; it is refuted, though, by O'Neill himself.

Writing to Bennett Cerf in 1951 (nearly a year after his son's suicide), O'Neill thanked him for returning some scripts that had been stored at Random House, and he added: "No, I do *not* [his underlining] want *Long Day's Journey Into Night*. That, as you know is to be published twenty-five years after my death—but never produced as a play."

* * *

Misnamed. The following photographs in *Gelb*, between pages 264 and 265, have erroneous captions:

Beneath the photo of the Barrett House, the child at the left, identified as Eugene aged two, is really his brother Jamie; the child in the center, identified as Eugene aged five, is Kenneth Macgowan, and the young man at the right, identified as Jamie, is Robert Edmond Jones.

The house identified as the Monte Cristo Cottage was the home of the Rippins, where the O'Neill family took their meals and where Eugene convalesced one winter after his discharge from the Gaylord Farm TB sanatorium.

At the sanatorium: The young woman at the left, identified as Kitty MacKay, the real-life model for the heroine of *The Straw*, is a nurse whose name is unknown. This photograph, with the same erroneous caption, appeared in *The New York Times* on October 18, 1982, with a story about Gaylord Farm. For a photo of Kitty MacKay, see *Sheaffer I*, p. 251).

In the beach party scene, between pages 552 and 553, the group is identified, from left to right, as follows: Henrietta Metcalf, holding Shane; Eugene, Edith. Shay, unidentified man, Agnes, Frank Shay and unidentified woman.

The caption should read: Mrs. Francesco Bianco, Agnes' aunt; Shane, Eugene, Edith Shay, Frank Shay, Agnes, Mr. Bianco, and Margery Boulton, Agnes' sister.

Erroneous caption in *Sheaffer I* (p. 427): The infant being held by Mrs. Fifine Clark is Oona in Nantucket in 1925, not Shane in Provincetown, 1920.

17:3 (Fall 1983)

WORKS CITED

Alexander	Alexander, Doris. *The Tempering of Eugene O'Neill*. New York: Harcourt, Brace, 1962.
Basso	Basso, Hamilton. "The Tragic Sense," *New Yorker*. February 28, March 6, and March 13, 1948.
Bowen	Bowen, Croswell. *The Curse of the Misbegotten*. New York: McGraw-Hill, 1959. (Although the title page says the book was written "with the assistance of Shane O'Neill," he had no hand in its composition.)
Carpenter	Carpenter, Frederic I. *Eugene O'Neill*. New York: Twayne, 1964.
Clark	Clark, Barrett H. *Eugene O'Neill: The Man and His Plays*. New York: Dover, 1947.
Gelb	Gelb, Arthur and Barbara. *O'Neill*. New York: Harper and Row, 1962.
Nathan	Nathan, George Jean. *The Intimate Notebooks of George Jean Nathan*. New York: Knopf, 1932.
Raleigh	Raleigh, John Henry. *The Plays of Eugene O'Neill*. Carbondale: Southern Illinois University Press, 1965.
San Francisco	O'Neill, Patrick. *James O'Neill*. History of the San Francisco Theater, Vol. 20: Writers' Program of the WPA in Northern California, 1942.
Sheaffer I	Sheaffer, Louis. *O'Neill: Son and Playwright*. Boston: Little, Brown, 1968.
Sheaffer II	Sheaffer, Louis. *O'Neill: Son and Artist*. Boston: Little, Brown, 1973.

Eugene O'Neill and the Creative
Process:
A Road to Xanadu

John H. Stroupe

Do I then strive after happiness?
I strive after my work!
—Nietzsche[1]

It is a commonplace of O'Neill criticism that the areas of action within his plays are coincident with his own moral universe—that as an obsessed dramatist, his entire canon is a search for meanings in a world he finds sterile and corrupt. Certainly the complexity of O'Neill's obsessions and their relationship to his well-known psychological difficulties are the sources of his unique virtues and defects as an artist; the author's psychological state is the catalyst bringing together artistry and idea, linking each play to his own core concerns.

It is also well known that O'Neill was an obsessive craftsman and that his plays are a consistent chronological record of a mind in torment. The creative process was for him a means of charting his own nature. And in order to carry out his task, he compelled himself, very courageously, to live on the very edge of his psychological strength. What is most important is that O'Neill used his personal life for his artistic life with a ruthlessness as unsparing as that of Strindberg, whom he so greatly admired. His conclusions are thus far less interesting than the various means he uses to analyze his material. This is as it should be in drama.

Marco Millions, first conceived in 1921 and completed in 1927, was written during the most productive years of O'Neill's life and provides a useful focus for a study of his artistry. What becomes important, then, in an examination of *Marco Millions*, knowing that O'Neill was attempting to dramatize once more oft-explored ideas, is an examination of

115

the steps involved in the creation of the play. Such an inquiry demonstrates not only how the action evolves from O'Neill's compelling criticism of American values, but also reveals the steps in the creative process which give power and shape to his dramatic work. Available for such a study are O'Neill's direct source for the play, his working notes (written during 1922 and the winter of 1923), his longhand first draft, a typescript of that draft—with O'Neill's extensive pencil cuts and revisions upon that text—and the Theatre Guild's prompt copy from its 1928 production of *Marco Millions.*[2]

I

While in prison at Genoa (1298-1299) following his years in the Orient, Marco Polo dictated his travels to a fellow prisoner, Rusticiano, the Pisan writer, and it is this account to which O'Neill turned for information regarding the Polos' journeys before he drafted *Marco Millions.* O'Neill's notes indicate that he worked directly from the most celebrated edition of the travels, *The Book of Ser Marco Polo*, edited by Sir Henry Yule, and that he approached his source with a clear idea of the *kind* of material he wanted to find there.[3]

O'Neill's preliminary notes for the play can be divided into two unequal sections.[4] The larger part consists entirely of material dealing with major characters, notes which O'Neill drew from Yule's lengthy Introduction to Marco Polo's own Prologue and Four Books of his travels, rather from a close reading of the travels themselves. O'Neill includes an outline of Marco's known career, a proposed cast of characters, the major dates of the Polo family's travels between 1254 and 1299, and data on the characters of Marco Polo and Kublai Khan. There are individual pages of notes on Rusticiano; outlines of Chinese history, particularly of the genealogy of Chinghiz, the Great Khan, including Kublai, his grandson; lists of Marco's missions, data on specific voyages, and information on his return to Venice.

O'Neill took notes in several different ways, varying in explicitness from direct quotation and almost verbatim paraphrase through condensed summarizations to bare notations of page references. He seemed content at this stage to rely fully upon his source. In Yule's Introduction, for example, there is a description of the elaborate feast given by the Polos upon their return to Venice from Persia:

> They invited a number of their kindred to an entertainment,
> which they took great care to have prepared with great state
> and splendour in that house of theirs; and when the hour
> arrived for sitting down to table they came forth of their
> chamber all three clothed in crimson satin, fashioned in long
> robes reaching to the ground. . . . Straightway they took
> sharp knives and began to rip up some of the seams and
> welts, and to take out of them jewels of the greatest value in
> vast quantities, such as rubies, sapphires, carbuncles,
> diamonds and emeralds, which had all been stitched up in
> those dresses in so artful a fashion that nobody could have
> suspected the fact. (*Yule*, I, p. 5)

In his notes, O'Neill merely lists the page reference where
this description can be found. But there is no doubt that he
returned to these introductory remarks when he later drafted
the play: for Act Three, Scene One repeats much of the
substance of this description. The Polos enter *"dressed in
long robes of embroidered crimson reaching almost to the
ground."* Finally, the three slit *"up the wide sleeves . . .
lower their opened sleeves, and . . . let pour from them a
perfect stream of precious stones which form a glittering
multicolored heap."*[5]

O'Neill's notes for the character of Marco are of course
the most important, for they indicate the nature of his
reliance on Yule's edition and his conception from the
beginning of his central character. O'Neill twice refers to
Marco in his notes as the living embodiment of twentieth-
century American man. First, in Yule's Introduction there is
this passage about Marco Polo:

> Still, some shadowy image of the man my be seen in the
> Book; a practical man, brave, shrewd, prudent, keen in
> affairs, and never losing his interest in mercantile details, very
> fond of the chase, sparing of speech; with a deep wondering
> respect for Saints, even though they be Pagan Saints, and
> their asceticism, but a contempt for Patarins and such like,
> whose consciences would not run in customary grooves, and
> on his own part a keen appreciation of the World's pomps
> and vanities. (*Yule*, I, p.108)

In a second passage, Yule, also evaluating the character of
Marco Polo as he emerges from the travels, comments:

> Besides intrinsic improbability, and positive indications of
> Marco's ignorance of Chinese, in no respect is his book so
> defective as in regard to Chinese manners and peculiarities.

The Great Wall is never mentioned . . . . The use of Tea . . .
is never mentioned; the compressed feet of the women . . .
artificial egg-hatching, printing of books . . . beside a score of
remarkable arts and customs which one would have expected
to recur to his memory, are never alluded to . . . . It is
difficult to account for these omissions . . . but the impression
remains that his associations in China were chiefly with
foreigners. (*Yule*, I, pp. 110-11)

In response to both passages O'Neill made entries in his
notes identifying Marco as the American ideal; the first
passage he repeated in his notes word for word; the second
he repeated, retaining Yule's phrasing, shortened merely
through the use of connectives. It is quite probable, on the
basis of O'Neill's notes on Yule's Introduction, the general
method in which he took his material and recorded it, that
O'Neill seized upon details which placed Marco Polo within
his own preestablished framework as an American ideal. It is
evident in *Marco Millions* that O'Neill consciously developed
Marco as an exponent of our society as he interpreted it. His
own *a priori* notions of America and of Marco as its
representative were so settled that he did not bother to
explore Marco's travels carefully: Marco was an O'Neill
character before he was created and takes his place alongside
Yank Smith and Billy Brown as O'Neill's vehicle for
presenting an idea. He is the embodiment of "virtuous
Western manhood amid all the levities of paganism" and
one who surely will be "worth a million wise men—in the
cause of wisdom " (p. 363).

The second section of O'Neill's preliminary notes consists
of background data on the geographical and economic
aspects of the Orient. There are sections on Persia, India,
Mongolia, and China, the four countries most prominent in
Marco's narrative (and which appear as the principal
countries within the play). His comments on Persia
(Trebizond, Mosul, Baku, Georgiana, Bagdad, Tariz,
Hormuz, Sapurgan, and Badasham), India (on Buddha, the
Brahmins, and the Jagis), Mongolia (Pein, the Gobi Desert,
Tangut, Camul, Chingintalas, Sukchu, Tibet, and
Caracoron), and China (Erguiul, Tenduc, Bacsi, Sensin, and
Cambaluc) are all taken from Marco's descriptions of these
countries and their peoples.

For example, in Marco Polo's narrative, O'Neill read that
"We're now passing through kingdoms where they worship

Mahomet," and that near Baki, "there is a fountain from which oil springs in great abundance."[6] In Persia, Marco observes: "And you must know that it is in this country Armenia that the Ark of Noah exists on top of a certain great mountain." Passing through Georgiana, Marco speaks of "A kingdom called Mausul," and recalls that the people there "weave the finest carpets in the world." And of Bagdad we learn, "It is the greatest city in these regions."

O'Neill's notes here reveal that he was looking at the travels for elements he could condemn in his portrayal of Marco Polo as a typical twentieth-century American success. He recorded only those elements which typical American tourists would observe—that which has commercial and monetary relevance, or the commonplace and pedestrian, or the trivially exotic. O'Neill's commentary, then, which he found in Marco's narration and recorded in his notes, shows him adopting, either consciously or unconsciously, the very attitude he was to condemn in his play. For O'Neill was simply not interested in Marco's occasional descriptions of the cultures of these lands, nor did he remark on the many Christian miracles which Marco accepts as true and repeats for our pleasure.

Marco's penchant for reciting facts, chamber-of-commerce fashion, is accentuated by O'Neill in *Marco Millions*. In Act One, Scene Three, Maffeo says, "we better read him [Marco] from the notes we made on our last trip all there is to remember about this corner of the world." And Nicolo responds, taking out *"note-books closely resembling a modern business man's date-book and read[s]*: 'We're now passing through kingdoms where they worship Mahomet.' " Maffeo follows: "There's one kingdom called Musul and in it a district of Baku where there's a great fountain of oil . . . . make a mental note of that" (p. 365). Just as Marco Polo kept notebooks of his travels and dictated to Rusticiano from them, so O'Neill took the above lines from Yule's edition of Marco's travels, set them down in his notes, and then allowed Nicolo and Maffeo to read these comments from their notebooks. And there are hundreds of similar examples where O'Neill recorded in his notes data taken from Marco Polo's narration, material which he would later incorporate into his final product. O'Neill depicts Marco, for example, arriving in Islam, rushing to his father and uncle with news that "A man told me that Noah's Ark is still somewhere around here on top of a mountain" (p. 364).

O'Neill's preliminary notes for *Marco Millions* indicate that as he approached a writing of the play, he sought information from Marco's travels and from Yule's introductory materials, frequently forming opinions from Yule rather than from a careful "crusading behind the lines of his [Marco's] book."[7] His intent was satirical, his focus economic. In forming Marco, he sought only that information which would allow him through a slanted projection of Marco Polo to satirize the American businessman and to show the tragedy inherent in American culture. He would depict the effect Marco would have upon Eastern culture and, by extension, the base corruption and soullessness of American society.

II

From his reading of *The Book of Ser Marco Polo*, O'Neill concluded that the most effective dramatic presentation of Marco's story could be achieved by following the structure of Marco's own narrative. Therefore he created the Venetian as author-narrator of his own play, dramatizing Marco's role in two scenes within the Genoese prison. In the first prison scene, Marco prepares to dictate his travels to Rusticiano; in the second, he concludes his narrative. Though these two scenes were later removed from the play, *Marco Millions* was first conceived as a play-within-a-play, one interscene demonstrating this intention: in it Marco dictates to the poet to remind the audience of the convention.

The first prison scene takes place in Marco Polo's cell in the fortress of the Malapaga, Genoa, and contains six characters: Marco, Donata, Nicolo and Maffeo Polo, Rusticiano, and Giovanni, the turnkey. Most of the scene is a dialogue between Marco and Rusticiano. Marco is drawn as direct, aggressive, and resolute in contrast to Rusticiano who is pale and sickly—a romantic, sentimental, ineffectual artist. (We are well-acquainted with this typical polar opposition of types in the O'Neill canon.) Marco and Rusticiano agree to combine efforts in an account of the Polo family travels, and Rusticiano recounts his past success as a man of letters, assuring Marco that he is well-qualified for the noble task. Finally, Marco states his humanitarian reasons for wanting to prepare the book: he wishes to provide useful data—mainly facts and statistics—as an educational influence for his people. Giovanni soon enters to announce three visitors—Marco's wife, father, and uncle— and following introductions, Marco explains his joint undertaking with the poet, the brothers delighting in the potential millions worth of advertising in the proposal. Nicolo and Maffeo tell of their attempts to bribe the Governor for Marco's freedom, and at the conclusion of the scene, Marco, nagged by Donata, blandly suggests that perhaps Rusticiano can someday devote an entire book—a romance—to the story of her faithful, twenty-three year wait for his return from the East.

The stage directions at the beginning of the second prison scene indicate that only a few months have passed since the initial prison scene and that two years have elapsed since the Polos' return to Venice from the Orient. The action involves only Marco, Rusticiano, Donata, and Giovanni. Marco completes his dictation to Rusticiano, reaffirms the desire that his story will help Venice capitalize upon his influence with the Khan, and tells his scheme to arrange an exclusive trade agreement with the East that will bankrupt Genoan merchants and importers. The scene, however, becomes one of low comedy with the entrance of Giovanni, who interrupts a domestic argument between Marco and his wife with great trumpeting raspberries, imitations of dogs barking, and suggestions that Marco must have enjoyed millions of loose women in the Khan's empire. Marco, of course, views Giovanni's mentality as merely typical of those narrow-minded few who will view his book as a tissue of lies. The scene concludes with Rusticiano questioning Marco about his relationship with the Princess Kukachin, while in the distance temple bells begin to ring, increasing in volume until the last scene of the play opens upon the funeral of Kukachin.

In all drafts of the play and in the published editions, *Marco Millions* begins and ends with scenes depicting the death of Princess Kukachin. In the opening scene, the audience witnesses the progression of her funeral cortege toward China: in the final scene, it participates in her funeral service at Cambaluc. These *funeral* scenes, then, provide a framework for the entire play. But in the drafts, the two *prison* scenes initially provided a second frame, appearing immediately after the first and before the 1st funeral scene:

Opening scene: Persia: Kukachin's funeral procession
First prison scene: Marco's cell in genoa: the same hour
                    intervening scenes depicting
                    the Polo's travels
Second prison scene: Marco's cell
Final scene: Kukachin's funeral: the same hour

Most important, this double framework illustrates O'Neill's desire to emphasize the disparity between the two worlds. The two "outside" scenes depict the Eastern world exemplified by Kukachin and Kublai Khan; the "inner" framework shows Marco as representative of the Western world. Marco, in prison, is an isolated specimen to be examined critically: the corrupt, materialistic opportunist who will even try to cheat Rusticiano out of his share of the profits from the publication of the travels. Thus, the double framework originally helped to project O'Neill's dual purpose in the play: to present a tragedy and moral satire— to condemn Marco as living representative of modern culture, to "dig at the roots of the sickness" of the modern world by presenting a soulless creature devoid of human understanding, a man "full of the gravity of material things," and one endowed with a "childish vanity and a sentimental credulity."

But while the double framework reveals much of O'Neill's intent, it presents numerous problems, for dramatically it is weak. In both prison scenes, Rusticiano appears only as a foil to Marco. He is such a romantic dreamer, ineffectual as an artist, naíve and unsophisticated, that Marco, with a large degree of natural wit and ability, becomes a sympathetic figure by comparison. Donata is maternal, a close-haggling housewife. Compared with these two and Giovanni, Marco emerges as the only sensible figure. Paradoxically, O'Neill, in his attempt to show Marco as soulless, worldly-wise, and corrupt, destroys part of his satiric intent in these scenes. Further, satire can best be displayed through dramatic action rather than by secondhand revelation through a narrative and two scenes written with blatantly satiric intent. Finally, these harshly "comic" prison scenes, juxtaposed to the high seriousness of the two funeral scenes, mar the dramatic effectiveness of the latter. O'Neill's instinctive feel for the dramatic is here richly apparent in his removal of these scenes from the play.

The omission of the inner framework for *Marco Millions*—the device of the distancing narrator—is but one of several changes O'Neill made. His second major structural change, also revealing his strong capacity for pointed dramatic action, alters the character of Princess Kukachin and directly affects the action within three different scenes. In the published play, Marco, together with Nicolo and Maffeo, journeys through Persia, India, and Mongolia, finally reaching the palace of the great Kublai Khan in Cathay after several years' travel. Their meeting with the Khan and his spiritual advisor, Chu-Yin, is described in Act One, Scene Six, a scene in which Princess Kukachin does not appear. She is first introduced (apart from the funeral scene framing the play) in the next scene, Act Two, Scene One, which takes place fifteen years later. There. Kukachin is *"a beautiful young girl of twenty, pale and delicate"* (p. 384), and has already fallen in love with Marco, although she is engaged and soon to marry the Arghun Khan in Persia. In O'Neill's drafts of the play, however, Kukachin appears in three scenes, first as a child of four, then at six, and later at eighteen—scenes later altered in his revisions.

As the child of four, Kukachin appears sitting at the foot of the Khan in a scene where he greets the Polos for the first time. To the gasping horror of the Court, Marco sets Kukachin on his knee to get better acquainted, and she exchanges confidences with her new friend, revealing among other things that the wart on her grandfather's nose wiggles when he is troubled. Throughout, Kukachin is thoroughly spoiled little royalty. When at the conclusion of the scene Marco steps into the courtyard for a breath of fresh air, Kukachin imperiously commands him to remain with her. In a fit of rage, she stamps her feet and orders a hungry tiger loosed into the yard. As her servants turn to obey, Kukachin hysterically rescinds her command, breaks into tears, crawls into her Nurse's arms, and asks for a piece of candy.

In the next scene, three years have elapsed since the Polos' arrival in Cambaluc. Princess Kukachin, now six years old, is discovered playing chess wtih Chu-Yin at Kublai's summer palace at Xanadu. About to lose the game, she orders it suppressed, since a princess of the blood may not lose. His education now complete after three years of schooling, Marco, together with Nicolo and Maffeo, turn to a discussion of Marco's future. But the scene quickly shifts as Kublai calls to his side the Classicist and the Scientist who have been Marco's teachers since his arrival at Court. We recall from the published play, Act One, Scene Two, that Tedaldo, the new Pope, had announced *"sardonically"* that he had "no hundred wise men—nor one!" (p. 362) to send to the Khan. Instead, with *"a sudden whimsicality,"* he decided that Marco's presence would be more instructive:

> Let him set an example of virtuous Western manhood amid all the levities of paganism—be oblivious and level-headed—shun the fraility of poetry—have a nest-egg million in the bank, as he so beautifully phrased it, and I will wager a million of something or other myself that the Khan will soon be driven to seek spiritual salvation somewhere! Mark my words, Marco will be worth a million wise men—in the cause of wisdom! (p. 363)

In the first draft, however, it is the Classicist and Scientist who first discern the truth of the Pope's perception. As Marco's tutors of Chinese, the Tartar dialects, history, and philosophy, they discover that he educates them. Wisdom stops, they report, where Marco begins. But the lengthy dialog between the tutors soon becomes digressive in its revelation of their intense rivalry: the Classicist finds Marco a grubber after the facts who would make a renowned scientist, while the Scientist discovers that Marco uses facts as a narcotic to escape from scientific truth and predicts that he will be a famous artist or philosopher. Later in the scene, Marco and Kukachin are playing jackstraws, observed by Kublai and Chu-Yin, both of whom sense Kukachin's love for Marco. Chu-Yin explains this attraction by suggesting that both are spiritually of the same age and that to Marco life is merely an earnest game of jackstraws. This is a truth Kublai hesitates to accept, but its truth becomes apparent before the play reaches its conclusion. The scene concludes as Marco comes before Kublai and decides upon a career as a Second Class Agent.

When we next meet Kukachin, it is in the following scene, twelve years later, but set again at Xanadu. She is here a young woman of eighteen, preparing to depart for Persia to marry Arghun Khan. The action of the scene is similar to the published Act Two, Scene One, and its function is to depict Marco's effect upon Kukachin. Further, the scene serves to expose Marco's reforms upon the city of Yang-Chau, which he governs, and to present his economic and social doctrines. Kukachin confesses her love for Marco to Kublai; Marco arrives from Yang-Chau; and Nicolo and Maffeo attempt to impress Kublai by reciting improvements Marco has made as Governor. Marco has given the city, they report, a marble court house, a granite jail, a swimming pool, a harem, and a racetrack. He has built a marble house for aged Venetian Christians and a magnificent asylum for members of the Chamber of Commerce. He has passed ten thousand laws, closed the theatres and houses of ill fame, cleaned the streets of the city, purged the police department, and licensed sacred concerts in the dance halls—not wishing to restrict legitimate entertainment. Marco, who returns from washing his hands and combing his hair, defends himself against a petition Kublai has received from the citizens protesting Marco's rule; Marco promises Kublai the means to conquer the world—the cannon—if he will promise never to destroy Venice and if he will allow the Polos to return home; Kublai agrees, and the Polos, accompanied by Kukachin, prepare to depart for Persia.

In his revisions, O'Neill cut all references to Kukachin in the first two scenes (Kukachin as a girl of four and six). In addition, he removed the figures of the Classicist and the Scientist from the second scene, and combined what remained with the third—the conflation of the two scenes bringing us immediately to Xanadu fifteen years after the Polos' arrival at Court.[8] O'Neill's changes again seem to be motivated by one dominant factor: all the alterations serve to emphasize the spirituality of Eastern culture and the crassness of the Western, widening the gulf between the two. At the same time, they heighten the dramatic effect by making the Western figures the corrupting influence upon the East. If Kukachin remains in the play as a child, she becomes humanized. She also appears as much Western as Eastern—spoiled, autocratic, and intemperate. Her imperious arrogance, though childish, wins no sympathy from an audience, and there is little difference between the child-like Marco and the actual child, Kukachin. Indeed, Chu-Yin views them both as of the same age spiritually; his comment postpones the emergence of Kukachin as a spiritual figure in the play, even though she does mature as the play progresses. Also, the portion of the scene in which Kukachin commands the tiger to be let loose in the yard is psychologically forced, implausible, and trite; the entire sequence is stagey and amateur; it is a dramatic cliché.

It is dramatically more effective to view Marco upon his arrival in China and then see him suddenly fifteen years later. The audience thereby witnesses the result of Marco's fifteen-year stay and reaches its own conclusions about his influence upon the culture and the culture's lack of influence upon him. Marco becomes by his own words and actions the personification of corruption and depravity. He is no longer a mere merchant of Venice, but a symbol of middle class America, a "lump of deformity" in full career.

The Classicist and Scientist, ostensibly representatives of Chinese wisdom and sagacity, emerge as typical western pendants, each quibbling over the value of his academic field. It is ironic that the "wise" scholars of the Eastern world would make the mistake of fragmenting knowledge, of trying to dissever the disciplines. After all, why should Marco, the narrow-minded man, have learned anything from such narrow-minded tutors?

Certainly *Marco Millions* benefits from such omissions. Most important, Kukachin thereby emerges as a spiritual figure, representative of Eastern beauty and nobility. Portrayed as a child she was too human, too perverse in her ways; and if the satirical and tragic elements are to be heightened, the gulf between East and West must be maintained. This new scene—the conflation of the second and third (Act Two, Scene One in the published play)— depicts Kublai as the exemplar of Eastern wisdom, a detached commentator upon Marco's behavior over the fifteen-year period, one in which Kublai becomes the eventual victim of the tragic fate which he himself has allowed. Marco's actions speak for themselves. His speeches justifying his reforms in Yang-Chau lead Kublai to recognize that Marco has no soul, only an "acquisitive instinct." Finally, Kublai begins to grow weary of Marco's "grotesque antics," and observes:

> A jester inspires mirth only so long as his deformity does not revolt one. Marco's spiritual hump begins to disgust me. . . . We have given him every opportunity to learn. He has memorized everything and learned nothing. He has looked at everything and seen nothing. He has lusted for everything and

loved nothing. He is only a shrewd and crafty greed. I shall
send him home to his own wallow.[9] (p. 387)

O'Neill shows Marco to be the epitome of corruption and
greed as the Venetian announces his two great contributions
to Eastern culture: paper money and the invention of the
cannon: "You conquer the world with this . . . and you pay
for it with this." "You become the bringer of peace on
earth and good-will to men, and it doesn't cost you a yen
hardly" (p. 396). Kublai can only say with *"weary
amazement"*: "Life is so stupid, it is mysterious" (p. 399).

While O'Neill's changes in *Marco Millions* are motivated
by his desire to depict the corrupting influence of the
Western image of God upon Eastern culture, the play at the
same time castigates the modern American's pursuit of
material goals; for the creation of a prideful, materially-
minded, corrupt human being will have a tragic effect upon
everyone who comes in contact with him. *Marco Millions*,
like so many of O'Neill's plays, is reminiscent of the
dramatized elements of pride in the medieval morality plays,
expressing the ethic of a Catholicism which O'Neill never
completely lost. Marco's new American denseness and blind
egoism are old spiritual pride writ large.

III

In the chronology of his plays supplied for Richard
Skinner's *Eugene O'Neill: A Poet's Quest* (New York,
1935), O'Neill records that in the summer of 1924, he
"finished 'Marco Millions' in its original two part two-play
form, each play short full length." He adds that in the
winter of 1925, he completed the "Final draft of 'Marco
Million,' condensed into one play." And in a letter
published in Barrett Clark's *Eugene O'Neill* (New York,
1947), O'Neill explained that as he revised the play, he chose
to "rewrite and condense the two nights into one long
night." Evidently, then, *Marco Millions*, had at first been
two plays, or one play in two parts, intended for production
on successive evenings. A quick review of the mechanical
arrangement and rearrangement of the parts which make up
the play will clarify these terms, for by reviewing O'Neill's
drafts we discover he initially conceived *Marco Millions* in
five parts, later altered it to five acts, then restructured the

play in eight acts, finally to publish it within a three-act structure.

O'Neill's handwritten first draft of *Marco Millions*, completed in the summer of 1924, reveals a structure of Five Parts divided into fifteen scenes:

First Draft in Five Parts

Part I, scene i:	A sacred tree in Persia: funeral cortege
Part I, scene ii:	Marco's cell in Genoa
Part II, scene i:	Donata's home: Venice
Part II, scene ii:	Palace of the Papal Legate: Syria
Part II, scene iii:	Marco's journey to Persia
Part II, scene iv:	India
Part II, scene v:	Mongolia
Part II, scene vi:	Arrival in China: Kublai's palace
Part III:	Kublai's palace: three years later
Part IV, scene i:	Same: twelve years later
Part IV, scene ii:	Royal warf: seaport of Zayton
Part IV, scene iii:	Harbor of Hormuz, Persia: the royal junk
Part V, scene i:	Kublai's palace: Cambaluc
Part V, scene ii:	Marco's cell in Genoa
Part V, scene iii:	Kublai's palace: funeral scene

Twelve of these fifteen scenes are substantially identical to the twelve scenes of the published play. The three additional scenes which appear here are the two prison scenes, the inner framework (Part I, scene ii and Part V, scene ii above), and the scene set in Kublai's palace three years after the Polos' arrival in China (Part III above; we recall that when O'Neill removed Kukachin from the scenes now labeled Part II, scene vi and Part III, most of the *content* of Part III appeared in the scene which followed, Part IV, scene i, and is set fifteen years after Part II, scene vi).

It is this draft which O'Neill described as his original "two part two-play form, each play short full length," intended for production on successive evenings. As O'Neill wrote to Kenneth Macgowan (12 October 1924): "The first draft 'Marco' play is now finished. . . . I should say the play is two good long plays of 2 1/2 hours each—at least! So you see it's really two plays I've done. Luckily, without premeditation, the piece falls into two very distinct—and exactly equal in length—halves."

While the division into two plays could have been a mechanical one based merely upon the temporal requirements of playing time upon a stage, O'Neill originally intended a break between Part Two, Scene Six and Part Three, and this division is so indicated upon the manuscript (between Acts One and Two in the published play). Since O'Neill saw the internal movement dividing into the progress of Marco to the East and then his effect upon the East, the action builds toward the eighth scene, Marco's arrival in China; the latter half of the play builds toward the funeral scene where the audience witnesses Marco's effect upon all of China, specifically upon Kublai and Kukachin.

Completing a first draft, O'Neill had his longhand manuscript typed, as was his custom, this typed draft substantially a complete transcript of the first draft except that the "Parts" had become "Acts." Only when O'Neill revised the typed script did he make two significant changes in the play. First, he revised the five-act structure into an eight-act form and placed the new act and scene designations over the old headings of the typescript. His second change was the removal of the character of Kukachin as a young girl with the resultant conflation of Act Four, Scenes One and Two (Part Four Scenes One and Two in the handwritten first draft). These two changes, then, resulted in an eight-act form in fourteen sections:

Typescript	*Revisions*
Ace I, scene i:	Act I, scene i
Act I, scene ii:	Act I, scene ii
Act II, scene i:	Act II, scene i
Act II, scene ii:	Act II, scene ii
Act II, scene iii:	Act III, scene i
Act II, scene iv:	Act III, scene ii
Act II, scene v:	Act III, scene iii
Act II, scene vi:	Act III, scene iv
Act III:	Act IV
Act IV, scene i:	Act V
Act IV, scene ii:	
Act IV, scene iii:	Act VI
Act V, scene i:	Act VII
Act V, scene ii:	Act VIII, scene i
Act V, scene iii:	Act VIII, scene ii

This revised draft, *with the prison scenes still in the play*, is O'Neill's "final draft" which he completed in March, 1925 (the manuscript is so dated), and does qualify as a "condensed version." There is, however, other evidence to support this conclusion, for Barrett Clark writes that in 1926, he read O'Neill's "condensed version" of the play and that it was "longer by at least two scenes" than the one ultimately acted (p. 108). If, as O'Neill tells us, he completed a final draft in the winter of 1925, and if Clark read this same draft, the "condensed version," in 1926 only to find the later acted version still shorter, then O'Neill's so-called final draft would appear to be simply another draft later to be revised and cut before the published version of the play appeared in 1927 and before the Theatre Guild production in January, 1928. Certainly Clark was not likely to remember two scenes by their numbering, or remember, as a number, the total scenes he read. But he would remember something outstanding or unusual in their substance or their setting. The two prison scenes seem eminently to qualify as the scenes Clark refers to, and the draft, now in fourteen sections, is a "condensed version."

Apparently O'Neill, in March, 1925, completed what he called his final draft, "condensed into one play," consisting of fourteen scenes. Finished with the manuscript, O'Neill put it aside and turned to work on *The Great God Brown*. David Belasco had acquired the rights to produce *Marco Millions* in 1925, but after a year's delay hesitated to do so, claiming that it would cost too much money. Finally, in September, 1926, O'Neill wrote George Jean Nathan that the Theatre Guild "has definitely decided that they want the play—but they could not do it for over a year" (Clark, p. 108). The prison scenes still remained in the play, then, in 1926 when Clark read O'Neill's final version; they were only omitted sometime before the published Boni and Liveright edition of 1927.[10]

That the Revised Draft could easily become the three acts of the published edition can be readily observed:

	Revisions	1927 Published Edition
	Act I, scene i:	Prologue
	Act I, scene ii:	Prison scene omitted
	Act II, scene i	Act I, scene i
	Act II, scene ii:	Act I, scene ii
	Act III, scene i	Act I, scene iii
	Act III, scene ii:	Act I, scene iv
	Act III, scene iii:	Act I, scene v
	Act III, scene iv:	Act I, scene vi
	Act IV:	Act II, scene i
	Act V:	Act II, scene ii

Revisions	1927 Published Edition
Act VI:	Act II, scene iii
Act VII:	Act III, scene i
Act VIII, scene i:	Prison scene omitted
Act VIII, scene ii:	Act III, scene ii

Let us review the progress of the manuscript thus far: O'Neill's handwritten first draft reveals that he initially conceived *Marco Millions* in five parts. Then the text of the fifteen scenes within the five-part structure was typed, the five parts becoming acts. O'Neill then altered the framework from five to eight acts, still in fifteen scenes, and only then did he revise the new structure by altering the scenes with Princess Kukachin. These two revisions resulted in an eight-act structure, consisting of fourteen scenes. This emergent draft was the author's "final draft," later typed to be sent to the Guild and to his publisher. Only during 1926, at least sometime prior to 1927 publication, did O'Neill omit the prison scenes, reducing the play to twelve sections. Finally, these twelve sections in eight acts were regrouped into a framework of three acts.

Although O'Neill changed the play, then, from five parts to five acts, to eight acts, and finally to three acts, he made, with the exception of two conflations and two excisions, no fundamental change either in the order of scenes or in basic substance, despite the variety of numbering systems by which the scenes were successively designated. The changes in labels do describe, however, the shifts in O'Neill's *pacing* of the play. Yet the structure of the *action*, in any real sense, is not significantly changed; O'Neill merely changed his mind several times about where best to have intermissions and how many.

Marco Millions was produced by the Theatre Guild in January, 1928, and O'Neill, as was his habit, attended the rehearsals of the play. Alfred Lunt, who played Marco Polo, remembers O'Neill sitting in the rear of the theatre during many of the rehearsals, relaying his wishes through the director, Rouben Mamoulian.[11] We also know that O'Neill approved the prompt copy which the Guild used during its rehearsals. But since the play had been published first because of the delay in production, O'Neill insisted that the performance adhere to the version already published, though his usual procedure was to insist that published editions of his plays adhere strictly to the performance. Thus, with remarkable closeness, the acted version of *Marco Millions* is similar to the printed text but for one change, approved by the author. In the acted version, there are only five scenes in Act One instead of six. Act One, Scene Five, the short scene in Mongolia, is omitted from the synopsis of scenes in the program notes and from the play itself, but most of the substance of the scene was added to Act One, Scene Four, Marco's visit to India. Because of the length of the play, the time necessary to change scenes, and the elaborate setting required for the foreign lands Marco visited, Mamoulian decided to omit one scene. While agreeing to the omission, O'Neill saw to it that most of that scene was incorporated in the preceding section. Thus, the presentation of *Marco Millions* by the Guild consisted of a Prologue and ten scenes within a three-act structure, and the actual performance, shortened only by the time required for a scene change, does not conflict with Barrett Clark's statement. Clark had noted, we recall, that the condensed draft he read was "longer by at least two scenes" than the acted version. The later omission of the prison scenes explains the discrepancy; this further shortening in the actual performance explains his words "at least."

In *Marco Millions*, Eugene O'Neill was experimenting with a form not employed earlier in his canon. Anticipating the nine-act structure of *Strange Interlude*, he wrote a play conceived in a "two part two-play" form, intended for production on successive evenings, the first two Parts depicting Marco's early travels and education, Parts Three through Five showing his corrupting influence upon Chinese society. Only when the play was condensed into three acts, however, did O'Neill find he could present his criticism of America's values most dramatically.[12]

Notes

[1] O'Neill's inscription on the title page of his first manuscript draft of the play, originally titled *Mr. Mark Millions*.

[2] O'Neill's working notes, his longhand first draft, and a typescript of that draft, were a gift from the author to Yale University in 1942 and are available in Yale's Collection of O'Neilliana. The Theatre Guild's prompt copy is in the Theatre Guild Collection, also at Yale.

[3] *The Book of Ser Marco Polo*, ed. Sir Henry Yule (New York, 1921). Hereafter, *Yule*. This two-volume edition was first published in 1871, reappeared in revised form in 1875. A third edition appeared in 1903 and was reprinted in 1921, the same year O'Neill conceived the idea for *Marco Millions*. See my "O'Neill's *Marco Millions*: A Road to Xanadu," *Modern Drama*, 12 (February 1970), 377-82, for a detailed examination of these notes.

⁴ My division. O'Neill's "Preliminary Material" for *Marco Millions* is available on microfilm (27 frames) in the Yale Collection and is labeled "O'Neill Film No. 3." Section One is on frames 1-18; Section Two on frames 19-27.

⁵ *Marco Millions*, in *The Plays of Eugene O'Neill*, 3 Vols. (New York: Random House, 1955), p. 429. All further references to the play, hereafter incorporated into the text, are from this edition.

⁶ O'Neill read these comments and the others cited in this paragraph in *Yule*, I, pp. 60, 46, 43, 50, and 63.

⁷ In a foreword to the first published edition (New York: Boni and Liveright, 1927), O'Neill wrote that *Marco Millions* was his attempt to render poetic justic to a famous traveler, "unjustly world-renowned as a liar," a "practical man of data" who "moves one to pity, to indignation, to a crusading between the lines of his book, the bars of his prison, in order to evoke the true ghost of that self-obscured Venetian." Virginia Floyd notes in *Eugene O'Neill at Work* (New York: Ungar, 1981) that the playwright "always read a considerable amount of material for the historical plays he either completed or contemplated," and that his extant notes for *Marco* "indicate none was so thoroughly researched" (p. 60).

⁸ When O'Neill omitted Kukachin and the tutors, the first of the three scenes under discussion was reduced to the initial meeting of the Polos with Kublai. When the second and third scenes were combined, O'Neill took the discussion of Marco's career and his decision to be a Second Class Agent and joined it to the first. As a result, the revised first scene allows the audience to see Marco meet Kublai and immediately choose a career. The new scene which follows fifteen years later introduces Kukachin to the play as a girl of twenty. See the published play, Act One, Scene Six, and Act Two, Scene One.

⁹ The passage is identical in both the published edition and the drafts.

¹⁰ Working from O'Neill's Work Diary, Virginia Floyd concludes that "Mr. Mark Millions" was initially a "six-part scenario" which the playwright then transformed into "a massive four-part first draft." Floyd also states that O'Neill eliminated the two prison scenes in January 1925 when he condensed the two "long plays" into "the drama's final form the present three-act" work. See *Eugene O'Neill at Work*, pp. 62-63.

Taoism and O'Neill's *Marco Millions*

James A. Robinson

It is common knowledge that Eugene O'Neill acquainted himself with Oriental religion during the 1920's. The climax of *The Fountain* (completed in 1922) dramatizes a mystical vision involving Buddhist and Moslem priests; *The Great God Brown* (1925) alludes to Nirvana and transmigration; the protagonist of *Lazarus Laughed* (1926) resembles Buddha in his serenity and non-egoism. Thus far, however, discussion of O'Neill's Orientalism has largely confined itself to exploring the influence of Hinduism and Buddhism on particular plays, neglecting the impact on his art of the Chinese religion of Taoism.[1] This is surprising, given the preference he expressed for this particular mystical philosophy in a 1932 letter to Frederic Carpenter about the "considerable reading in Oriental philosophy and religion" he confessed to doing "many years ago." "The mysticism of Lao-tse and Chuang-Tzu," O'Neill continued, "probably interested me more than any other Oriental writing."[2] The influence of these two major Taoist philosophers is especially apparent in *Marco Millions,* which concerns the conflict between the Western materialism of Marco Polo and the serene spirituality of the Chinese society he encounters. Taoist teachings on life, death, and the illusory nature of the ego are reflected in the speeches of the play's Chinese characters. Moreover, its central figures demonstrate in their personalities or relationships the rhythms of the Tao, the cosmic force around which Taoist thought revolves. This play about East meeting West remains, in the final analysis, within Western theatrical and philosophical traditions; but a Taoist counterpoint adds tension and depth to the play's vision, and offers insight into O'Neill's mystical temper.

The playwright's interest in China was not confined to its religions. In 1922 (a year before beginning work on *Marco Millions*) he wrote Kenneth Macgowan that his family's "plans

135

for the winter remain chaotic," and fantasized that "we will probably, in a fit of desperation, wind up in China. I'd like that, too, while Europe somehow means nothing to me."3 Six years later, O'Neill and Carlotta Monterey (a life-long collector of Oriental art) realized that fantasy by taking a cruise to China. But when he researched and composed *Marco Millions* between 1923 and 1925, the playwright contented himself with journeying to the Orient in his imagination by means of the books he read on China at that time. While Sir Henry Yule's edition of *The Book of Ser Marco Polo* constituted the play's primary source,4 other volumes acquainted O'Neill more fully with the medieval Chinese society where most of the action takes place.5 Several of these books were themselves informed by Taoist thought. O'Neill's personal edition of Li Po's poetry, for example, recurrently revealed that poet's Taoistic suspicion that life was a dream.6 Another work, Laurence Binyon's *The Flight of the Dragon,* focuses on the "rhythmic vitality" of Chinese art that is patterned on the "great cosmic rhythm of the spirit" that Chinese term the Tao.7 The major source of O'Neill's knowledge of this ancient mystical religion, however, was the James Legge translation of *The Texts of Taoism,* volume 39 in the *Sacred Books of the East* series edited by Max Müller. Including translations of Lao Tse's *Tao Te Ching* and the first seventeen of the 35 books (chapters) composed by Chuang Tse, this edition offered both the sacred texts and a scholarly analysis of this obscure philosophy, courtesy of an outstanding authority on Chinese thought.

This article's scope obviously does not permit detailed recapitulation of Legge's translation and commentary; but the following brief synopsis highlights the fundamental features of Taoism that pertain to *Marco Millions.* Like the Indian religions that O'Neill also studied around this time, Taoism posits that an impersonal, mysterious ultimate reality offers man liberation from the sufferings of existence. Buddhism calls this state Nirvana; Taoism locates it in the dynamic cosmic force known as the Tao, described by Legge as "the spontaneously operating cause of all movement in the phenomena of the universe."8 Like Buddhism and Hinduism, Taoism perceives the phenomenal world in a constant state of flux that repudiates man's conventional, rationalistic beliefs about reality and individual identity. Chuang Tse (in Taoism's most famous parable) dreams he is a butterfly, and awakes to discover "myself again, the veritable Kau. I did not know whether it had formerly been Kau dreaming that he was a butterfly, or it was now a butterfly dreaming that it was Kau. . . . This is a case of what is called the Transformation of things."9 Dismissing the notion of the unique ego, Taoism also questions the "reality" of life itself, and perceives death as "the great awaking, after which we shall know that this life was a great dream."10 Consequently, Taoism proposes a policy of *wu wei* (inaction) by which man detaches himself from this illusory life through renouncing all activity and desire. Through passivity, one avoids interference with the spontaneous movements of the Tao, and thereby realizes the bliss that union with this cosmic force offers.

As indicated, many Taoist beliefs correspond to Indian religious teachings; but in *Marco Millions* (as we shall see), the speeches that refer to these beliefs frequently allude to *The Texts of Taoism* in particular. The personalities of the play's major characters, moreover, point to a more exclusively Taoist influence. Chinese philosophy views existence as a series of apparent oppositions that relate to the two poles of *yin* and *yang*. The *yin* is dark, receptive, female, intuitive and still; the *yang* is light, aggressive, male, rational and active. But as the *Tao Te Ching* asserts, "the movement of the Tao/ By contraries proceeds."11 That is, within the Tao *yin* and *yang* alternate and interpenetrate in an eternal cycle that represents the hidden, dynamic unity behind all superficial contrasts and conflicts. The Tao, then, is above all a monistic force that rhythmically harmonizes polar oppositions, including that between life and death. In *Marco Millions* the emperor Kublai Khan is portrayed as one who (like the Taoist sage) reconciles opposites within his own personality. Furthermore, the contrasting personalities of Kukachin and Marco Polo correspond to *yin* and *yang,* subtly suggesting that they—and the East and West they symbolize— may in fact be united by larger cosmic cycles.12

This monistic Taoist strain in the play, however, must contend with more traditional Western elements in O'Neill's vision. In the plot, Kukachin falls in love with Marco Polo, who is so blinded to her love by his materialistic preoccupations that he unwittingly brings about her death. *Marco Millions* thus follows the lines of conventional Western tragedy, which assumes a dualistic universe of irreconcilable conflict—though here, rather than God or nature defeating man, it is West destroying East. Indeed, underlying the East-West conflict of the action is a similar conflict within O'Neill, whereby Western dualism ultimately triumphs over the harmonic view of the universe O'Neill discovered in Taoist thought. The play's Eastern elements represent the dramatist's suspicion that at the deepest level, man and world and cosmos were integrated and serene; but his pessimistic modern-Western side seems reluctantly convinced that man and universe are in hopeless conflict, a conflict reflected in the irreconcilable opposition of Oriental and Occidental cultures.

The play's early scenes reproduce this deeper conflict between dualistic and monistic world views, though the monism is not presented along Taoist lines. The final four scenes of Act I follow young Marco Polo, his father and his uncle through Persia, India and Mongolia to China. Uniting these scenes are common structural elements that hint at the universality of certain human patterns, despite superficial cultural differences. The differences are exotic and striking: the Persian setting features a *"jeweled, high-colored, gorgeous background"*;[13] the Indian scene contains a snakecharmer; the Mongolian episode offers a Tartar kettledrum accompanying a wordless chant. But in stage groupings, the three scenes are identical. Each contains a ruler seated before a place of worship, surrounded by attendants and a larger semicircle of squatting figures who represent various stages of life from infancy to death. In each scene (and also in scenes two and six, set respectively in a Papal Legate's Persian palace and in Kublai Khan's court), the ruler in the center is flanked by a warrior and a spiritual advisor. The sequence of events in scenes three, four and five is also identical. The Polos enter carrying sample cases and read their notes about the area; young Marco observes the natives and encounters a prostitute (the same actress in three different costumes); a brief exchange unfavorably compares the local religion to Christianity; the Polos depart as the natives pray.

The similar stage groupings and character types symbolize the profound identity between different cultures that makes understanding possible. The response of the protagonist, however, emphasizes cross-cultural conflict. The farther he journeys East—through lands whose mystical creeds preach tolerance and renunciation—the more intolerant, ethnocentric and materialistic Marco becomes. Before the journey began, the teenaged Marco displayed enthusiastic curiosity about the Orient. But by the time he reaches India, the maturing Marco glances at a sacred statue and mutters, "so that is Buddha!" in *"a smart-Aleck tone"* (234). In Mongolia, he *"hardly glances"* at the local people in the background (238). And when Marco departs for China from Mongolia, the stage directions highlight his emerging mythic status as the quintessential Western businessman. As he struggles through a gate, *"for a second he is framed in it, outlined against the brilliant sky, tugging a sample case in each hand"* (241). Having gained his manhood, Marco is now prepared to assume the larger symbolic role ironically assigned him by the Papal Legate (and future pope) in scene three: to "set an example of virtuous Western manhood amid all the levities of paganism, shun the frailty of poetry, have a million to [your] credit" (227).

As a prime "example of virtuous Western manhood," Marco learns nothing from fifteen years in China, pointing up an apparently unbridgeable gap between East and West. His materialism intensifies: through taxing necessities rather than luxuries, he proudly delivers to the Emperor Kublai Khan "the unprecedented amount" he has "sweated out of" the city he rules (255). His intolerance deepens: 500,000 inhabitants of the city sign a petition accusing him of "endeavoring to stamp out their ancient culture" (256). Marco also dabbles in weaponry, inventing a cannon that (he claims) will save the Khan money, and (incidentally) bring Polo Brothers and Son one million yen. This behavior confirms the scepticism of Kublai Khan and his counselor Chu Yin about Marco's possession of "that thing called soul which the West dreams lives after death" (243)—a Christian teaching Marco had promised to demonstrate to the Chinese ruler during their initial audience. Only Kukachin, who falls in love with him, believes in his soul. When Marco sails with her to Persia, the Khan orders him to gaze daily into her eyes, believing that his "soul" cannot ignore Kukachin's despairing love. The Venetian remains blind. Only on the final night does he glimpse her desire, and respond with a *"voice thrilling for this second with oblivious passion"*; but the next instant, his uncle Maffeo is seen *"slapping a stack of coins into the chest with a resounding clunk,"* which instantly returns Marco to his true beloved (280).

The relationship between Kukachin and Marco dramatizes

the polarity of the conflict between East and West. Marco exudes intolerance, while Kukachin radiates the supreme tolerance of one who loves a totally different person. Marco loves the treasures of this world, while Kukachin transcends them. Hence, her final lines bid farewell to Marco *"in a voice which is a final, complete renunciation."* As with Marco earlier, a silhouetted pose here illustrates her symbolic status: on the upper deck, she *"stands outlined against the sky, her arms outstretched,"* looking away from the earth (285). Within a short time, she perishes. The fact that Marco cannot perceive her love, causing her initial anguish and eventual demise, would seem to offer the final proof that West and East are doomed to incomprehension, struggle and destruction. These qualities also typify Western tragedy, and Kukachin's death allies her with numerous O'Neill tragic protagonists who strive against impossible odds and fail. Like Yank in *The Hairy Ape,* she confronts a dualistic cosmos where man is doomed to battle larger forces and lose. In this instance, however, the tragedy is more international than cosmic, in the manner of a Henry James novel. Kukachin herself represents one larger force, the Orient; her defeat is by a more powerful antagonist, progressive Western civilization.

Behind the dominant dualism, though, the mystic in O'Neill—influenced by Taoism—strives to discover unity. The Oriental Kukachin, who is feminine, passive, and spiritual, corresponds to the *yin* principle in Chinese thought. The Occidental Marco corresponds to *yang,* the masculine, rational and active principle. The latter association is made explicit in the second act, when Marco is about to speak off-stage to a crowd. Chu Yin reports that one of his hands "rests upon—and pats—the head of a bronze dragon, our ancient symbol of Yang, the celestial, male principle of the cosmos" (253). Marco's behavior consistently underlines this identification. His countless clever schemes evidence a rational, technological mind that needs to keep busy. This obsessive activism is even announced, in his departing lines to Chu Yin before sailing to Persia: "If you look before you leap, you'll decide to sit down. Keep on going ahead and you can't help being right! You're bound to get somewhere!" (271).

If the opposing personalities parallel *yin* and *yang,* so does their relationship. While Marco's insensitivity blinds him to

Kukachin's passion, her love suggests an attraction corresponding to the subtle bonds uniting *yin* and *yang*. The two figures also interpenetrate. Marco remains alive and successful after Kukachin perishes, but Kukachin finds life after death due to love. In the prologue, the dead Kukachin temporarily revives to proclaim, "I loved, and died; Now I am love, and live" (218). That line quietly underscores the secret unity of the two characters: the soul's immortality was the very thing Marco had promised to prove. In addition, Marco and Kukachin sail away together on a sea voyage, like Christ and Matt in *Anna Christie*. In the earlier play, the journey implied the secret union of all sailors in a transcendent force oblivious to individual differences. In *Marco Millions* the voyage instead suggests that Marco and Kukachin participate in the same large, unifying process. If this is so, then the same may be said of the opposing cultures they represent—and, by analogy, of all the oppositions in existence itself.

The monistic Taoist influence on the play also extends to O'Neill's portrait of Kublai Khan. The Emperor, called "son of Heaven, Lord of the Earth," harmonizes not only these realms but also the masculine rationality and aggressiveness of the West, and the feminine intuition and passivity of the East. An effective ruler of a vast empire, he periodically retreats to Xanadu to contemplate *"the vanity of his authority"* (248), indicating a balance between active and passive, public and private, pragmatic and spiritual in his personality. His opening description also emphasizes the harmony of opposites, picturing *"his expression tinged with an ironic humor and bitterness yet full of a sympathetic humanity. In his person are combined the conquering indomitable force of a descendant of Chinghiz with the humanizing culture of the conquered Chinese who have already begun to absorb their conquerors"* (241). In this Oriental despot, O'Neill pictures both the integrated personality he himself lacked, and the harmonic universe assumed by Taoist thought. But the Khan's Taoist harmony is upset by Marco and his effect upon Kukachin. Deeply attached to his grand-daughter, the Khan cannot remain serene when he contemplates her love for Marco, whom he recognizes as "only a shrewd and crafty greed" (251). In his attachment, the Khan violates Taoist precepts urging abstinence from relationship with anything but the Tao, and he suffers as a consequence.

In fact, only one Chinese character remains unperturbed, and consistently maintains the detachment of the Oriental sage: Chu Yin, the Khan's advisor. Not surprisingly, his advice accords with (sometimes even paraphrases) the teaching of Lao Tse and Chuang Tse. Thus, Chu Yin advises the Emperor after their initial encounter with Marco to "let him develop according to his own inclination," reflecting the Taoist policy of non-interference with the spontaneous operations of nature (246). Later, when Kublai Khan threatens to kill Marco rather than let Kukachin sail with him, Chu Yin recites *"in a calm, soothing tone"* that "the noble man ignores self. The wise man ignores action. His truth acts without deeds" (265). Legge's translation of the *Chuang Tse* similarly observes that "the Perfect Man has no thought of Self," while Lao Tse expresses the doctrine of *wu wei* in his statement that "the sage manages affairs without doing anything."[14] In the same scene, Chu Yin tells the sorrowful Kukachin that "life is perhaps most wisely regarded as a bad dream between two awakenings" (266), alluding to several passages in Taoist texts. Chuang Tse maintains that "we are born as from a quiet sleep, and we die to a calm awaking"; and as mentioned earlier, he regards death as "the great awaking, after which we shall know that this life was a great dream."[15]

This Taoist connection of life to dream appears again in Kukachin's poetic lament preceding her final departure from Marco.

> I am not.
> Life is.
> A cloud hides the sun.
> A life is lived.
> The sun shines again.
> Nothing has changed.
> Centuries wither into tired dust.
> A new dew freshens the grass.
> Somewhere this dream is being dreamed. (282)

The final line faintly echoes the concluding sentence in Chuang Tse's butterfly dream, where he admits that "I who say that you are dreaming am dreaming myself."[16] Viewing existence as illusion, Taoism is sceptical about the unique, separate personality: Chuang Tse realizes he may actually be a butterfly dreaming he is Chuang Tse. Similarly, Kukachin here proclaims "I am not," and wonders if she participates in another's dream. Other lines of the poem also reflect Taoist teachings. The cloud hiding the sun while "a life is lived" hints again at the obscure, dream-like nature of existence, and suggests the larger natural cycle formed by life and death, which alternate like cloudy and sunny days. The expression "nothing has changed" likewise points to eternal cycles in which all apparent transformations— e.g., from life to death—mask the changeless nature of the Tao. And lines 7 and 8, with an image of decay ("tired dust") followed by one of renewal ("new dew"), once more call attention to the merging of opposites into a larger divine rhythm.

Marco Millions' final scene brings together the Taoist motifs of complementary polarities and life's illusory nature. The *yin/yang* symbolism is rendered visually. Before the entrance of Kukachin's corpse, nine aged masked singers appear, *"dressed in deep black with white edging to their robes. After them comes a troupe of young girls and boys, dressed in white with black edging,"* their costumes reversing the pattern of the elder's robes (299). The complementary opposition resembles that found in the Taoist *mandala,* where a light dot surrounded by a dark semicircle complements an adjacent semicircle in which the pattern is reversed. The Khan's remark in the middle of his oration, "contain the harmony of womb and grave within you," relates to the symbolism of these costumes (301). Just as the apparel of the old and young complement each other, so do birth and death harmonize in the rhythm of the Tao. The Emperor's final speech recalls another related Taoist teaching, since he (like Chuang Tse above) suggests that life and death may be opposite to what we believe: Kukachin's death may actually be life, while Khan's life may be death. Kublai Khan softly accuses Kukachin of feigning death. "Open your eyes and laugh," he pleads, "laugh now that the game is over. Take the blindfold from my dim eyes. Whisper your secret in my ear. I—I am dead and you are living!" (303). His pathetic final lines, in which he bids Kukachin "welcome home," allude to a particular passage in the *Chuang Tse.* The Taoist sage asks, "how do I know that the love of life is not a delusion? and that the dislike of death is not like a young person's losing his way, and not knowing that he is (really) going home?"17 From this perspective, the Khan's apparent confusion about life and death contains wisdom as well as grief; and his final lines may token his knowledge of her awakening.

Marco Millions, however, does not conclude on this Eastern note. In the epilogue, as the house lights come up, the audience sees a fellow theatregoer who is *"none other than Marco Polo himself, looking a bit sleepy, a trifle puzzled"* until he arrives in the lobby, where *"his face begins to clear of all disturbing memories of what had happened on stage."* As he enters his luxurious limousine, he heaves *"a satisfied sigh at the sheer comfort of it all,"* and the car pulls away (304). The protagonist's obtuse complacency and materialism is thereby projected onto the Western audience, and juxtaposed one final time with the Oriental beauty and wisdom displayed in the previous scene. The juxtaposition reveals the divided vision of O'Neill. He focuses on two characters, a wise Emperor who harmonizes opposites, and a spiritual advisor who expresses Taoist wisdom; and he suggests via costume and dialogue that apparent dualities—including that of life and death—may in fact be complementary, unified by a larger cosmic cycle. But O'Neill's Western side has the final word. The Eastern loveliness Marco has witnessed briefly baffles, then bores, him; and his incomprehension seems both inevitable and common to Westerners. From this angle, East and West represent antagonistic approaches to life. Moreover, from the perspective of O'Neill's tragic sense of life, this antagonism does not simply govern the relations between Occident and Orient—it lies at the heart of the universe. However much O'Neill may satirize the Western greed and insensitivity of his protagonist, the playwright cannot divorce himself from the dualistic Western world view, since it constitutes the essence of his dramatic, tragic vision.

Finally, despite its numerous allusions to Oriental wisdom, *Marco Millions* seems sceptical about modern Western man's ability to embrace Eastern truths. A speech toward the end of the play indicates that the monistic philosophies of the East had not furnished O'Neill with the healing unity he sought. "My hideous suspicion," laments the grieving Kublai Khan, "is that God is only an infinite, insane energy which creates and destroys without other purpose than to pass eternity in avoiding thought" (291). The American playwright remained trapped within a Western consciousness that led not to liberation, but despair: the prophet behind these words is not Lao Tse, but Schopenhauer. Nonetheless, O'Neill's interest in Taoism continued long after this particular play was completed. It would wax and wane over the next fifteen years, reappearing in the polarities of

Lazarus Laughed, and expressing itself again in the cycles of *The Iceman Cometh, Long Day's Journey Into Night,* and *Hughie*—three plays composed in the O'Neills' California residence known as Tao House. In no other O'Neill work, however, were its teachings presented as directly as in *Marco Millions.* This in itself does not justify elevating this largely neglected drama into the first ranks of the O'Neill canon; but it does suggest that this unique blend of tragedy, romance and satire has more depth and complexity than has previously been acknowledged.

14:3 (Fall 1980)

NOTES

1 See Doris Alexander, *"Light on the Path* and *The Fountain,"* *Modern Drama,* 3 (1960), 260-67, and *"Lazarus Laughed* and Buddha," *Modern Language Quarterly,* 17 (1956), 357-65; I. M. Raghavacharyulu, *Eugene O'Neill: A Study* (Bombay: Popular Prakashan Press, 1965), chapters three and four *passim;* and Frederic I. Carpenter, "Eugene O'Neill, the Orient and American Transcendentalism," in *Transcendentalism and Its Legacy,* ed. Myron Simon and T. H. Parsons (Ann Arbor: Univ. of Michigan Press, 1966), pp. 204-13. Also see Carpenter's book *Eugene O'Neill,* 2nd. ed. (Boston: Twayne, 1979), which suggests correspondences between O'Neill's "theory of tragedy" (as exemplified in the late tragedies especially) and Indian religious thought (pp. 78-79, 175-79).

2 O'Neill letter to Carpenter, quoted in "Eugene O'Neill, the Orient and American Transcendentalism," p. 210.

3 O'Neill letter to Macgowan, dated 23 September 1922; File Folder Za/O'Neill/ to Macgowan, O'Neill Collection, Beinecke Library, Yale University.

4 See John Stroupe, "O'Neill's *'Marco Millions':* A Road to Xanadu," *Modern Drama,* 12 (1970), 377-78.

5 The precise date of acquisition of the three volumes mentioned below (all currently housed in the O'Neill Collection at the C. W. Post Center of Long Island University), is impossible to determine; but circumstantial evidence points strongly to O'Neill's reading them prior to completing *Marco Millions* in 1925. All are inscribed by O'Neill in the signature style he employed prior to wedding Carlotta Monterey in 1929, indicating purchase in the 1920's. Given O'Neill's 1932 remark to Carpenter about reading Oriental material "many years ago," and the fact that the books' copyright dates are all prior to 1923, it is likely he read them in the early 20's. And since these books and *Marco Millions* are concerned with Chinese culture, O'Neill probably consulted the former while doing background research for the latter.

6 *The Works of Li Po, the Chinese Poet,* trans. Shigeyoshi Obata (New York: Dutton, 1922).

7 *The Flight of the Dragon: An Essay on the Theory and Practice of Art in China* (London: John Murray, 1922), pp. 11-12.

8 *The Texts of Taoism*, tr. James Legge (London: Oxford Univ. Press, 1891), p. 15.

9 *Taoism*, p. 197.

10 *Taoism*, p. 95.

11 *Taoism*, p. 83.

12 In regard to the concept of complementary polarities, Taoism was not O'Neill's only source. Carl G. Jung also asserted that every personality contains contrasting feminine and masculine features that must be integrated; but Jung himself was strongly influenced by Taoism in regard to this concept.

13 O'Neill, *Nine Plays* (New York: Random House, 1954), p. 228. Hereafter documented informally.

14 *Taoism*, pp. 169, 48.

15 *Taoism*, pp. 250, 95.

16 *Taoism*, p. 193.

17 *Taoism*, p. 194; Legge's parenthesis.

O'Neill's Transcendence of Melodrama
in *A Touch of the Poet* and
A Moon for the Misbegotten

Michael Manheim

I have limited this discussion to a pair of late O'Neill plays which transcend melodrama by means of their comparable plots, themes, and characterizations. They are similar chiefly in that both begin with formulaic melodramatic intrigues which are spoofed or actually displaced as the plays develop. I intend in time to explore this theme in all O'Neill's later drama.

Melodrama, just about everyone is agreed, is indefinable, though that has not stopped people from attempting to define it.1 In Europe of the mid-nineteenth century, it meant a serious play with much scenic spectacle, musical background, a set of "stock" characters (which usually included a hero, heroine, and a villain), and an ending in which the "right" (the definition of which was not subject to discussion) always triumphed. Later, it was broadened to include any play, serious or comic, which was built around an elaborate set of intrigues; which contained a good deal of secrecy, deception, and evasion; in which the dialogue was full of explosive outburst and unexpected revelation; and which was peopled by the old stock characters supplemented by a variety of secondary figures. According to Frank Rahill, under the influence of several American dramatists—notably David Belasco and William Gillette—American melodrama near the turn of the century was being "modernized." These playwrights, says Rahill, sought to make melodrama "plausible, adult, and even intellectually respectable."2

Melodrama continues to be seen as a kind of drama in which

good and evil are self-evident entities. As Robert B. Heilman points out, its characters are invariably "whole," undivided as to right and wrong, and "free from the agony of choosing between conflicting imperatives and desires."3 This "wholeness," of course, is opposed to the chief quality of the leading characters in tragedy, which is their frequent agony over conflicting imperatives, their essentially divided natures. "In melodrama," says Heilman, "man is seen in his strength or in his weakness; in tragedy, in his strength and his weakness at once."4 It follows that melodrama so conceived need not be resolved happily. While right and wrong may be clear cut, there is no assurance in much melodrama that right will necessarily triumph. Recent studies have also focused on the pre-eminence of plot over characterization in melodrama.5

Eugene O'Neill grew up on a diet of melodrama provided by the theatre of his youth, especially as it was represented in his father's famous *The Count of Monte Cristo,* a classic nineteenth-century melodrama. John Henry Raleigh makes amply clear the degree to which that play—with its theme of ravaged innocence, its complicated intrigues and revenges, and the undivided personalities of its heroes and villains—was ground into O'Neill's consciousness from earliest memory and influences almost every play in his entire canon.6 O'Neill's attempts to overcome the influence of the image of theatre his father's work projected were less successful than he hoped they would be until quite late in his career. He did not easily forsake his theatrical heritage.

At the same time, a melodrama was critically associated with O'Neill's heritage in another way. As we know from *Long Day's Journey Into Night* and from two highly detailed biographies,7 O'Neill's family home had all the characteristics of a real-life melodrama. The O'Neill home in New London was shrouded in secrecy, suspicion, deception, and evasion all surrounding Ella Quinlan O'Neill's now well-known drug addiction. It was a setting of endless intrigue, in which mother sought to deceive father and sons, and father and sons plotted against mother. Paralleling the story of young Edmond Dantes in *The Count of Monte Cristo,* the story of young Eugene O'Neill (significantly called *Edmund* Tyrone in the later play) was one of rejection, intrigue, deception, escape, and if not violent revenge then certainly violent feelings growing out of a deeply vengeful spirit. Further, the characters of O'Neill's personal domestic melodrama viewed one another as "wholly" good, or "wholly" bad—usually the latter. That *Long Day's Journey* itself, written so many years after the events it dramatizes, is finally not a melodrama, is a subject I have recently explored and shall be exploring further.8

In his most famous plays of the 1920's and 1930's O'Neill obviously sought to avoid traditional conceptions of melodrama. He blurred clear distinctions between good and evil, and seemed determined to avoid heavy dependence on undivided characters and on intrigue. For example, his early sea plays, in particular *Moon of the Caribees* of the SS Glencairn series, prefigure *The Hairy Ape* and *The Emperor Jones* as dramatic explorations of the psychological complexity of their characters. These plays all but abandon intrigue—at least of the *Monte Cristo* variety. But as the 1920's progressed, and O'Neill experienced the loss of father, mother, and brother in rapid succession, the characteristics of melodrama became increasingly evident in his plays. Even O'Neill's admirers of that period acknowledge this.9 While O'Neill clearly *hoped* his plays would generate interest in the psychological states of his characters, the interest that is generated has more to do with their intrigue and their explosive dialogue than with any conflicting motives lying beneath the surfaces of their characters.10

Several plays which might not at first appear to substantiate this view actually do substantiate it. In *Strange Interlude*, O'Neill's use of the "interior monologue" is clearly designed to reveal the complexity of the play's characters. Similarly, in *The Great God Brown*, O'Neill reveals deep divisions in his characters through the use of masks. Deep divisions do not seem to fit the characters of melodrama. But the interior monologues and the masks have a more melodramatic effect than O'Neill might have imagined. What we see ànd hear on stage often suggests *two* undivided and opposing personalities rather than the single divided personality of Heilman's tragic hero, two personalities which often feel more like the hero and villain of melodrama than the conflicting forces within a single individual. This distinction is particularly evident in a play of the early 1930's, *Days Without End*, in which the hero John Loving is divided into two characters, John (the hero) and Loving (the villain). Each of these two characters is quite undivided in his stage personality, and much of the effect of their dialogue is melodramatic. Interestingly, however, in a scene from the second act of that play, when John's lover Lucy describes the single person John Loving she has had an affair with, the effect of her description is more genuinely probing than the scenes in which we encounter the doubled character. Her described John Loving seems more truly a single, divided individual. We find a similar split of a single personality into two dramatic characters, with similar melodramatic effect, in the figures of Lavinia and Orin Mannon in *Mourning Becomes Electra.*

Beyond characterization, what has kept audiences attentive to these plays, some of which are quite long, is their complex melodramatic plots. Despite O'Neill's efforts to the contrary, plot takes precedence over characterization in them. In the nine-hour-long *Strange Interlude,* for example, a gothic tale of hidden family insanity is introduced, with a father who died mentally ill and a mad old aunt locked away in an upstairs bedroom. Out of this intrigue about inherited madness there emerges the second and more famous of the play's intrigues, a tale totally dependent on secrecy, deception, and revenge for the interest it achieves. It is a story of forbidden love, with secret assignations, the expenditure of great efforts to deceive an unsuspecting husband, and the birth of a child whose illegitimacy is known only to its parents. This intrigue in turn leads to a new intrigue involving the attempt to hide that illegitimacy until the child's adulthood.

In the same way, while enigmas associated with sensitive individuals are important in two other well-known plays of the period—*Desire Under the Elms* and the aforementioned *Mourning Become Electra*—their melodramatic plots are still more important. The deception of old Ephraim Cabot in *Desire Under the Elms,* which grows out of the lust Eben and Abbie Cabot submit to, engages audience attention more than Eben's adolescent moodiness, though Eben is a genuinely divided figure. And the most engaging aspects of *Mourning Becomes Electra*—its secrecies, deceptions, suicides, revenges, and scenes of madness—are clearly melodramatic. Raleigh attributes these qualities to the influence of *Monte Cristo,* citing Robert Benchley's review of the play, in which the reviewer "conjures up an old actor with a white wig and sword standing in the wings and exhorting: 'That's good, son! Give 'em the old Theatre!' "[11] I would simply add that O'Neill's home life, which Benchley probably knew nothing about, has as much to do with the blatant melodrama of this play as the influence of old *Monte Cristo.* Like all

O'Neill's earlier plays, *Mourning Becomes Electra* disguises O'Neill's compulsion to reveal (while carefully hiding) the personal melodrama of his family home.12 The events and emotions centering on Ella O'Neill's addiction and later death are its much-varied theme. While O'Neill's hostility toward his mother is in the ascendancy, she is represented by the sinning Christine Mannon and he is represented by the outraged Lavinia. When O'Neill's guilt is in the ascendancy, however, his mother becomes the suicidal Christine and he becomes the guilt-ridden Orin.

And so it goes in O'Neill's other earlier plays—the pattern of unspeakable crimes committed by guilt-ridden women set against young men oscillating between fierce hostility and equally fierce guilt, or of deaths which heroes or heroines cannot face or (with similar effect) cannot bear. Throughout the entire earlier canon there is an unbroken rhythm of hostility followed by guilt followed by new hostility followed by renewed guilt— all taking place in an atmosphere of plotting and counter-plotting, suspicion and spying, vengefulness and accusatory out-burst, sudden reversal and angry defensiveness—in short, all the characteristics customarily associated with melodrama.

Toward the end of the 1930's, O'Neill's plays begin to sug-gest a coming-to-terms with his memories of his family. Con-comitantly, the plays reveal a new attitude toward melodrama. The new attitude is first reflected in the essential lightness with which very noticeable melodrama is treated in *A Touch of the Poet*.13 Raleigh notes that this play parodies *The Count of Monte Cristo*.14 Con Melody, like the outraged Edmond Dantes, wears Napoleonic period military garb, broods endlessly on past wrongs done him, and constantly plots revenge. But Raleigh fails to note the degree to which Con's characterization is a loving satire of James O'Neill, Sr., and his famous role. Con's personality is clearly the most important element in this play, and that personality is equally clearly that of the old campaigner both on stage and off. *A Touch of the Poet* shows O'Neill's understanding of his father while demonstrating the excesses of both his father's personality and his theatre.

But that the treatment of the melodrama in this play is comic is also important in understanding O'Neill's own artistic development. Throughout the play, Con sees his melodrama in serious terms while we take it in comic terms. When his daughter, for example, cannot marry her lover because the lover's father refuses his son permission to marry into Con's family, Con is described angrily journeying to the rich Yankee's home to get revenge. Needless to say, he takes this very seriously, though we do not. Further, when we hear that Con has been refused admission and beaten by the police for his efforts, the action approaches farce. O'Neill is thus revealing a growing sophistication not only about his father's art but about his own. As in *The Count of Monte Cristo,* so in O'Neill's earlier plays we took the characters as seriously as they took themselves. In this play we take the characters less seriously than they take themselves. As O'Neill began to put his family in perspective, he was becoming more able to put his own melodramatic excesses in perspective.

O'Neill's transcendence of melodrama in this play may also be explored from another point of view. Con's daughter Sara, at her father's suggestion, plots melodramatically and with great singleness of purpose to entice Simon Harford to sleep with her so that she may trap him into marrying her. At a crucial point late in the play, however, she suddenly loses her melodramatic certainty about what she has been doing. She becomes undecided over whether her enticements have been the result of her desire to trap Simon or the result of her genuine love for Simon, and her indecision is never resolved in the play. She moves quite suddenly from undivided character to divided character. By the end of the play, in fact, her indecision becomes so great that she seems about to become a genuinely tragic figure. She perceives through her own divided feelings a new image of her father. Con has throughout the play been posing as the aristocrat, speaking in lordly tones and treating everyone, including Sara, in a distinctly haughty manner. Late in the play, as a result of his humiliation by Simon Harford's father, Con "reverts" to his "peasant" origins, carousing loudly with low companions and speaking with a thick brogue. What Sara observes is that this peasant nature is but a second pose, that Con is no more truly a peasant than he was an aristocrat. She panics at the realization that Con is caught between two irreconcilable natures—both genuine yet at the same time both poses. Her panic unexpectedly introduces a tragic cast to a play which has appeared anything but tragic because the new feeling shifts audience interest away from the story of Con's revenge and toward a serious consideration of the contradictions in human personality. Sara can never know whether he is an aristocrat or a clown. The tragedy is inherent in the fear that neither she nor her father has a true self, the fear that human personalities may be entirely façades.

A Touch of the Poet thus begins to explore issues which are central to O'Neill's next two plays—*More Stately Mansions* and *The Iceman Cometh*—issues which are too varied and complex to explore in detail here.15 The central struggles of these two plays—which immediately precede his last, great plays, directly concerning O'Neill's own family—are struggles between the avoidance of self and the facing of self. They attest potently man's heavy dependence on illusion, but at the same time they recognize the heroic in the individual who is capable of facing an existence without illusion, who will accept the heavy contradictions and seeming emptiness that constitutes self-knowledge. Their transcendence of melodrama is very much tied with self-knowledge in ways that more than ever pertain to O'Neill's coming to terms with himself and with his past.

A Moon for the Misbegotten, which deals with the last days of O'Neill's brother, goes beyond the gentle mocking of melodrama in *A Touch of the Poet* to an actual displacement of it as the play's basis of construction. That O'Neill was probably thinking about melodrama when he was writing the play is suggested by a reference late in the play to David Belasco.16 Belasco, referred to earlier, was, of course, an important writer and producer of American melodrama spanning a period from the time James O'Neill was at the height of his successful career until the time Eugene O'Neill was making his first efforts as a playwright. His attempts to up-date melodrama fit O'Neill's earlier drama rather well. While undeniably melodramatic, O'Neill's earlier plays are certainly plausible, adult, and intellectually respectable—the terms used at the opening of this paper to describe Belasco's modernization. Thus, late in his career, O'Neill could be identifying the melodrama of his own earlier works with the work of a modernizer like Belasco, who took melodrama a few steps beyond that of the *Monte Cristo* variety.

That O'Neill had melodrama in mind in writing this play is also evident from the nature of its plot. As in *A Touch of the Poet,* the play starts out as a comic intrigue. The scheming Irishman Phil Hogan tries to trap his landlord, the "rich" Jim Tyrone, into marrying his oversize but not unattractive daughter Josie. This directly parallels the second intrigue referred to in *A Touch of the Poet,* both intrigues of course involving the oldest of melodramatic routines, with a father (shotgun in hand) discovering his daughter and her lover in bed together. Much more involved than this element of the plot in the earlier play, here this intrigue actually takes up more than half the action. A revenge theme is also introduced here. Believing her father's story that Jim is trying to cheat them out of their farm by selling it to a "Standard Oil millionaire," Josie goes along with the entrapment routine as a means of getting revenge on the unsuspecting Jim. Throughout a large portion of Jim's and Josie's late-night dialogue, Josie seeks to carry out what she sees as her bluffing seduction of Jim. Almost an hour and a half of this play, in other words, strikes its audience as good, old-fashioned melodrama—with tricks, deceptions, outbursts, and revelations of supposed villainy. Some viewers of the play never do get the point that melodramatic intrigue is not finally the central interest of this play.

Rather early following Jim's first-act entrance, we are made to sense that something quite removed from the activity at hand is occupying Jim's mind. Facial expression and seemingly irrelevant remarks on his part indicate—first quite subtly, then with increasing frequency and intensity—that something is haunting Jim Tyrone, something which may ultimately make Phil's intrigue and Josie's revenge seem insignificant. Jim is haunted, of course, by the memory of his recently dead mother (never specifically named Mary Tyrone) and by his personal behavior following her death. Having watched his mother die of a stroke during a trip to California, Jim, a supposedly reformed alcoholic, has abruptly and vengefully returned to his drink. He brought his mother's body back to New York by train, during which ride he consumed close to a case of whiskey and had nightly relations with a whore, for whose services, he pointedly observes, he paid "fifty bucks a night!"17 Upon his return, he had to be carried off the train and did not attend his mother's funeral. Since then, he has regularly suffered violent DT's while trying to sleep, and feelings of unbearable guilt while awake and sober. He has also unsuccessfully been trying to drown his sorrows in ever huger quantities of alcohol.

On the surface during the first act, Jim appears the friendly drunken Irish wit, providing and receiving great bursts of laughter in the company of his tenant Phil Hogan and Phil's buxom daughter. Under these circumstances, Jim's repeated assertions that he loves that large colleen seem unconvincing, especially to Josie. But, on the contrary, we come to learn by the middle of the play that everything *except* that love is Jim's bluff. His humorous manner is but the deceptive tip of a large iceberg of pain. He says he loves Josie "in his fashion"; and that fashion involves her capacity to provide him the immense forgiveness which will allow him to die at peace with himself. Jim has already destroyed himself irrecoverably through his drink.

Jim and Josie, throughout a large part of their long midnight meeting, speak tantalizingly at cross-purposes. Josie is playing her game, of course, deceptively saying things that will arouse Jim's sexual interest, though her deep affection for him makes her have to keep reminding herself that she is playing a part in a melodramatic deception. She really wants to make love to him. For his part, Jim begins by acknowledging his guilt only in truncated asides; then he does so more openly as he drunkenly forgets where he is and who Josie is. As she becomes more brazen, Jim begins to confuse her with the whore on the train, and thus with his monumental guilt. At one point, he does in fact behave as though he intends to rape her, which only adds to his guilt when he recalls who she is. His statements become extremely self-accusing and self-pitying—to Josie's growing amazement. Finally the subject turns to Phil's false accusation that Jim intends to sell the farm out from under them, which Jim dismisses with surprised contempt at Josie's gullibility. With Josie's realization that her father has made a fool of her, the intrigue is over, and all semblance of the play's original melodrama disappears. The play assumes a new shape built around its central characters' attempts to be totally honest with one another about their deepest feelings. Although there remains the question about what is disturbing Jim so critically, the interest of the play arises not out of that question but out of its characters' determination to give full expression to their until now unspoken pain. From being a play about the entrapment of a rich suitor, it becomes quite unexpectedly a play about confession, forgiveness, and freely given love. The play's interest moves from that associated with melodramatic intrigue to that associated with the total release of pent-up feeling—to a catharsis not unlike that associated with classical tragedy.

While the climax of the scene in question is Jim's long confession, the first of the two to speak openly about what for years has been her shame is Josie. She loves Jim because he sees through her coarse posturing. He gets her to confess quite simply that she is a virgin, and that her playing "the whore" has been her means of arousing sexual interest in men because she feels her size makes her physically unattractive. Jim brings her to realize that her pose has been damaging both to her suitors and herself, to them because of their resentment of inevitable rebuffs, and to herself because of the feelings of personal debasement her behavior arouses.

Jim then fully opens up Josie's feelings by telling her that while his love for her certainly includes sexual attraction, at the moment he desperately needs her help. Josie, abruptly realizing that sex has nothing to do with what Jim came for, must learn the terrible nature and extent of his shame and self-hatred. Jim's confession is something more than simply the story of his mother's death, his renewed drinking, and the whore on the train. It is a full reliving of the emotions associated with those events—the awesome fear which followed the loss of his mother, and the equally awesome hostility toward her for leaving him, the loss which prompted his renewed drinking and his taking up with the whore. These in turn have prompted the vengeance his personal furies are taking on him, drunk or sober. Josie's reactions are at first those of extreme disgust, but these change quickly to feelings of great affection. She is prepared to give him what he really came for, and her capacity for forgiveness is of a size proportionate to her body's. She first lets him fall asleep on her breast, then holds him between her legs for the remaining hours of their long night.

Jim Tyrone's fear and shame, when it is finally released, create the pity and terror Aristotle speaks of because his experience is made so immediate and familiar. His confession—like Hickey's in *The Iceman Cometh*—and his own confession as Jamie Tyrone in *Long Day's Journey* assumes the proportions of Lear's great, agonized periods in Shakespeare, or of the rich outbursts of pain and suffering in Greek tragedy. He becomes Oedipus expressing his overwhelming agony late in Sophocles' play, or Theseus giving expression to his pain at losing his son in Euripides' *Hippolytus*. He becomes bare, unaccommodated man proclaiming his agony to the universe.

Jim's reference to David Belasco referred to earlier drives home the point I have been making about this play's transcendence of melodrama. During the last act, following his night-long alliance with Josie, Jim observes the dawn, associating its beauty with that of his new-found (though soon-to-be-ended) love for Josie. She has just made renewed reference to his earlier, whorish lovers:

> Don't remind me of that now, Josie. Don't spoil this dawn! *(A pause. She watches him tensely. He turns slowly to face the east, where the sky is now glowing with all the colors of an exceptionally beautiful sunrise. He stares, drawing a deep breath. He is profoundly moved but immediately becomes self-conscious and tries to sneer it off—cynically).* God seems to be putting on quite a display. I like Belasco better. Rise of curtain, Act-Four stuff. *(Her face has fallen into lines of bitter hurt, but he adds quickly and angrily)* God damn it! Why do I have to pull that lousy stuff? *(With genuine feeling)* God, it's beautiful, Josie! I—I'll never forget it—here with you.[18]

When we recall Belasco's association with melodrama, we recognize that Jim is here identifying the false theatrical dawn of melodrama with his past cynicism and self-loathing, and the real dawn he is viewing with his transcendence of his own melodramatic fear through his love for Josie. The Belasco dawn is associated in Jim's mind with his great sins and guilt—and that dawn for O'Neill (seeing it in terms of his own life) has to do with the melodrama of his past, with its secrecies, deceptions, and excessive outbursts. The dawn at hand is an untheatrical new dawn—a dawn associated with openly confessed shame fully forgiven.

O'Neill had sought to recreate Greek tragedy ten years earlier in *Mourning Becomes Electra* and achieved there what is for many a prolonged and heavy melodrama. He finally did recreate the essential effect of classical tragedy, however, in a play where a fake melodrama is displaced by a mimesis rooted in the total release of the deepest emotions. He could write only melodrama—with its mysteries, disguises, secrets, and deceptions—while his plays of the 1920's and early 1930's served as suitable disguises for the circumstances of his personal hell. He came to control his art as he came to understand himself, and that artistic control is best represented in his rejection of melodrama in favor of the free and open pathos of traditional tragedy.

NOTES

1 There has been a flourishing interest in the study of melodrama over the past two decades covering a considerable gamut of perspectives. At one extreme are historical studies which consider the forms and look at examples of typical nineteenth-century melodrama. Michael R. Booth, *English Melodrama* (London: Herbert Jenkins, 1965); and Frank Rahill, *The World of Melodrama* (University Park, Pennsylvania, and London: The Pennsylvania State Univ. Press, 1967) are two such studies. At the other extreme are works which use the term much more generally, examining how melodrama and tragedy create the basic categories of all serious drama. Such a work is Robert Bechtold Heilman, *Tragedy and Melodrama: Versions of Experience* (Seattle: Univ. of Washington Press, 1968). A brief work which lucidly summarizes the different approaches is James L. Smith, *Melodrama* (London: Methuen, 1973).

2 Rahill, *The World of Melodrama*, p. 268.

3 Quotation is taken from James L. Smith's summarizing of Heilman's ideas, in *Melodrama*, p. 7. Heilman defines the undivided nature of the characters in melodrama versus the divided nature of the characters in tragedy in *Tragedy and Melodrama*, pp. 79-81.

4 *Tragedy and Melodrama*, p. 90.

5 Joseph Wood Krutch stated succinctly the idea that plot is more important than character in melodrama in "What is Melodrama?" *The Nation*, 138 (9 May 1934). 544, 546. Recent discussions of the importance of plot in melodrama are Earl F. Bargainnier, "Melodrama as Formula," *Journal of Popular Culture*, 9 (Winter 1975), 726-33; and Daniel Gerould, "Russian Formalist Theories of Melodrama," *Journal of American Culture*, 1 (Spring 1978), 151-68. Gerould and others demonstrate that melodramatic plot formulas provide much raw material for formalist literary analysis.

6 See John Henry Raleigh, "Eugene O'Neill and the Escape from the Chateau D'If," in *O'Neill: A Collection of Critical Essays*, ed. John Gassner (Englewood Cliffs: Prentice-Hall, 1964), pp. 7-22.

7 Louis Sheaffer, *O'Neill: Son and Playwright* (Boston: Little, Brown, 1968); and Arthur and Barbara Gelb, *O'Neill* (New York: Harper and Row, 1973). In *Eugene O'Neill's New Language of Kinship* (Syracuse, N.Y.: Syracuse Univ. Press, 1982), I survey in detail the pervasive influence of O'Neill's home life throughout his drama. See also Virginia Floyd, *Eugene O'Neill At Work* (New York: Frederick Ungar, 1981).

8 My chapter on *Long Day's Journey* in *O'Neill's New Language of Kinship* (pp. 164-90) emphasizes the forthright confessional nature of the play, suggesting its overall subordination of intrigue. I plan shortly to study the play's relationship to melodrama more specifically.

9 One of O'Neill's most outspoken admirers of the 1930's, Homer E. Woodbridge, made clear in an essay interestingly entitled "Beyond Melodrama" that O'Neill's plays up to that point missed being great tragedy largely because he was indeed "at times melodramatic." The essay is reprinted in *O'Neill and His Plays*, ed. Oscar Cargill *et al.* (New York: New York Univ. Press, 1961), pp. 307-20. O'Neill's denigrators on those grounds are well represented by Francis Fergusson, "Melodramatist," in *O'Neill and His Plays*, pp. 271-83.

10 On the "failure of language" in O'Neill's plays of this period, see Jean Chothia, *Forging a Language: A Study of the Plays of Eugene O'Neill* (Cambridge: Cambridge Univ. Press, 1979), pp. 84-110.

11 Raleigh,". . . Escape from the Chateau D'If," p. 12. In the same review Raleigh refers to, Benchley also concludes that while he could not figure out what the play meant, "It sure did scare the bejeezus out of you!"—which is perhaps the most typical of all responses to melodrama. See *The New Yorker*, 7 November 1931, p. 28.

12 I discuss reflections in *Mourning Becomes Electra* of O'Neill's family crises in *Eugene O'Neill's New Language of Kinship*, pp. 76-88.

13 While some might view *Ah, Wilderness* from this perspective, I feel the sentimentality of that play outweighs its lightness of tone. Instead of reflecting O'Neill's understanding of troubled memories, *Ah, Wilderness* attempts to cover them over. See *Eugene O'Neill's New Language of Kinship*, pp. 101-05.

14 Raleigh, ". . . Escape from the Chateau D'If," p. 21.

15 See *Eugene O'Neill's New Language of Kinship*, pp. 116-56.

16 Eugene O'Neill, *A Moon for the Misbegotten* (New York: Random House, 1974), p. 111.

17 *Ibid.*, p. 97.

18 *Ibid.*, p. 111.

"Daddy Spoke to Me!": Gods Lost and Found in *Long Day's Journey Into Night* and *Through a Glass Darkly*

Thomas P. Adler

> "In our family we stammer unless,
> half mad,
> we come to speech at last."
> William Carlos Williams,
> "To Daphne and Virginia"

Stockholm's Dramatiska Teatern has indeed been a very congenial stage away from home for America's only Nobel Prize-winning dramatist, mounting not just the premiere of *Long Day's Journey Into Night* in 1956, but also the first productions of *A Touch of the Poet* (1957), of "Hughie" (1958), and of *More Stately Mansions* (1962). Although Ingmar Bergman, Sweden's leading filmmaker as well as a theatre director of some renown, has never yet directed an O'Neill work for either stage or screen, he has "often quoted"—and therefore apparently values—the playwright's belief that "drama that doesn't deal with man's relation to God is worthless." As Bergman goes on to explain in a 1969 interview, "Today we say all art is political. But I'd say all art has to do with ethics. Which after all really comes down to the same thing. It's a matter of attitudes. That's what O'Neill meant."[1] As Paisley Livingston comments, "In Bergman's reading of the O'Neill dictum, man's relation to God passes through man's relation to man."[2] No one, however, has begun to explore fully the possible relationships (over and above their common indebtedness to Strindberg)

between O'Neill's plays and Bergman's films, although Michael
Manheim does suggest in passing that Bergman's *Autumn Sonata*
(1978) "may well have been influenced by O'Neill's later plays,
given their well-known popularity and availability in contemporary Sweden."3 Along with establishing some connections
between O'Neill's *Long Day's Journey* and Bergman's *Through
a Glass Darkly* which might particularize Manheim's general
intuition that O'Neill be seen as influential on Bergman's art,
an intertextual perspective, the later work seen as re-interpreting
the earlier, can help audiences resee the play from the vantage
point of its focus upon faith—losing faith, searching for and,
perhaps, finding faith.

Each work, *Long Day's Journey* and *Through a Glass
Darkly*, is a play of four figures: three men, one of them father
to the other two, and one of those two considerably younger
than the other; and a woman, who is wife and either mother
or daughter/sister. Both works are set by the sea. The young
man in each—an incipient artist—has an inordinately close
attachment to the woman (mother or sister), while the old man
is a popularly successful but failed artist of a sort. In both, too,
there is inherited illness or the threat of it: Edmund's consumption from his maternal grandfather and his tendency towards
suicide from his paternal; Karin's mental instability through her
mother. Of greater concern here, and ultimately what this essay
works towards, are the links between the two women, which
are underscored by certain physical and psychological symptoms: the nervous gestures; the over-sensitivity to sounds; the
retreat to the upstairs room; the guilty turning away from others
into the self; the living in two worlds.

In previous discussions of both works, but maybe more
especially so with *Long Day's Journey*, the *centrality* of the
female character and of her faith (or crisis of faith) experience
has been downplayed, perhaps in part because of the presence
of an autobiographical and/or authorial figure who commands
attention. If Karin's near continuous presence and her climactic
vision, because of its disturbingly late placement in the film,
help to confirm Bergman's focus upon her, Mary's virtual
absence from the long last act of *Journey*—she comes on stage
only in the ineffably beautiful yet unsettling coda—might tend
to make us overlook the fact that, for the first three acts, *it is
Mary Tyrone's play*. For her alone is this an unrelieved journey
into the dark night of the psyche, into what Yasuko Oku calls

"the nightside of self."4 For the three men, on the other hand, though it is too late for change and too soon for forgetfulness, it is an opportunity for truthfulness and understanding and perhaps even forgiveness. Father speaks to son, son to father, brother to brother. But no one can break through to the mother lost in her own private hell of self-recrimination.

For virtually all of the characters in these two works, the crisis in faith is bound up with a failure in vocation. This is particularly so for the two older men, the failed-artist/fathers who realize the painful disparity between what might have been and what is. James Tyrone comes to understand too late that, for a complex of reasons, he sold his soul to money rather than dedicating it to art by choosing commercial success and popular adulation instead of stretching his gifts as a classical actor. Likewise David, a financial success as a novelist, has never been recognized for the genius he so covets. Like that early novelist of surfaces in O'Neill, Charlie Marsden in *Strange Interlude*, he has not "married the word to life"; David's son-in-law Martin chides him for being a writer of "monstrous inventiveness" who crafts "lies [that] are so refined they resemble truth" and who is "absolutely perverted in [his] frigid lack of feeling": "You know how everything should be expressed. At every moment you have the right word. There's only *one* phenomenon you haven't an inkling of: life itself."5

What is more, David cannibalizes life for his fiction, preying unfeelingly on his daughter's mental illness as a possible subject for his writing. Unlike the altered Marsden, who finally composes "the book of us" as an avenue of penitence and reconciliation, or, indeed, unlike O'Neill himself who penned *Journey* "in tears and blood. . . . with deep pity and understanding and forgiveness for *all* the four haunted Tyrones"—that is, writers who relive and recreate the past in order somehow to transcend it, even though there seems to remain in *Journey* a residue of hatred on the part of the son towards the mother who made him feel so guilty—David would "use" and destroy others.6 His "art" has imprisoned, and he can only escape back into life by renouncing it. Before the action of the film opens, David had actually attempted suicide, saved only by the "inscrutable grace" of a stalled engine; in that action, all façades were stripped away so that he could "see [him]self." And "out of [his] emptiness something was born which [he] hardly dare touch or give a name to. A love" (*Glass*, p. 47). Late in the film, as part of the recurrent structure of confession it shares with *Long Day's Journey*, David seeks, and finds, forgiveness from Karin for sacrificing her life "to [his] so-called art"; afterwards, he burns the manuscript of his novel almost as an act of expiation.

While the older "sons" in each of these families hide from life—Jamie in drink that has always prevented him from committing himself to any vocation; Martin in a medical profession that not only permits but demands a certain defensive detachment—the younger sons are actively searching for meaning. Both journey through darkness into light, or at least a momentary glimpse of it. As an apprentice artist, Bergman's Minus deprecates his own efforts at playwriting as "shit." His playlet-within-the-film, entitled "The Artistic Haunting or, The Funeral Vault of Illusion" and presented as part of the celebration welcoming David home, raises, but leaves unresolved, the issue of the relationship between art and life. In Minus' "morality play, intended only for poets and authors," a Princess dies in childbirth, eventually to be forgotten by her young husband; later she returns to seek out an artist of evidently no achievement, one who "despise[s] . . . completed work[s as] banal," to love her. Though tempted to achieve his goal of transforming his life into a work of art, the young artist finally refuses to follow his Princess to death and eternity in order to complete his "masterpiece." Yet if the artist is to write about his experience with the ghost of the dead Princess, he knows that the ending would require "a more heroic twist." And so Minus' play ends in tension: can one reach through the finality of art what one refused during the flow of life?

Edmund, too, wonders at his capacity to render in words what is revealed to the imagination. In a lengthy monologue in Act Four that draws upon the same passage in St. Paul's First Letter to the Corinthians that provides Bergman with the title for his screenplay, Edmund recounts his experiences aboard ship when he was suffused by an ecstatic sense of belonging and oneness with "something greater than [his] own life . . . to Life itself! To God"; or, again near the sea, when with something "Like a saint's vision of beatitude" he saw face to face: "Like the veil of things as they seem drawn back by an unseen hand. For a second you see. . . . For a second there is meaning!" (*Journey*, p. 153) as art breaks through the fog that is life. Yet in spite of Tyrone Senior's recognition that his younger son possesses a touch of the poet, Edmund doubts that his words have been able to approximate the transitory vision; he "just stammered" and reduced things to a "faithful realism" at best, he thinks. The audience's judgment, however, is more apt to coincide (albeit bolstered by hindsight) with the father's, and the promise of art in the offing overwhelms even the pervasive death wish—the pull towards becoming lost in the fog "where truth is untrue and life can hide from itself" (p. 131) that links the younger son's predilection with his mother's.

If O'Neill's autobiographical play understandably examines Edmund primarily from the viewpoint of the artist's journey through darkness into an attainable—if rarely achieved— mystical, aesthetic light, Bergman's treatment of Minus mainly concerns itself instead with the movement from sexual innocence to experience and the achieving of, or at least the beginnings of, an emotional, psychological wholeness. Apparently living casually and closely with an older sister (and her husband), with no mother and an often absent father, Minus feels "shut up in[side] himself . . . in his own box" (*Glass*, p. 40) and deeply confused by his sexuality, particularly by his obvious attraction towards Karin—the sounds of her and Martin making love are equivalent to the primal scene and evoke not only embarrassment but jealousy. Her seduction of him in the womblike hull of the schooner seems to be *paired visually* with the earlier play-within-the film acted out in front of an inner stage summerhouse/tomb. The artist in Minus' playlet, it is true, finally chooses life over art by refusing love-in-death with the Princess; this scene, on the other hand, asks that the viewer somehow see the violation of the sexual taboo as ultimately positive for Minus rather than completely debilitating as it might at first appear. The conclusion of Bergman's film implies that the incestuous encounter between Minus and Karin is finally an essential release of tension for the boy, guaranteeing that he will not be sexually and psychologically fixated at that point.

After Minus' almost despairing entreaties to God go unanswered, he comforts the trancelike Karin (in a Pietà pose with the genders significantly reversed) as "the evening sun breaks through" the rain and "shafts of light . . . crisscross the darkness" (p. 51). Bergman imagistically establishes the potentially liberating and regenerative aspect of the consummation by the huge shadow in the shape of a crucifix cast on the schooner's floor as Minus cradles Karin in his arms. If "reality burst in pieces for [Minus]" (p. 59) in "the torment of insight," it is

David the father who helps him put those pieces back together again. If God as transcendent being seems to have gone out of Minus' world—just as he has from Edmund's "God is dead" universe—David counsels him to find "proof" for God's existence in the fact of *"Every* sort of love . . . the highest and the lowest . . . the most ridiculous and the most sublime . . . the obsessive and the banal . . . in the world of men." Man loves, and therefore God exists, providing "a pardon . . . from sentence of death." The human supplants the divine. As Bergman said in 1964 of his "trilogy" (*Through a Glass Darkly, Winter Light,* and *The Silence*): "They are not concerned—as many critics have theorized—with God or His absence, but with the saving force of love"—a value that Mary Tyrone desperately insists upon as well.7 For Minus, the loving presence of the human father substitutes for, or is equivalent to, the existence of God; he discovers—to borrow Cornelius Ernst's words in writing about Wittgenstein—"God's presence-in-absence in the world."

For the women in both works, on the other hand, any image of God in which the notion of *maleness* inheres is immediately suspect and threatening. Karin, suffering from an incurable mental disease, reveals her illness and instability in ways similar to Mary: the nervous gesture of running her hands over her hair; the extreme sensitivity to noises. And just as Mary retreats to the spare room upstairs for the drugs that will take her back before the pain and guilt began, Karin ascends the steps to the wallpapered-room; there she can, like Mary, leave behind her men (though the turning away from Martin's love causes her to feel guilty) and escape to a different, *real* world, apart, she claims, from the dreamworld of her illness. She tells Minus she can "walk straight through [the] wall, entering a "lovely . . . safe" room filled with people whose "faces are radiant with light," bonded together in "love," and "waiting for him who is to come" (p. 42) And that advent, Karin believes, will be "God . . . reveal[ing] himself to us."

Yet when she escapes back to the room just before she is to be taken to the asylum, the insect God who finally reveals himself to her and whom she sees as attempting to violate her sexually is associated visually with the machine, a "gigantic dark" heliocopter whose engines make "a tremendous roar," come to take her away: "The door opened. But the god who came out was a spider. . . . He came up to me and I saw his face, a loathsome, evil face. And he clambered up onto me and tried to force himself into me. But I protected myself. All the time I saw his eyes. They were cold and calm. . . . I've seen God" (pp. 58-59). Karin's chosen solipsistic "reality," the distorted vision of God with which she must live—whatever its genesis in the psychological traumas she has suffered in the past—turns out to be much more forbidding than the now altered realities of David and Minus that frame it and thereby temper it. David's decision to confess and seek forgiveness, and later his ability to talk to Minus and convince him of the power of love, though they cannot cancel out the forcefulness of the dark vision within which Karin is locked, offer alternatives for change and growth, at whatever point—even late—in life, that seem totally absent from *Long Day's Journey*, finally rendering *Through a Glass Darkly* less fatalistic in its outlook.

Mary's choice of the morphine-induced fog instead of her present reality of pain and guilt isolates her from the three men in *Journey* in much the same way as Karin's mental state separates her. Mary may have sold her soul for surcease from physical discomfort, but her real betrayal, she thinks, occurred much earlier when she turned her back on her dual vocation as pianist and nun to fall in love with and marry the dashing James Tyrone, with whom she "was so happy for a time" (*Journey*, p. 176). If Edmund searches through the fog for some visionary moment (art), Mary searches through the morphine for her lost faith. Failed by the men in her life—husband, doctor, older son, perhaps even the father whom she idolized and who introduced her to James—she never prays, however, to a father God, but always to the Virgin Mary to restore her to faith. It is as if *only a mother God*—a virgin free from sexuality who, like Mary Tyrone herself, suffered the loss of her son(s)—can save her. (This rejection of the burden and responsibility of married sexuality recurs frequently in O'Neill's plays—e.g., Nina and Lavinia at the close of *Strange Interlude* and *Mourning Becomes Electra*, respectively, especially when there has been an Oedipal or incestuous attachment.)

Though in life Ella O'Neill evidently refound that faith, in art she does not: the cycle, once initiated by one unwise, romantic choice, compounded by still other choices through time, is finally impossible to break free of. Character has become fate; Mary has "lost [her] true self forever" (p. 61) and can no longer call her soul her own. And so while the men can speak to and listen to one another, when they talk to her, she cannot hear. Trailing the gown in which she was wedded to James—but which she would also have worn in the convent ceremony during which she would have taken vows as a bride of Christ—Mary has not lost herself so completely in a drugged euphoria that she can forget the difference between romantic dream and disappointing reality. Like Edmund who experienced the momentary vision only to understand its intractability to ordinary language, Mary glimpsed happiness only to lose it. At the final curtain, she seems perpetually locked in that moment when happiness turned into pain. Unable to get back beyond that moment when she "fell in love with James Tyrone" and, as yet, unable to regain her faith in the Blessed Virgin, she is as irreparably cut off from her husband and sons, and from any certainty of human—let alone divine—love, as Karin is.

20:4 (Winter 1986–87)

NOTES

1 *Bergman on Bergman: Interviews with Ingmar Bergman*, ed. Stig Bjorkman, Torsten Manns, and Jonas Sima (New York: Simon and Schuster, 1973), p. 177.

2 Paisley Livingston, *Ingmar Bergman and the Rituals of Art* (Ithaca: Cornell Univ. Press, 1982), p. 251.

3 Michael Manheim, *O'Neill's New Language of Kinship* (Syracuse: Syracuse Univ. Press, 1982), p. 231.

4 Yasuko Oku, "An Analysis of the Fourth Act of O'Neill's *Long Day's Journey Into Night*: Mainly of His Application of the Comic Perspective," *Studies in English Literature*, 58 (1982), 48.

5 Ingmar Bergman, *Through a Glass Darkly*, in *Three Films*, trans. Paul Britten Austin (New York: Grove Press, 1970), pp. 45-46. Further references appear within parentheses in the text.

6 Eugene O'Neill, *Long Day's Journey Into Night* (New Haven: Yale Univ. Press, 1956), p. 9. Further references appear within parentheses in the text.

7 "Playboy Interview: Ingmar Bergman," *Playboy Magazine*, June 1964, p. 68.

The Defense of Psychoanalysis in Literature:
Long Day's Journey Into Night
and
A View From The Bridge

Albert Rothenberg and Eugene D. Shapiro

I

Psychoanalysis and literary criticism were made for each other, if ever two endeavors were.* A psychoanalytic approach to literary criticism merges two intuitive and analytic pathways to the human heart. But this type of criticism has often proved banal and repetitious, reducing literary themes to the ubiquitous Oedipus complex and ignoring form, flux or language. Despite some notable exceptions, there have been serious sins. Psychoanalytic criticism has often ignored the aesthetic integrity of a literary work, focusing exclusively on limited elements of plot and theme. Or, it has aimed at extraneous and scientifically unjustified analyses of the personality of the author in relation to his work.

There is really no reason to challenge the validity of psychoanalysis or to look for some special theoretical flaw accounting for the unsatisfactory showing with respect to literature. Current clinical practice of psychoanalysis involves a type of formal analysis of patients' behavior that lends itself directly to literary criticism. Practicing phychoanalysts routinely analyze formal properties of a patient's behavior called psychological defenses. Curiously, no one has ever applied such an analysis directly to literature, despite the fact that literature contains the everyday

* This investigation was supported by a Public Health Service Research Scientist Development Award number MH 23621 from the National Institute of Mental Health.

stuff of clinical practice—verbal representation of feelings, thoughts, personality patterns and interpersonal interactions. Analysis of specific psychological defenses is clearly analogous in literature and in life. We will support this categorical statement by presenting a concrete example of such a defense analysis applied to literature. This analysis will be our defense of the use of psychoanalysis in literary criticism.

Before we provoke an argument over whether psychological defenses are only present in sick people—emotionally sick, that is —or whether it is appropriate to discuss characters in literature as though they were real people, several assertions are useful. First, psychological defenses operate in all people, sick or healthy. Psychological defenses are specific unconscious or semiconscious patterns of behavior used to avoid internal or external threat. They are universal modes of dealing with anxiety and are intrinsic to personality and character. Defenses are more obvious in emotional illness because they are more overdeveloped and rigid there. Second, we feel there *are* problems in analyzing literary characters as though they were real people. Aesthetic form and statement, author's intent, use of imagery, symbol and many other factors must be taken into account. But rather than pause too long with this theoretical problem now, we will go directly to our test example, the discussion of psychological defenses in Eugene O'Neill's great play, *Long Day's Journey Into Night*. We chose this play because psychological realism is a major factor in its appeal.

Long Day's Journey Into Night depicts a day in the life of an Irish-American family named Tyrone. It takes place in the early part of the twentieth century on a summer's day in a small New England town. The family consists of the father, James Tyrone, who is a famous actor; the mother, Mary; and the two brothers, Jamie and Edmund. As is well known, these characters directly represent the author Eugene O'Neill's own family, and the author is represented in the play by the character Edmund, the youngest. The two major events of the play are the return of the mother to her morphine addiction and the discovery that young Edmund is stricken with tuberculosis.

Some passages taken directly from the play illustrate almost all of the classical defenses:

> *Mary:*   It makes it so much harder, living in this atmosphere of constant suspicion, knowing everyone is

> spying on me, and none of you believe in me, or
> trust me.

This is an example of the defense of projection. *Projection* is a defense against unconscious or preconscious drives, fantasies, or conflicts through which these internal psychic products are perceived and represented as coming from outside the self. Mary does not trust herself and feels guilty about beginning to take morphine again, but she defends herself by blaming those around her.

> *Mary:* . . . Of course, there's nothing takes away your ap-
> petite like a bad summer cold. I know he'll be all
> right in a few days if he takes care of himself. . . .
> I'm not upset. There's nothing to be upset about.

Denial: A total repudiation of an internal or external threat in spite of clear evidence of its existence. It is clear that Mary semiconsciously thinks that Edmund has consumption, the disease that killed her father, but she vigorously denies it.

> *Tyrone:* Hardy's treated him whenever he was sick up here,
> since he was knee high. He knows his constitution
> as no other doctor could. It's not a question of my
> being miserly, as you'd like to make out [Jamie].
> And what could the finest specialist in America do
> for Edmund, after he'd deliberately ruined his health
> by the mad life he's led ever since he was fired from
> college? Even before that when he was in prep
> school, he began dissipating and playing the Broad-
> way sport to imitate you, when he's never had your
> constitution to stand it. You're a healthy hulk like
> me—or you were at his age—but he's always been
> a bundle of nerves like his mother. I've warned him
> for years his body couldn't stand it, but he wouldn't
> heed me, and now it's too late.

Rationalization: Personally unacceptable thoughts, feelings, or actions are justified by reasons that distort facts and logic. Usually, the reasons given are socially acceptable ones. Tyrone defends against his guilt at having hired a cheap doctor for Edmund by finding reasons to justify or dismiss the hiring of Doctor Hardy.

> *Jamie:* (sneering jealously again) . . . they tell me he's a
> pretty bum reporter. If he weren't your son—
> (ashamed again) No, that's not true! They're glad to
> have him, but it's the special stuff that gets him by.

> Some of the poems and parodies he's written are
> damned good. (grudgingly again) Not that they'd
> ever get him anywhere on the big time. (hastily)
> But he's certainly made a damned good start.

Undoing: An attempt to "wipe out" or "take back" something
the person has done or is doing, including feelings and thoughts
relating to the act. This taking back is often repetitive and
cyclical. Jamie criticizes his brother sharply and repeatedly re-
tracts his criticism because of his intense ambivalence about
his brother's success.

> Mary: Why do you look at me like that? Is it my hair com-
>   ing down? I was so worn out from last night. I
>   thought I'd better lie down this morning. I drowsed
>   off and had a nice refreshing nap. But I'm sure I
>   fixed my hair again when I woke up.

Displacement: Personally unacceptable impulses or fantasies appropriate to some person or thing are shifted onto another person or thing. Mary has just returned to her morphine addiction
and her sons look at her suspiciously. She shifts her own concern
about her addiction to concern about her hair.

> Mary: What are you talking about? What drugstore? What
>   prescription?

Repression: The basic defense against unconscious or preconscious drives, fantasies, or conflicts. Unacceptable and anxiety-
provoking feelings and thoughts are kept out of consciousness
and forgotten. Mary has, for the moment, completely forgotten
about her anxiety-laden return to the drugstore for more
morphine.

> Jamie: And then this stuff of your getting consumption. It's
>   got me licked. We've been more than brothers.
>   You're the only pal I've ever had. I love your guts,
>   I'd do anything for you.

Reaction Formation: Turning unacceptable and unconscious
drives, attitudes, or feelings into their opposites. Just prior to
this passage, Jamie had confessed hatred and jealousy for his
brother. The protests of love are unconvincing and are an unconscious turnabout.

> Jamie: What are you trying to do, accuse me? Don't play
>   the wise guy with me! I've learned more of life than
>   you'll ever know! Just because you've read a lot of
>   highbrow junk, don't think you can fool me!

Identification: Unconsciously modelling oneself after another person in order to ward off unacceptable feelings toward that person, i.e., it may take the form of identification with a loved person or persons (which alleviates anxiety or tensions resulting from hostility), identification with a feared person or persons (which overcomes fear by assuming the threatening qualities), or identification with a hated person or persons (which alleviates anxiety about feelings of hate and/or ambivalent love feelings). Jamie is identifying with his father, using precisely his father's words to rebut an accusation from Edmund.

> *Jamie:* I want to warn you—against me. Mama and Papa are right. I've been a rotten bad influence. And worst of it is, I did it on purpose.

Introjection: The opposite of projection, this defense operates by taking something outside the self and representing it as though it were an internal product or aspect of the self; it is often marked by a definite change in a certain behavior or attitude. Jamie has incorporated his parents' accusations about him and elaborates on them as though they were his own.

> *Mary:* I play so badly now. I'm all out of practice. Sister Theresa will give me a dreadful scolding. She'll tell me it isn't fair to my father when he spends so much money for extra lessons. She's quite right. . . . I'll practice every day from now on. But something horrible has happened to my hands. The fingers have gotten so stiff—the knuckles are all swollen. They're so ugly. I'll have to go and show Sister Martha. She's old and a little cranky, but I love her just the same. . . . She'll give me something to rub on my hands and tell me to pray to the Blessed Virgin, and they'll be well again in no time.

Regression: The reversion to behavior, thoughts, or feelings appropriate to an earlier stage of emotional development. Mary has regressed to her early days in a convent instead of facing Edmund's illness and her own return to morphine.

> [There are no examples of the following defense in *Long Day's Journey Into Night*.]

Isolation: Thoughts and emotions are unconsciously separated from each other. Unacceptable emotions are thereby excluded from consciousness. Thoughts of murder, for example, are not accompanied by conscious feelings of hatred or hostility.

Long Day's Journey Into Night is a vibrant exposition of a family's reaction to physical and psychological threat. Edmund's tuberculosis, the physical threat, was considered to be inevitably fatal by Irish-American families of the time. It is suspected from the first and becomes a reality as the play progresses. Mary's relapse into morphine addiction, the psychological threat, is also suspected early and all the members of the family—including Mary herself—flounder helplessly to prevent it. One of the great psychological ironies unfolded within the play is that the family's particular way of floundering inexorably helps to bring the relapse about: Mary's addiction continues as a result of her own and her family's characteristic ways of interacting with each other. And their reactions on this particular day vividly represent the structure of the family relationships. They react to the physical and psychological threats with characteristic defenses and reveal long-standing inner concerns and tensions. The play is a condensation and extract of the entire psychological history of the family.

II

Psychological defenses are portrayed in this play with unerring and extraordinary clarity. All but one of the classical defenses are portrayed at least once, giving the play a psychological range and universality that is rare in literature. And an actual counting of the instances of specific defenses portrayed reveals an intricate and illuminating pattern of defensive themes. We first carried out this counting of defenses ourselves, using a random sampling of passages throughout the play. Then we corroborated our judgments by submitting the same passages to an independent group of psychiatrists and psychologists.

The major defenses manifested throughout the play were denial, projection, and rationalization or intellectualization. Through denial, there is blank nonacceptance of reality; through projection, inner guilts are blamed on others; through rationalization, distortion of truth is made to appear reasonable. What does the listing of these three defenses tell about the structure of psychological relationships among the characters in the play? What is the relationship between this structure and the aesthetic form of the play?

When denial and projection are prominent defenses in a family interaction, when members of a family tend to deny both internal and external reality and to project their inner wishes and guilts upon each other (as well as upon others outside the family), there are insuperable barriers to effective family communication. When rationalization and intellectualization are also used as prominent defenses in a family, an air of reasonableness and intellectuality is superimposed upon these barriers and makes the atmosphere of noncommunication appear insuperable. After all, if lack of contact and communication is treated with a veneer of reasonableness or intellectual appropriateness, how can intelligent human beings ever hope to supercede it or overcome it?

The characteristic use of these three defenses, primarily by the mother, father and younger son, directly contributes to the mother's disturbance. Although she herself tries to deny the reality of her illness, her husband's and son's denial does not reassure her but increases her panic. She feels that her suffering is too frightening to be accepted by others and that she is hopelessly ill. She feels lonely and misunderstood. Since her family members deny the reality of her illness, they neither exert effort to get help for her nor do they try in any serious and concerted way to prevent her deterioration. Also, their rationalizations serve to minimize their own responsibility, and their projections serve to shift blame and paralyze each other. In short, the family as a whole is responsible for the mother's illness; the illness itself is partly a manifestation of a family disturbance, not just the disorder of a single member. Emotionally and aesthetically, the play presents three defensive themes interacting in intricate contrapuntal polyphony, an interaction finally culminating in a single cacaphonous theme.

Only one family member, the older brother Jamie, does not use the particular denial and projection defenses at all throughout the play. But Jamie's defensive interaction also contributes to the overall difficulty in the family and provides an important psychological and thematic contrast. Jamie's characteristic defense is *undoing,* the undoing of thought and action. His defensive behavior clashes with the characteristic defenses of the other members of the family and directly produces some of the upheaval: considered by everyone as the black sheep of the family or as the person who doesn't fit in, he sees the truth and brings it to everyone's attention. From early on, he recognizes the signs of his mother's deterioration and the family's disordered and defensive reactions to it. But, hoist on the petard of his own defensive undoing, he acts and then takes his action back. Rather than producing effective communication and action, he only causes trouble.

Jamie's defensive clash with the other members of the family has an important dramatic effect. In some ways, his conflicts make him the most interesting character in the play. A thirty-three-year-old failure, he has done nothing but depend on his father to find work for him and support him. In spite of his awareness of the family's problems, he is paralyzed. He sees the truth but is unable to act on it or even grow from his knowledge. Responding to his father's demand that he pretend to his mother that his brother Edmund is not sick, Jamie says: "All right. Have it your own way. I think it's the wrong idea to let Mama go on kidding herself. It will only make the shock worse when she has to face it." Although most critics have considered Mary, or possibly Edmund, as the major tragic figure in this play, Jamie, in his particular type of defensiveness, has an important tragic role. As the family member who sees the truth but cannot act, he is a modern incarnation of Hamlet. When Hamlet decides to kill Claudius at prayer and then immediately argues himself out of it, he, like Jamie, demonstrates the undoing defense.

Jamie's defensive undoing is also important because it provides a structural boundedness to the play. Although Jamie is physically present throughout the play, his undoing defense appears primarily in the first and last acts. As in a musical composition, the theme of undoing is stated at the beginning and appears as a restatement at the end. In an emotionally violent sequence of interactions with his brother in the penultimate scene, his doing—"I love your guts"—and his undoing—"I can't help hating your guts," throbs and beats like a tragic drum of despair. Like any great musical composition, however—we are really discussing O'Neill's construction of an emotional tone poem or symphony—the theme of undoing does not return completely unchanged at the end. Jamie displays other defenses along with undoing, notably defensive identification: an identification with his feared and hated father.

Interestingly, Jamie's use of identification represents psychological progress for him. Identification tends to integrate one's personality and is a more constructive defense than many other defenses. Though Jamie is still ridden with self doubts and anxiety at the end, his use of identification is a shift to an improved level of defensive functioning. Subtle and slight as this shift is, it represents a movement toward resolution of Jamie's defensive theme—such is O'Neill's consummate artistry.

Looking at relationships between defenses and considering them in a purely formal sense without referring too much to content can be a risky business. But this approach reveals an aspect of the psychological structure of the play that would not otherwise be apparent. Carrying a purely formal analysis of defenses further, extracting defenses from specific content and looking at their temporal distribution throughout the play, will be very revealing indeed.

Bear in mind that defenses are responses to psychological tension. Therefore, the intensity of defensiveness at any point in the play indirectly reflects the degree of psychological tension among the characters. Like music, the emotional impact of drama fluctuates and varies over a considerable period of time. Tracing defensive interaction and psychological tension in drama, therefore, is analogous to the tracing of dissonances and consonances in a musical composition. High degrees of defensive interaction are psychological dissonances among the characters in the play that are periodically relieved or resolved by reduction in defensive interaction.

Charting defensive interaction is a more accurate and specific way of describing tension in a play than simply indicating that tension is high because two characters are having an argument or, according to an earlier model of psychoanalytic criticism, that they are manifesting aspects of an Oedipal interaction. In everyday life, a good deal of our response to other people is dictated by interpersonal defensive reactions. When other persons are defensive, we ourselves become tense, and when their defenses relax, we relax. It is an interesting and important paradox in human interaction that we become irritated when we experience others using our own characteristic defenses. Primarily, this is because we are reminded of our own weaknesses. At the same time as we are irritated, we are drawn to those who are similar to ourselves and they often intrigue us. Therefore, defenses have a good deal to do with feelings of attraction and repulsion for other people. Although characters in a play aren't real people, where do our feelings of attraction and revulsion come from? Isn't it reasonable to assume that we react to their defenses—even when they are stylized, condensed or designed to make an aesthetic statement—as though they were defenses in living people?

A major difference between a play and everyday life is that characters in a play have no direct effect on our lives. Consequently, our irritation with their defensiveness does not overwhelm us but engages us and stimulates us. We expect a work of art to throw us off balance, and we court the experience of successive stimulation and relaxation again and again. Our reactions to defenses and our experience of tension reduction play a large role in our aesthetic response to the drama.

The following curve illustrates the patterns of tension and tension reduction in *Long Day's Journey Into Night*. It is derived from a graph of the numerical distribution of all types of defenses throughout the course of the play.

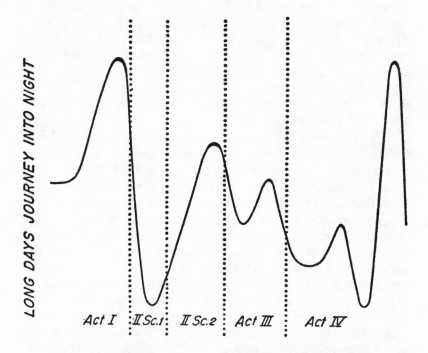

The play starts with a high level of defensiveness among the characters and a high level tension in the very first act. There are some rather sharp peaks of increased defensiveness at several points throughout the remainder of the play but the overall level of defensive interaction—imagine a straight line representing an average of all the peaks and crannies throughout—declines steadily. Despite the rather sharp peak of defensiveness near the end, the average defensiveness in the last act is quite a bit below the average defensiveness in the first. Of special interest is the fact that there is a sharp reduction of defensiveness in the first scene of the second act after the high level in the first act and a return to a high level in the second scene of the second act. Also, the transitory sharp increase of defensiveness in the last act of the play is followed—the very last point of the graph line—by a degree of defensiveness that is below the level of the first act. It is a complex pattern of declining defensive interaction in a complex play.

Since this is a play about disordered and tragic psychological interaction within a family group, it is not surprising to find a high concentration of defensiveness in the first act. The first act sets the stage and demonstrates the basic dynamisms within the family and within the play as a whole. Also, by engendering a high degree of tension in the beginning, it intrigues and engages the audience. The sharp reduction in defensive interaction in the first scene of the second act indicates some relief of tension among the characters and, we believe, produces an important relief from the intensity of the first act for the audience as well. Although there is nothing like the comic relief of classical tragedy in this scene, the defensive relief seems to serve a similar purpose. Following this relief, there is a heightened intensity of defensiveness. This high intensity serves primarily to re-engage the audience after the interlude and it is followed by the slow unravelling and relaxation of tension in the last two acts.

The marked reduction of tension due to defensiveness in the last act of the play helps account, we think, for some of the dramatic effect of the act. In a family situation where there is a high degree of defensiveness, particularly the use of such defenses as denial, projection and rationalization, one possible outcome is that members of the family give up their defenses and achieve psychological insight. If this were true for all the members of the family, or even for one, the play might have an essentially happy outcome rather than a tragic one. Insight reduces anxiety and defensiveness and promotes harmony and accord. In *Long Day's Journey Into Night,* however, there is a shift in the type of defenses used but there is little giving up of defenses or achievement of insight for any of the characters. In the important and dramatic confrontation between Jamie and his brother Edmund toward the end of the play, Jamie seems to achieve psychological insight at certain moments. He seems to understand that some of his destructive behavior toward Edmund results from his own intensely ambivalent feelings. At that point, Jamie almost succeeds in becoming a hero, if not a tragic hero, at least a psychological one. But ultimately he fails. He has not really overcome his defenses in this scene because in using the defense of undoing, his confession of hatred is rapidly taken back and invalidated.

Edmund comes closer than any of the characters to achieving real insight. In a dramatic outburst close to the end of the play, he admits he is ill and attempts to break through his mother's denial of his illness. As Mary has withdrawn almost totally into her drugged defensive state in the last act, Edmund desperately says to her (with, as O'Neill says, "the quality of a bewilderedly hurt little boy"): "Mama! It isn't a summer cold! I've got consumption!" These are powerful words, because in saying them aloud, Edmund accepts his illness and gives up his own tendency to denial. But the insight is weakened because the plaintive words are primarily addressed to his mother—he is more concerned with breaking through her denial than with understanding or changing himself. There is insight but not triumph because his breakthrough is primarily a cry of despair and rage at a withdrawn, rejecting mother.

The intense defensiveness in this family interaction depicted at the start of the play could have been resolved by a movement of all characters toward insight at the end, but it is not. The major alternative, then, is turmoil, because defenses are broken down rather than given up. In most cases, when people's defenses break down, a high degree of anxiety results and new defenses are set up to take their place. And this is precisely what happens for Mary, the most defensive character in the play. Mary's defenses break down and she shifts to less effective ones. Throughout the course of the play, Mary's defenses had been breaking down, partly because they were intrinsically inadequate and inappropriate and partly because of the family's distorted response to her.

Mary's most frequent and intense denial was her denial of

Edmund's sickness: it was not consumption but "just a summer cold," she repeated over and over again. Her own father died of consumption, and Mary was simply unable to accept the idea that Edmund was sick; she became upset and was driven back to her morphine addiction because of her inability to deal with her fears.

Her addiction to morphine was the other condition she denied, but here her defense was not so firmly entrenched. She never was able to acknowledge Edmund's illness, but at times she did relinquish denial of her addiction and was able to confess and plead for understanding. But even as she admitted the horror of the situation, she still felt a strong need to defend herself, and replaced denial with the more primitive defenses of projection and rationalization: she blamed her addiction on a cheap doctor who first gave her morphine at the time of Edmund's birth; she played on Tyrone's guilt for having hired an inexpensive doctor, and reproached Edmund by insisting that his birth caused her addiction.

At the end of Act III, when Edmund plaintively asked her to stop taking morphine before it was too late, she said, "Anyway, I don't know what you're referring to. But I do know you should be the last one—. Right after I returned from the sanatorium you began to be ill. The doctor there had warned me. I must have peace at home with nothing to upset me, and all I've done is worry about you." In these words, her beginning denial ("I don't know what you're referring to") shifted into a combination of rationalization and projection; she constructed a reason for her anxiety and projected the guilt onto Edmund.

But the defenses of projection and rationalization were insufficient protection against her overwhelming anxiety. Shortly after the previous reproach to Edmund, she moved to her ultimate and most primitive defense, regression: "But some day, dear, I will find it again—some day when you're all well, and I see you healthy and happy and successful, and I don't have to feel guilty any more—some day when the Blessed Virgin Mary forgives me and gives me back the faith in her love and pity I used to have in my convent days, and I can pray to her again— when she sees no one in the world can believe in me even for a moment any more, then she will believe in me, and with her help it will be so easy. I will hear myself scream with agony, and at the same time I will laugh because I will be so sure of myself."

The negative kind of development of defenses in these passages is carried through to the end of the play and it reflects the hopelessness, not only of Mary's plight, but of the entire family situation. At the very end she abandons herself to regression, the most insidious defense of all; her journey into night is completed with a movement into psychological darkness, or, if you will, death of the soul. In the face of overwhelming anxiety, she reverts to an earlier level of psychological adaptation, that of a virtually helpless child.

How does Mary's breakdown of defenses and reversion to regression pertain to the reduction of overall intensity of defensiveness in the last act? Ordinarily, viewing such disintegration and overwhelming anxiety in another human being would be highly terrifying and disturbing. But somehow, in this play, it is tolerable for the audience. The gradual reduction in overall intensity of defensiveness, from the first act to the last and the transitory sharp increase followed by reduction of defensiveness close to the end provide an explanation.

The gradual reduction of defensiveness during the course of the play indicates a slow and continual decrease of psychological tension. Although there is a sharp increase close to the end, relaxation follows almost immediately. This rapid alternation helps prepare for the terrifying scene at the very end. In other words, the play moves to a kind of psychological consonance or reduction in tension despite the feelings of helplessness engendered by Mary's collapse. The audience is strongly moved but not unnerved when the play is over.

For the purposes of comparison, we did a similar type of analysis on a shorter and simpler play, *A View From the Bridge* by Arthur Miller. Miller's play is also somewhat of a family story, portraying an event in the lives of an immigrant Sicilian family from the Red Hook section of Brooklyn. The family consists of Eddie, a longshoreman, his wife Beatrice, and their niece who lives with them, Katherine. Eddie and his wife became Katherine's legal guardians after the deaths of Eddie's sister and her husband. After accepting two illegal immigrants from his native Sicily into his home, Eddie becomes concerned about the relationship of the younger man, Rudolpho, to Katherine, a concern that clearly has incestuous overtones. Because of his involvement with Katherine, Eddie commits the greatest kind of treachery—according to unwritten law of Sicilian and longshoreman culture—he reports the illegal presence of the two men in this country to the immigration authorities. The play ends with Eddie's death at the hand of the older of the two men, Marco. Like *Long Day's Journey Into Night*, this play is a psychological drama. Although there are overtones of classical tragic drama, *A View From the Bridge* is primarily concerned with psychological interaction.

In this play, the major defenses are projection, rationalization and repression. Projection, in fact, may be characteristically associated with psychological tragedy because people who project and blame others for their own failings almost invariably come to grief. Although other classical defenses beside these three major ones are represented in *A View From the Bridge,* the extensive variety of defenses in *Long Day's Journey Into Night* is notably absent. Length may be a factor, but there are fewer contrapuntal defensive themes and no defensive development or resolution in *A View From the Bridge*.

The graph of defensiveness in *A View From the Bridge* shows a relatively uncomplicated pattern:

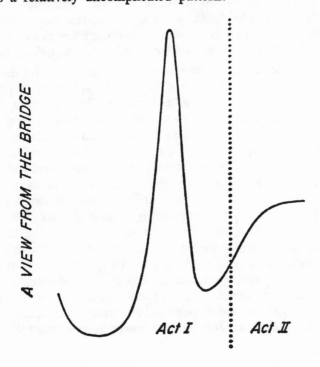

There is a slight overall increase from beginning to end with one point of sharp intensification approximately three-quarters into the first act. This intensification of defenses toward the end of the first act is great but rather brief and there is a rapid return to a baseline rate of defensiveness for the remainder of the act. The second act is considerably shorter than the first and it contains no point of sharp intensification of defenses. Therefore, the overall graph line shows little fluctuation except for one major peak of intensification in the first act.

As might be expected, the two most defensive characters in the play are Eddie and Katherine. Eddie characteristically projects his sexual feelings for Katherine onto Katherine herself or onto the young man, Rudolpho, accusing them both of lascivious behavior. Katherine characteristically uses repression, never becoming aware of the way that she is subtly seductive to Eddie. Both Eddie and Katherine's defensive patterns remain basically the same throughout the play, and they complement and intensify each other. Neither person achieves any insight nor is there any breakdown or shifting of defenses. Eddie's defensive projection becomes more intense and, at the point when his defenses might have broken down, he is killed. Interestingly, he is killed with his own knife, accidentally turned back into him by Marco. His defensive projection is repudiated in death when the deadly knife he turns on Marco lodges inside Eddie himself.

The defensive structure of the Miller play is quite different from *Long Day's Journey Into Night*. The sequence of psychological tension and tension reduction in *A View From the Bridge* has a simple bi-phasic quality—moving from consonance directly to dissonance and back to consonance again—in distinction to the slow and complex defensive sequence of *Long Day's Journey Into Night*. This linear and static graphic sequence parallels the lack of psychological development in the content of the tragedy: the psychological evil and illness in Eddie move to destroy those around him but, in the end, destroy Eddie himself. We would like to insist, in fact, that the psychological structure of this play requires an inherently exciting event such as Eddie's death for an emotional climax. The sharp peak of tension late in the first act is followed by a gradually increasing level of tension in the second act that demands resolution; Eddie's explosive death provides this resolution through sudden tension and relief. Unlike *Long Day's Journey Into Night,* however, this relief is rather shallow because it is produced by sudden action and a sense of moral retribution in his death rather than a gradual reduction of defensive tension and a slow movement of dissonance and consonance. There is little complexity to the emotional experience and no really moving involvement at the end.

Discussion of defenses in plays like *Long Day's Journey Into Night* and *A View From the Bridge* may seem like gilding the lily. Psychological plays will, of course, lend themselves to psychological discussion. Also, such a discussion cannot hope to exhaust all the aesthetic and emotional issues in these plays or even to do justice to the simple poignancy of such lines as Mary's final ones in *Long Day's Journey Into Night:* "I married James Tyrone and was so happy for a time." But human interaction is a constant feature in all types of literature and where there is human interaction, there are defenses. Analysis of these defenses unearths themes that run like musical refrains throughout a literary work and reveals other structural patterns. Much can be learned from careful attention to these structural features. They are the building blocks of psychological form.

Jean Anouilh and Eugene O'Neill: Repetition as Negativity

Joseph J. Moleski and John H. Stroupe

The true and false are both species of repetition.
> Jacques Derrida, "Plato's Pharmacy"

Orpheus. I hate death.
M. Henry (*gently*). You're unfair. Why should you hate death? She alone can create the proper setting for love.
> Jean Anouilh, *Eurydice*

Only art penetrates what pride, passion, intelligence, and habit erect on all sides—the seeming realities of this world. There is another reality, the genuine one, which we lose sight of. . . . The true impressions, our persistent intuitions, will, without art, be hidden from us, and we will be left with nothing but a 'terminology for practical ends which we falsely call life.'
> Saul Bellow, 1976 Nobel Prize Speech

Ultimately it is repetition that destroys the characters of Jean Anouilh. Mask and ritual are merely the accessories of a force of displacement as tragic as it is inexorable. Its names are various: society, religion, language. It is a movement never sensed as liberating, never affirmed, and its discovery is the single peripeteia of Anouilh's drama. The self comes to be seen as doubled, exported beyond itself, dispersed; the moment—Orpheus and Eurydice's, for example—is found to be itself a repetition that will be repeated by yet other moments, with a resultant hollowing out and draining away of apparent presence. Self and moment are always "contaminated" by the trace of the others, other times, and other selves: the present is the lovers' hotel room shot through with the comings and goings of others, who inevitably mark it. This face of repetition is that of "life going out of itself beyond return. Death rehearsal. . . . The irreducible excess . . . of any self-intimacy of the living, the good, the true."1 Repetition is the true antagonist of Anouilh's world, and it is insuperable.

In O'Neill's theater of compulsion, repetition's other face dominates. There, symmetrically, repetition is the meaningless source of meaning, not only that which betrays truth, as in Anouilh, but equally that which constitutes it. With no meaning, no self preceding, subtending repetition, existence means succumbing to monotonous, iterative, numbing attempts to accede to some stability, clarity, definition, or identity. These "rituals" finally dominate and subvert what they were meant to produce. O'Neill's repetition is "that without which there would be no truth: the truth of being in the intelligible form of ideality discovers in the *eidos* that which can be repeated, being the same, the clear, the stable, the identifiable in its equality with itself." Repetition as "death rehearsal" in Anouilh is, in O'Neill, "repetition of life" (Derrida, p. 168).

Different as they may seem at first glance, both Anouilh and O'Neill remain steeped in the negativity of repetition, obsessed with tracing the implications of repetition and of strategies that seek to master or eliminate repetition, with equal fatality. Anouilh situates meaning only in the transcendence of a world of hollow, ritualistic exchanges and self-deception, where external social forces mutilate, compromise, and pervert individual integrity, while O'Neill explores a vision of life wherein adherence to the ritual demands instilled by society provides the only meaning to be found. Neither, however, posits any inherent correspondence between meaning and reality. Anouilh's Antigone, Becket, and Orpheus (in *Antigone, Becket,* and *Eurydice*), for example, create significance for themselves only by refusing to compromise the self-embraced roles through which they have preserved their personal integrity; yet Becket has never believed in God, Antigone acknowledges to Haemon that she does not know why she is dying, and Orpheus joins Eurydice in death because only there can the perfect love they tried to create have permanence. Yank Smith's quest to belong (*The Hairy Ape*), Nina Leeds' search for happiness (*Strange Interlude*), and the pipe dreams and illusions of Harry Hope and his friends (*The Iceman Cometh*) become patterns which give meaning to life, yet it is a meaning O'Neill equates with illusion. Reality has no direct bearing on the meaning an individual is able to create or sustain in the vision of either playwright. Explicit support for these observations is supplied by the plays themselves.

Many of Jean Anouilh's dramas present a vision of the world in which life becomes a meaningless pattern characterized by adherence to false values, beliefs, and attitudes. His dramas explore a world in which some characters create a transitory meaning by embracing an illusion of selfhood and where others continue to live only through compromise with the purity of their dreams. Since the roles his heroes and heroines embrace inevitably reject such compromise, the dramatic intensity of Anouilh's plays often grows from just this gnostic conflict between the demand for purity and the impossibility of achieving it in life. His protagonists share a conception of death as a transient, vivifying, and authenticating act which makes it, when its conditions have been selected and simplified, the very meaning of unadulterated selfhood. To Anouilh's central figures, selfhood, if available at all, consists in a fundamental purity in the sense of homogeneity and isolation, which life constantly jeopardizes if not necessarily renders impossible.

When Creon shows Antigone the sordid truth about the brother whose right to burial gave Antigone a pretext to die, he takes away only her excuse and not her determination. Unless she can be sure that "everything will be as beautiful as when I was a little girl," Antigone wants to die.[2] Nothing less than a life of complete non-difference, of innocence and purity unsoiled by the harshness of inevitable maturation, will satisfy her. But life, or at least survival, is the acquiescence in repetition, in the belief that "life must go on, come what may." Antigone's demand is for plenitude, for a consummation beyond repetition, consummation that would itself be consumed, in an instant: "What," she asks, "are the unimportant little sins [sin is repetition, evil or dead or mechanical repetition] that I shall have to commit before I am allowed to sink my teeth into life and tear happiness from it? Upon whom shall I have to fawn? To whom must I sell myself?" Rejecting a life based on compromise, she "spits on" the hollow rituals of "humdrum happiness"—even happiness itself, repeated, is de-natured, emptied of itself—and "kitchen politics." She has never had to say "yes" to life. "I can say no to anything I think vile, and I don't have to count the cost."

At one level, "Little Antigone," scratching in the dirt with her toy shovel, wandering through the morning dew barefoot, is a striking contrast to the king who asks, "what sort of game are you playing?"[3] At another level, she displays a profound kinship with the Creon who admonishes her for believing in "priestly abracadabra." By stressing the absurdity of the "shuffling, mumbling ministrations of the priests," and decrying the "wretched consolation of that mass-production of jibber-jabber," Creon acknowledges that life degenerates into mere mechanical repetition. Seeking nobility through destruction, timelessness not through but out of time, Antigone cries, "I want everything out of life, I do; and I want it now! I want it total, complete: otherwise I reject it!" As R. J. Kaufmann observes: "We need acquaintance with someone who shouts 'No' to expediency and has the spiritual obstinacy to hold out against common sense— all the common sense prated so beautifully by the chorus in Greek tragedy."[4] And in her assertion of what she feels to be her real self in opposition to Creon's introduction of "a little order into this absurd kingdom," Antigone shouts "No" and creates her death as one might a work of art, fashions it, attempts to make it the consummation of life become timeless and absolute. Here as in *Becket* the true affirmation of the reality first and then the dignity of life are encountered only in death. But at least verbally, even in the heat of her insistence on death, she places the same symbolic kiss on the brow of life as Orpheus will upon his sleeping father.

Becket's heightened sense of aesthetics in Anouilh's *Becket* teaches him that—astonishing notion—the role he studies to give meaning to his existence must finally protect the pure and uncompromising honor of God at all costs. Formerly docile to the random quality of life, willing to play whatever role is offered him, without an honor of his own to value, agnostic if not atheistic, Becket determines finally to consummate his life in the role of Archbishop of Canterbury. Though King Henry argues that the Church and Crown go "hand in hand to conquer, pillage, and ransom," and one of the bishops, Oxford, reminds him of the delicate balance between heaven and earth: "excommunication . . . [is] bad policy," Becket refuses to play the games that have always characterized the relationship between church and state; bargains and compromises that allow the two to exist side by side with greatest advantage to both and dignity to neither. Becket, finally, is concerned only with the survival of the church, for "The kingdom of God must be defended just like any other."

Becket's negation of life, however, is at least an affirmation of something beyond himself. He says gently to Henry, "I felt for the first time that I was being entrusted with something . . . when you ordered me to take up this burden. I was a man without honor. And suddenly I found it—one I never imagined would ever become mine—the honor of God." He stands firm in defense of this honor because "We must only do—absurdly— what we have been given to do—right to the end." Becket does not go to his death with Antigone's eagerness, scorning filthy hope and happiness. Becket accepts death because it is a necessary part of his role. He says simply, "Here it comes. The supreme folly. This is its hour." He is destroyed in the performance of the Vespers ritual, performing to the last implication his adopted role. It is not a death which draws upon adamant convictions about the truth of the church's position in the conflict, nor is martyrdom as a means of self-glorification his object: his criterion is an aesthetic view of human morality, and what gives his role authenticity, what makes its artificial behavior timelessly Becket's behavior, is his selection of death as the sole means to fulfillment, or entelechy. For Anouilh deliberately depicts Becket as experiencing a sense of isolation from his context throughout the play, as an actor on a stage assuming the given role, utilizing the props at hand, his self shaped by the exegencies of the moment, until mask and self, life and role become one. Becket's willing submission to the ultimate consequence of his final role, an act which is the proof that what he finally represents himself as being is what he "really" is, removes the self's fear that honor and value and conscience are illusory and confirms it in a lasting attitude in which it is immune to change and life's adulterating ways.

In *Eurydice*, Orpheus and Eurydice create a pure, trans- cendent love for one day and one night, but it lasts no longer. Given the nature of the world and the people within it, such a love cannot long remain untarnished. The beautiful scene in the hotel room, where the lovers lie on the bed, happy and content, becomes an intense moment of epiphany and shatters, for Eurydice, the illusion they have created. Orpheus explains

to her the irreversible effect of experience. He says of the people
they have met, the subordinates in their drama: "They have
happened now, the good with the evil. They've danced their
little pirouettes, said their three words in your life . . . and
there they are, inside you, as they are, forever."

Eurydice is silent, then, fearfully, acknowledges the intrusion of the social world into their private consciousness:

> Then we can never really be alone, with all that around us. We
> can never be sincere, even when we mean what we say with all
> our strength . . . if all the words are there, all the filthy bursts of
> laughter, if all the hands that have ever touched you are still
> sticking to your flesh, none of us can really change . . . the first
> day all you have to do is invent . . . perhaps you thought I was
> someone else. And when you see me as I am. . . .

Temporarily she had believed in the permanence of their love,
but in this moment she realizes that she cannot escape her past.
Inexorably experience accumulates, leaving its impression as
the fingerprints on the dress and body of Eurydice accumulate,
remaining forever visible to the eye of Orpheus. "Put on the
lights," she tells Orpheus, and their day and night of happiness
is over. Although she desires it with all her strength, Eurydice
cannot play the role assigned to her, the "little silent companion
who takes on all the chores and at night, is warm and beautiful
beside you. Tender and secret, a woman for you alone."

Orpheus, who has created the role for her which she cannot
accept, cannot himself acknowledge the picture of the selfish,
cowardly, and casually promiscuous Eurydice that Dulac colors
for him. "She is as I know her to be," he shouts—and when
they are given their second chance, when he knows he will lose
her again if he looks at her, he will refuse to compromise his
ideal picture of their love. "Wait, wait, please wait . . . it will
soon be morning," Eurydice cries. "Let me live." But before
morning he will have decided. "It's too long to wait until we're
old," he says as he turns to look at her. To let Eurydice live
would mean, Orpheus reasons, accepting a life of casual infidel-
ities and hollow illusions, repeating a life of words and emotions
"the most conventional, the most vulgar, the ones we hate the
most." For Orpheus, the knot is repetition, the unintelligibility
of the superaddition of the copy to the archetype, of the 'second'
to the 'first': "What I don't understand," he confesses, "is why
they invented the second chair." Yet, despite the evil of sheer
number, Orpheus does not want to die, that is, until he sees his

father—a man "clinging to existence, with his poor snoring carcass sprawled over there" with the "fear of life" etched on his face—as a paradigm for life. Consistent in his role, Orpheus goes to join the Eurydice of their first meeting, "eternally pure and young, eternally herself."

Solidarity, purity, veracity, and fidelity are equally impossible in a world subject to time, in a life whose artifice is equated with adaptation, and adaptation is, in fact, life itself. Social living, at its most intense form in a love relationship between two people, demands for these protagonists when they meet their Henry or Creon or their Orpheus, or, in another sense, their former or future selves, the recognition of mutability, that one's life is to a degree shaped by and one's values scorched by the interaction; one only becomes inviolable, immune to the destructive force of repetition, in death. These Anouilh characters are driven by ideals of a flawless identity between their vision of self and the finite act in which it is expressed and find themselves finally incapable of tolerating the compromise inevitable when a being of infinite desire is manifested in finite terms. Ultimately death as Anouilh's antagonists achieve it is but the last intensification of the moment to moment confrontations with the finite which make of each moment and each other self a minor death. Doomed to finite acts, to the erosive force of society, a man can, if his image of himself as he should like to remain or become is sufficiently idealized, be driven to an acute sense of role playing, to insisting on the provisional and artificial quality of his behavior. Macbeth, we recall, unable to look back without anguish, also found life a "shadow" and a "tale."

While Anouilh concentrates on some individuals who reject and transcend life and society—characterized by attitudes structured by external social forces—O'Neill often focuses on the necessity of subscribing to the goals, desires, and forms which society postulates as valid and important—forms which O'Neill castigates, yet which, if embraced, allow for life itself to continue. Where the one conceives being as difference, the other defines difference as illusion (cf. O'Neill's *Diff'rent*) and repetition as the prison-house from which escape is impossible. Many of O'Neill's characters search for meaning, but even in those rare instances where they succeed, they discover that they have exchanged their individual identity for a social identity defined in terms of obedience and conformity to society, to custom or tradition—in short, to the exegencies of repetition as source of order and value. The searcher for stable meaning, completeness, "happiness" knows the while that ultimately even his most affirmative gesture is merely ritualized performance.

In *Strange Interlude* Nina Leeds directs all actions to her idol "Happiness," an illusion of a plentitude both deriving from and obviated by social institution. The compulsive search for it is her attempt to create meaning and an excuse for existence. "Being happy, that's the nearest we can ever come to knowing what's good! The rest is just talk," Mrs. Evans tells Nina, advising her to abort Sam's baby and commit adultery.5 "It's your rightful duty!" Nina's frantic search—which yields to ritualistic process—becomes a pattern in what would otherwise have been, after Gordon's death, a pointless existence, and infects each person with whom she comes in contact. Nina tempts Darrell from the cool, analytical position from which he had safely observed the passions of the world, but in the process he becomes weakened by the intensity of Nina's search and unable to continue his medical career.

Charlie Marsden, too, is caught in Nina's obsession, but the world he considers a "cool green shade" becomes a death in life where there is only sterility and where he will wait doggedly for Nina to join him in a world "passed beyond desire." Only Darrell finally seizes identity that depends, not on others' love, but on "my cells—sensible unicellular life that floats in the sea and has never learned the cry for happiness!" Nina represents the blindness of the human condition, for—even with a lifetime of suffering and anguish—she cries out to the son who is about to begin the cycle anew: "Be happy, dear! You've got to be happy!"

In *The Hairy Ape* O'Neill depicted his negative view of mechanized America, signifying senseless, unchecked repetition, where the best adjusted worker becomes a hairy ape, and where the society, in the vein of Plato of the *Laws*, becomes a procession of marionettes, having lost all connection with life itself. The government and the police function to isolate the classes, to keep the wealthy from being disturbed by Yank, and to prevent any opposition to the status quo. All facets of the state are focused upon regimenting and dehumanizing the citizens. The wealthy churchgoers are a chorused caricature of social-materialistic successful men and women; their mask-like faces, puppet-like gestures, and unison movements express their natures without words or commentary and in terms consonant with the total concept of the play.

The Hairy Ape is a psychological study of the disintegration of Yank Smith—who symbolizes the dreams of usefulness and power which may glorify a substratum of society—when he no longer feels that he "belongs." Yank had been egotistical, even happy in his ignorance, but once aware of the hiatus between his self-conception and others' belittling opinion of his labor, he becomes a pitiful creature who sees the forces which condemn him but is never able to understand them. For Yank is, writes O'Neill, "a symbol of man who has lost his old harmony with nature, the harmony which he used to have as an animal and has not yet acquired in a spiritual way."6 "Sure, you're de best off!" Yank says to the ape: "You can't tink, can yuh? Yuh can't talk neider. But I kin make a bluff at talkin' and tinkin'— a'most git away wit it—a'most—and dat's where de joker comes in."

"De joker" in many of O'Neill's plays is the fact that mimesis is the source of survival, yet it corrupts and destroys: the almost imperceptible difference between or non-coincidence of imitation and model, ritual and act persists as it by definition must. Repetition betrays itself as repetition—hence it cannot "succeed" or only succeed when it fails. Ultimately, all that individual man can do, suggests O'Neill, is to try to "belong to himself," for as soon as he accepts external rewards as truth, he seeks to escape responsibility. Social commitment is, for O'Neill, a substitution of external for internal authority to escape from personal fears of inadequacy.

While Nina Leeds' life was a continual quest for happiness and Yank sought to "belong," Harry Hope and his friends in *The Iceman Cometh* exist in a state of fixity, in the hell of repetition, for they oxymoronically desire only what they presently possess. While Nina failed to achieve her illusory goal, Harry and the others succeed completely: their pipedreams provide a state of imprisonment, of narcosis, inhibiting them from any self-consciousness. "Truth," says Larry Slade, "has no bearing on anything." Because "there is no farther they can go," the repetition which creates and sustains their own dreams gives life meaning by masking the absolute futility of their position. Into this "End of the Line Cafe" comes Hickey, the hardware drummer, the false prophet and self-appointed meddler-messiah who chooses to interfere to "save" them. Hickey's own illusion is that he has broken the round of repetition, the cycle of transgression and forgiveness, through violence. Convinced that peace comes only when there's "not a single damned hope or dream left to nag you" and when "you're rid of the damned guilt that makes you lie to yourself you're something you're not," Hickey confronts each with the truth he evades, and one by one sends them out to meet their failures. In this setting, *Iceman*, perhaps more clearly than any of O'Neill's other plays, is a morality play, a variation on the ancient motif of the Dance of Death with its modern paradoxical twist of willed chance and desired catastrophe, "where each man kills the thing he loves because he feels guilty of his inability to love enough."7

The quality of the "peace" Hickey thought to bring them is indicated by his own reaction to the destruction of the largest illusion of them all—his certainty that he killed Evelyn with "love in my heart." Hickey fancies himself unafraid of death, but truth would shatter him, just as it almost shatters the others. He cannot confront the "little truths"—like Anouilh's "little sins"—along his way, and cannot therefore see the relation between those and that ultimate truth which is death. The other members of the group, except for Larry Slade, rebuild their "Palace of Pipe Dreams," free themselves from Hickey's "peace of death," and slip back into the positive oblivion of their dreams and drunkenness. But Larry is the "only real convert to death Hickey made." He had masked his compassionate commitment to life and his fear of death in the belief that he was "finished with life," that he had taken "a seat in the grandstand of philosophical detachment to fall asleep observing the cannibals do their death dance." Parritt's death, however, to which Larry was the judge, brings home the futility of his position. Realizing that "I'll never be a success in the grandstand—or anywhere else!" he admits that life is "too much for me! I'll be a weak fool looking with pity at the two sides of everything till the day I die," and relinquishes the patterns of repetition through which he had imposed design upon his life. Isolating and freeing himself through this realization, he can at last say truthfully of his death, "May that day come soon." In O'Neill's world, all wait for the symbolic iceman, deadened by patterns of repetition, except those who acknowledge that life is false, pain is preeminent, and that death is mankind's only appeasement. In O'Neill's parable on the destiny of all mankind, these isolated heroes are engaged in the act of committing suicide.

In *Strange Interlude, The Hairy Ape,* and *The Iceman Cometh,* individuals compulsively engage in a process through which they seek to create meaning. This participation provides a design within which Nina Leeds is able to exist. For Harry Hope and the others, it becomes their entire life, the masks and illusions enabling them to continue to exist. In their lives, illusion itself becomes the ultimate pattern necessary for survival. Yank and Parritt die—and presumably Larry Slade as well—for they are in opposition to the survival of the dreaming and drunken world, the Nina Leeds, Charley Marsdens, Mildred Douglases, and Harry Hopes of this life. In O'Neill's world, those who capitulate before the force of repetition literally survive, even though they are spiritually dead and live in a world of protective illusion.

Both Anouilh and O'Neill, then, create meaning in a world not possessing it as an inherent attribute and where the very forms from which meaning derives destroy it. Generally, O'Neill's characters find such meaning in the world which Anouilh's are forced to reject. However, both subscribe to one basic truth: man cannot live, however miserably, outside the forms established by society. Anouilh's heroes and heroines refuse to adhere to those rituals if that adherence includes a compromise with their conceptions of themselves. Since Anouilh's vision of the world is one in which compromise and self-deception are a way of life, rejection of this life is inevitable. O'Neill's emphasis differs; his concern is not with the quality of a way of life but with life itself. His characters accept the values of their society and try to exist within its forms. While in Anouilh's theater, the self and temporality are conceived as presence and the present above and beyond the destructive instance of a repetition which comes to befall them; in O'Neill's drama, the self and temporality, in their essentiality and meaning, are produced by repetition or ritual.[8] As argued above—and the quoted phrases here are Derrida's—repetition as "death rehearsal" in Anouilh is, in O'Neill, "repetition of life."[9] Neither Anouilh nor O'Neill can envision an affirmation of repetition as radical play, as play in which everyone who wins loses, wins and loses, all the time, joyously.

NOTES

1 Jacques Derrida, "Plato's Pharmacy," in *Dissemination*, trans. Barbara Johnson (Chicago: Univ. of Chicago Press, 1981), p. 169. Originally: *La dissemination* (Paris: Editions Seuil, 1972).

2 For convenience, we have chosen to use the Anouilh translations most widely available: for *Antigone*, the translation by Lewis Galantière; for *Becket*, the Lucienne Hill translation; *Eurydice*, the translation by Kitty Black.

3 The phrase "la petite Antigone" is Antigone's own term to articulate her private sense of being. We evoke it here to refer also to Michael Spingler's sensible argument, "Anouilh's Little Antigone: Tragedy, Theatricalism, and the Romantic Self," in *Drama in the Twentieth Century: Comparative and Critical Essays*, ed. Clifford Davidson, C. J. Gianakaris, and John H. Stroupe (New York: AMS Press, 1984), pp. 173-83.

4 See "Tragedy and Its Validating Conditions," *Comparative Drama*, 1 (Spring 1967), 3-18.

5 Quotations from the O'Neill plays are from *The Plays of Eugene O'Neill*, 3 vols. (New York: Random House, 1955).

6 Barrett H. Clark, *Eugene O'Neill: The Man and His Plays* (New York: Dover. 1947), p. 84.

7 See Helen Muchnic, "Circe's Swine: Plays by Gorky and O'Neill," *Comparative Literature*, 3 (1951), 119-28, esp. 126.

8 See "The Abandonment of Ritual: Jean Anouilh and Eugene O'Neill," *Renascence: Essays on Values in Literature*, 28 (1976), 147-54, for a different version of the present argument—there cast in Eric Berne's terminology (*Games People Play*) rather than in the Derridian framework established here.

9 For additional commentary on this problem, see Gilles Deleuze, *Difference et Répétition* (Paris: Presses Universitaires de France, 1968). For a perspective on Derrida's statement "The true and false are both species of repetition," and the argument of this essay, see Elinor Fuchs, "The Death of Character," *Theatre Communications*, 5 (March 1983), 1-6.

When Playwrights Talk To God: Peter Shaffer and the Legacy of O'Neill

Michael Hinden

Eugene O'Neill's contributions to the modern theater are by now beyond dispute, and it is time for critics to assess his impact on more recent dramatists. "Most modern plays are concerned with the relation between man and man," O'Neill once remarked in conversation, "but that doesn't interest me at all. I am interested only in the relation between man and God."[1] In order to explore this monumental theme, O'Neill borrowed, transformed, and in good part invented a grammar of stage presentation that mixed naturalistic and expressionistic means and that embraced a variety of techniques, including masks, mechanical sounds, pantomime, music, song, elaborate stage directions, powerful visual and auditory images, and a vast, flexible array of language—slang, poetry, choric voices, thought-asides, soliloquies, expletives, rhetorical persuasion, searing condemnations, and occasional flights of rhapsody. Numerous dramatists on both sides of the Atlantic owe him an enormous debt. But because O'Neill did so much that was new, and because he did it so convincingly, he does not, strictly speaking, have a contemporary peer. He does, however, have a variety of successors. Already Williams, Miller, and Albee have secured their reputations, and there are other perhaps equally important playwrights who are just now reaching their prime. Of these, Peter Shaffer increasingly comes to mind.

I

Considering thematic concerns, dramaturgical techniques,

and the all-important power to rivet the attention of an audience, Shaffer is the playwright now writing in English who has benefitted most from O'Neill's legacy. Eschewing the bare settings and minimalist abstractions of the theater of the absurd, Shaffer traces his lineage directly to O'Neill and to the tradition of robust expansiveness that he inspired. Following O'Neill, Shaffer experiments with such devices as thought-asides or audible thinking *(Strange Interlude, The White Liars)*, the split protagonist *(The Great God Brown, Equus)*, masks, mime and spectacle *(Lazarus Laughed, The Royal Hunt of the Sun)*, and the extended monologue as a means of revelation *(The Iceman Cometh, Shrivings, Amadeus)*. Indeed, compared to Beckett, Pinter, and Stoppard, who may be called postmodernist playwrights in terms of their self-reflexive attitude toward form, Shaffer does appear "old-fashioned," which is to say that he places himself squarely in the tradition of modernism that was established—largely by O'Neill—in the American theater of the twenties.2

Even more significant is O'Neill's legacy to Shaffer in regard to theme. For many of the postmodernists, the passing of God, philosophy, and religious institutions is no longer a matter of concern so much as it is a foregone conclusion, but that is not the case with Shaffer. Like O'Neill, he is obsessed with man's longing for divinity, and like O'Neill, he is determined to do "big work." Indeed, he is drawn specifically to O'Neill's subjects and to his metaphysical themes. In *The Royal Hunt of the Sun,* the Spanish conquest of the New World serves him as the setting for a clash between Catholic and Pagan visions of the world, a subject first assayed by O'Neill in his early play, *The Fountain.* In *Equus,* Shaffer builds upon O'Neill's idea, developed in *The Great God Brown,* that modern life destroys our capacity for union with divinity. And in *Amadeus,* he expands upon O'Neill's perception in *The Iceman Cometh* that man's disillusionment with God can poison the relation of the self to others.

It is tempting to speculate that Shaffer and O'Neill's interest in religious questions may stem in part from parallel events in their experience. At least, both playwrights depict characters who in their youth witness a glimpse of mystical revelation, a sense of oneness with the universe. Curiously, in both instances the experience is associated with the sea. Here Edmund speaks in Act IV of *Long Day's Journey Into Night:*

> I lay on the bowsprit, facing astern, with the water foaming into
> spume under me, the masts with every sail white in the moonlight,
> towering high above me. . . . I belonged without past or future,
> within peace and unity and a wild joy, within something greater
> than my own life, or the life of man, to Life itself! To God, if
> you want to put it that way. . . . For a second there is meaning!
> Then the hand lets the veil fall and you are alone, lost in the fog
> again, and you stumble on toward nowhere, for no good reason![3]

In O'Neill's case, it has long been assumed that Edmund's speech
is autobiographical. Now here is Pizarro's recollection in *The
Royal Hunt of the Sun:*

> I had a girl once, on a rock by the Southern Ocean. I lay with her
> one afternoon in winter, wrapped up in her against the cold, and
> the sea-fowl screaming, and it was the best hour of my life. I felt
> then that sea-water, and bird-droppings and the little pits in human
> flesh were all linked together for some great end right out of the
> net of words to catch. Not just my words, but anyone's. Then I
> lost it. Time came back, For always.[4]

Both characters report that in later life the vision has been
unrecoverable; whether Shaffer here is speaking of his own
experience, we can only guess. Certainly O'Neill and Shaffer,
when speaking in their public voices, sound very much alike.
O'Neill: "The playwright today must dig at the roots of the
sickness of today as he feels it—the death of the old God and
the failure of science and materialism to give any satisfying new
One for the surviving religious instinct to find a meaning for
life in, and to comfort its fears of death with."[5] In Shaffer's
words, the issue lies in "the fact that I have never actually
been able to buy anything of official religion—and the inescapable fact that to me a life without a sense of the divine is per-
fectly meaningless."[6]

   In this context it is no accident that the two dramatists
employ similar techniques; rather, their use arises naturally from
the playwrights' mutual concern. For example, both writers' use
of the extended monologue is painfully appropriate: in the work
of Shaffer and O'Neill man talks to God but is answered only
by his silence. During that extended silence, the monologue
turns back upon the speaker and his memories, uncovering the
fragmentary nature of his being. It is for this reason, too, perhaps, that both dramatists are fascinated by the concept of the
split character. In *Equus* and *The Great God Brown,* the
speeches of both characters actually are components of a long

soliloquy, articulations of a divided self. Such inner divisions suggest an additional motive for the monologue, for it is a means by which one half of the split character attempts to communicate with his counterpart. In each case there appears a third term above the debate to which the characters appeal·in vain, an absent mediator: the silent God.

But although Shaffer has reasons of his own to discover these devices, his debt to O'Neill in this area is extensive. O'Neill did not invent the technique of the split character, but he was the first to popularize it in such works as *Welded, The Great God Brown, Strange Interlude,* and *Days Without End.* In addition, it is O'Neill who might be credited with reviving the possibility of the soliloquy on the modern stage. According to Kenneth Macgowan, O'Neill's success in conveying the unspoken words of his characters was his "outstanding contribution to modern dramaturgy."[7] It is true that O'Neill explores the monologue in his earliest work *(The Web, Bound East for Cardiff, Before Breakfast, The Emperor Jones, The Hairy Ape),* and he increases his reliance on the device toward the end of his career, notably in *The Iceman Cometh, Long Day's Journey Into Night, A Moon For the Misbegotten,* and *Hughie,* which contains perhaps the finest example of the form in modern drama.[8] In some instances O'Neill's monologists actually believe that they have spoken to the Deity and that they have heard His voice in reply; Cabot, for example, says as much in his fine monologue in Part II, scene ii of *Desire Under the Elms.* However, such occurrences are remembered through a glass and darkly. In the present tense of O'Neill's plays the protagonists are spiritually and metaphysically isolated, whether or not they are physically alone on stage. Cabot, Dion Anthony in *The Great God Brown,* Tiberius in *Lazarus Laughed,* Hickey in *The Iceman Cometh,* Mary Tyrone in *Long Day's Journey Into Night*—and others—speak mainly to the air, for they no longer hear the voice of God and care little for the compensation of the small human voices that address them. In this respect O'Neill's monologists are indeed the forerunners of Shaffer's voluble, God-driven protagonists— Pizarro, Dysart, Mark Askelon, Salieri—whose soliloquies on the silence of divinity have electrified the contemporary stage.

II

To flesh out the relation between Shaffer and O'Neill, let

us consider now two pairs of plays: *Equus* and *The Great God Brown; Amadeus* and *The Iceman Cometh.* These plays reflect an important thematic progression for both dramatists, and they also serve to illustrate their handling of the specific technical devices mentioned above. It may prove particularly useful to compare the relative success of the two dramatists in treating similar material. For instance, in *Equus* Shaffer finally overcomes the problem that defeated O'Neill in *The Great God Brown:* how to mount a play about man's primitive religious instinct in a form that could be grasped by modern audiences. But in *Amadeus,* as we shall see, he seems to forget an important tenet of characterization that O'Neill incorporated most successfully in *The Iceman Cometh.*

The parallels between *Equus* and *The Great God Brown* are particularly striking, so much so that the question of a direct influence is raised. Both plays depict a search for God by characters who are divided internally as well as externally so that they appear almost as halves of a single personality; both trace the repressive effects of puritanism on the sexual and religious instincts; both employ ritualistic elements such as masks, mime, and choric voices; and both rely on the extended monologue as the principal means of revelation.

In *Equus,* Alan (whose name in Greek ironically means "harmony") finds himself divided between two incompatible desires: his longing for union with the pagan Godhead symbolized by Equus, and his masochistic identification with the suffering and accusing Jesus, whose portrait stares down at him. His internal division has resulted in spiritual dis-harmony, sexual malfunction (his impotence with Jill), and violence (the blinding of the horses). Thus, his soaring dithyramb at the conclusion of Act I—

> *I'm raw! Raw!*
> Feel me on you! *On* you! *On* you! *On* you!
> I want to be *in* you
> I want to *BE* you forever and ever!—
> *Equus, I love you!*
> Now!—
> Bear me away!
> Make us One Person!
> *One Person! One Person! One Person! One Person!*9

—is counterbalanced by his babbling of TV advertising jingles and by the disabling guilt that renders him impotent:

No one ever says to cowboys 'Receive my meaning'! They
wouldn't dare. Or 'God' all the time. [*mimicking his mother*]
'God sees you, Alan. God's got eyes everywhere—'
                              (I.13; p. 56)
Eyes! . . . white eyes—never closed!
Eyes like flames—coming—coming! . . . God
seest! God seest! . . . NO! . . .
                            (II.34; p. 121)

In precisely the same way, Dion Anthony in O'Neill's play is
divided in his nature by a wish for pagan ecstasy and by a
repressive conscience shaped by social mores and the weight of
Christian guilt.

Now! Be born! Awake! Love! Dissolve into dew—into silence—
into night—into earth—into space—into peace—into meaning—
into joy—into God—into the Great God Pan! . . . Wake up! Time
to get up! Time to exist! Time for school! Time to learn! Learn
to pretend! Cover your nakedness! Learn to lie! Learn to keep
step! Join the procession! Great Pan is dead! Be ashamed!10

His name, according to O'Neill, derives from "Dionysus and
St. Anthony—the creative pagan acceptance of life, fighting
eternal war with the masochistic, life-denying spirit of Christianity as represented by St. Anthony—the whole struggle resulting in the modern day mutual exhaustion—creative joy in
life for life's sake frustrated, rendered abortive, distorted by
morality from Pan into Satan, into a Mephistopheles mocking
himself in order to feel alive."11

Similarly, O'Neill's description of Billy Brown, who at first
appears to be Dion's opposite but who later in the play quite
literally becomes his double, might be applied with relevance to
Martin Dysart. According to O'Neill, Brown is "the visionless
demi-god of our new materialistic myth—a Success—building
his life of exterior things, inwardly empty and resourceless, an
uncreative creature of superficial pre-ordained social grooves,
a by-product forced aside into slack waters by the deep main
current of life-desire. . . ."12 Dysart (whose name suggests dys-
function of the healing art) represents on the surface Alan's
opposite, the sexless apostle of reason and society, the Priest
of the Great God "Normal," as he puts it. But in a mysterious
way, Dysart is Alan's double, too. Just as in O'Neill's play Brown
suffers Dion's inner division as he becomes his alter ego, so
Dysart grows internally divided as he increasingly identifies with
Alan and his agonizing quest for union with the One: "I tell

everyone Margaret's the puritan, I'm the pagan. Some pagan! . . .
I . . . touch my reproduction statue of Dionysus for luck—and
go off to the hospital to treat him for insanity. Do you see?"
(II.25; p. 95)

Brown's function in the O'Neill play, like Dysart's, is to
dissuade his counterpart from his destructive course. But when
Dion drinks himself to death, Brown willingly exchanges masks
with him, discarding his own identity in order to impersonate
his "brother." So doing, he becomes the vehicle of an apotheosis
sought by Dion. An almost identical process of transference takes
place at the conclusion of *Equus*: Dysart stands on the verge of
becoming the new vehicle of the god's epiphany.

> And now for me it never stops: that voice of Equus out of the
> cave—'Why me? . . . Why me? . . . Account for me!' . . . All
> right—I surrender! . . . I stand in the dark with a pick in my
> hand, striking at heads. . . . *What dark is this?* . . . I cannot call
> it ordained of God: I can't get that far. I will however pay it so
> much homage. There is now, in my mouth, this sharp chain. And
> it never comes out. (II.35; p. 125)

Thus, the apostle of Normalcy in each play ends by becoming
the ritual substitute for the tortured god-seeker. In O'Neill's
play, the transference of Dion's pain to Brown has the effect of
purification; in Shaffer's play the result of Alan's transference
of pain to Dysart is more tentative. Although Brown has no
monologues to speak until after he takes up Dion's mask, his
dying speech is a reaffirmation of Dion's vision of primordial
oneness: "Only he that has wept can laugh! The laughter of
Heaven sows earth with a rain of tears, and out of Earth's
transfigured birth-pain the laughter of Man returns to bless and
play again in innumerable dancing gales of flame upon the
knees of God!" (IV.ii; p. 374). Dysart is not granted this ecstatic
vision, but Alan's transcendent laughter in the epiphany at the
end of Act I in *Equus* is a direct analogue: "*He rises up on the
horse's back, and calls like a trumpet. Ha-HA! . . . Ha-HA . . .
Ha-HA!*" (I.21; p. 85). In both plays, the veil is parted briefly
and a sense of mystery is celebrated in defiance of societal
restraints.

So far it may seem that I have been accusing Shaffer silently
of plagiarism, but that is far from my intention. Some of the
similarities may be attributed to what I suspect is the common
source for each play, Nietzsche's *The Birth of Tragedy*. It has

been established that O'Neill drew much of his inspiration from Nietzsche's work, and Shaffer, too, appears to be indebted to the great philosopher.13 Yet even if Shaffer did borrow significantly from O'Neill, in certain ways he has improved upon his model. For all its inventiveness, *The Great God Brown* is marred by serious inconsistencies resulting from an imperfect synthesis of naturalistic and symbolic levels. O'Neill's celebrated use of masks in the play is especially problematic; during the course of the action, some masks change in their appearance while others remain fixed, and the pattern of their use is arbitrary. In order to explain these convolutions, O'Neill is forced to waste several of Brown's monologues in exposition, which seems awkward coming as late as the third act of the play.

By contrast, Dysart's monologues are, without exception, dramatic; they are revelatory of character as well as thematically progressive. Dysart is more articulate, more self-aware than Brown. Significantly, Shaffer confines the use of masks to the Equus Chorus, and while this still provides a striking ritualistic atmosphere, it frees the principal characters to develop naturalistically. Finally, Shaffer provides a popular "psychiatric" subplot with all the turns and pacing of a Hitchcock thriller (*Spellbound* comes to mind) in order to balance the abstractions. We can piece together Alan's story without recourse to Nietzsche's metaphysics, whereas Dion's actions do not easily stand alone. It is telling that Dion's monologue on the death of his mother, which by far is the best speech in the play, filled with penetrating psychological insight, seems oddly out of character for him: "And my mother? I remember a sweet, strange girl, with affectionate, bewildered eyes as if God had locked her in a dark closet without any explanation. . . . I watched her die with the shy pride of one who has lengthened her dress and put up her hair . . ." (I.iii; p. 333). It is a measure of Shaffer's success that Alan's psychological and theological problems conjoin at moments of high intensity and blend into a seamless whole.

III

In relation to *Equus, Amadeus* marks a transition for Shaffer, even though at first glance the plays appear to be continuous. It is true that in *Amadeus* Shaffer repeats the pattern of much of his earlier work in which a male protagonist is motivated by jealousy to strike out against his adversary (*The Private Ear*,

The White Liars, The Royal Hunt of the Sun). It is true, moreover, that the play borrows the central relationship of *Equus,* pitting a socially prominent middle-aged man against an inspired youth—almost a demon—whose gifts shake the protagonist's faith in himself and his career. Like Alan, Mozart is a galling vessel of splendor; yet at the piano his becomes the voice of God. So in the dark of a Hampshire field is Alan's gift of divinity transmitted, though with far less happy consequences. Alan and Mozart both bespeak a mystery, but Dysart and Salieri perversely set out to destroy these vessels of authentic power (Dysart for reasons more altruistic than Salieri's). Both men see themselves as murderers, carving their victims as though with knives. As a consequence, Dysart and Salieri vent their guilt through a series of brilliantly conceived monologues in which they question the relationship of man to God.

Yet here the similarities end. In *Amadeus* a major shift has taken place thematically: the protagonist now abandons his quest for union with divinity and becomes the antagonist of the God, setting himself against the Deity in personal confrontation and defiance. To be sure, in Mozart Salieri hears the strange "laughter of God" that Dysart hears in Alan, but now it seems a mocking laughter shorn of transcendence and described only as a "dreadful giggle."[14] Nor are Mozart and Salieri truly halves of a split character, ritualistically interchangeable, each longing for the other's peace. A gap has opened between the seeker and the God Salieri:

> Spiteful, sniggering, conceited, infantine Mozart—who has never worked one minute to help another man! Shit-talking Mozart, with his botty-smacking wife! *Him* You have chosen to be Your sole conduct! And *my* only reward—my sublime privilege—is to be the sole man alive in this time who shall clearly recognize Your Incarnation! (I.12; p. 47)

Mozart is Salieri's rival, not his double, and he retreats into the background, notably during the second half of the play, when in fact he becomes Salieri's victim. Correspondingly, Salieri's role increases until there is only one voice audible in the theater: Salieri the enemy of God subsuming the entire dramatic action in one extraordinary monologue.

In this respect, it seems to me that Salieri comes more and more to resemble Hickey in *The Iceman Cometh* preaching his bleak philosophy of disillusionment. Salieri and Hickey are the two great monologists of our theater, and both are uncompromising in their pessimism. Indeed, *The Iceman Cometh* marks a bitter conclusion to O'Neill's quest for union with divinity; it is a work far distant in spirit from *The Great God Brown.* Whether *Amadeus* occupies a similar position in the Shaffer canon remains to be seen. But since Shaffer and O'Neill have pursued parallel careers in so many other respects, the possibility is an intriguing one. For the moment it can be said that our theater has not heard a barrage of anguished speech comparable to Hickey's monologue until these great soliloquies of Antonio Salieri.

Besides long speeches, Hickey and Salieri have a good deal in common, although here it would be forcing the issue to suppose an influence. Rather, the comparison allows further commentary on the deep affinity between these writers. Hickey and Salieri are, of course, both murderers (Hickey in fact, Salieri in spirit). Both are plotters and manipulators, modern Iagos with complicated schemes to engineer; in this lies much of their vitality. Both men have lost their trust in God, both suffer guilt, and both use the stage as a confessional. Hickey foists himself upon the lodgers at Harry Hope's saloon; Salieri imposes himself upon posterity, speaking directly to the audience. Ironically, no one believes these monumental confessions. The roomers in Hope's saloon conclude that Hickey has gone mad, and history refuses Salieri's confession for the same reason: *"No one believes it in the world!"* (II.19; p. 96). Neither, therefore, is permitted to atone, and in this sense the great monologues are failures.

Moreover, as psychological types Hickey and Salieri share a common weakness. Both pretend to superiority over their fellows, but when linked with a truly superior being, neither can bear the existence of the rival. Salieri knows this about himself from the beginning; indeed, he knows everything from the beginning, and he tells us all. With Hickey the truth lies hidden. Nonetheless, Evelyn is Hickey's rival just as surely as Mozart is Salieri's. If Mozart has a talent for the keyboard, Evelyn has a talent for the Good. Like Mozart's, the talent seems to cost her nothing. It is perfect, effortless. It grates on Hickey, who is consumed by self-loathing when he compares himself to her.

> I couldn't forgive her for forgiving me. I even caught myself hating her for making me hate myself so much. There's a limit to the

guilt you can feel and the forgiveness and the pity you can take!
You have to begin blaming someone else, too. I got so sometimes
when she'd kiss me it was like she did it on purpose to humiliate
me, as if she'd spit in my face! But all the time I saw how crazy
and rotten of me that was, and it made me hate myself all the
more.[15]

Salieri and Hickey both want their rivals to fail (Hickey: "If she
only hadn't been so damn good—if she'd been the same kind
of wife I was a husband" [IV, p. 238]), and both feel the same
mixture of pity and contempt. Salieri: "What did I feel? Relief,
of course: I confess it. And pity, too, for the man I helped to
destroy" (II.16; p. 91).

But chiefly both Hickey and Salieri want to reach through
their rivals to strike back at God. Salieri determines openly that
inasmuch as God has spurned *him* by favoring Mozart with
divine inspiration, so he will spurn God by destroying His creature's worldly progress: "My quarrel now wasn't with Mozart—
it was *through* him! Through him to God, who loved him so.
[Scornfully] *Amadeus!* . . . *Amadeus!*" (II.i; p. 51). Although
he does not articulate it so directly, Hickey also senses that
Evelyn is one of God's "beloveds," a "lover of God" (the meanings of "Amadeus"), a chosen one. And there is a sense of an
old wound opening in him when he tells how he set out to destroy the pipe dream of her faith—"She was a sucker for a pipe
dream" (IV, p. 233)—even as he had been forced to relinquish
his own illusions in his youth.

You've heard that old saying, 'Ministers' sons are sons of guns.'
Well, that was me, and then some. Home was like a jail. I didn't
fall for that religious bunk. Listening to my old man whooping up
hell and fire and scaring those Hoosier suckers into shelling out
their dough only handed me a laugh, although I had to hand it to
him, the way he sold them nothing for something.

(IV, p. 232)

Yet Evelyn was Hickey's last connection with the realm of the
divine, or at least with his habit of thinking about it: "Why,
Evelyn was the only thing on God's earth I ever loved!" (IV,
p. 246). Thus, in plotting to destroy her faith, Hickey renews
and focuses his own lifelong quarrel with the Deity.

Hickey's relationship with Evelyn is mirrored in the larger
context of the play by his relationship with Hope's barflies:
"Listen, everybody. I've made up my mind the only way I can
clear things up for you, so you'll realize how contented and

carefree you ought to feel, now I've made you get rid of your
pipe dreams, is to show you what a pipe dream did to me and
Evelyn" (IV, p. 228). This scheme has the formulaic ring of
Salieri's project against Mozart: "Reduce the man: reduce the
God. Behold my vow fulfilled" (II.16; p. 89). Hickey has made
a career of selling pipe dreams, Salieri, peddling inferior music
(neither respects his wares). But as both plays unfold, each
discovers a new dimension to his talent for deceiving others.
Salieri sets out to block Mozart's career at every turn and then,
when that fails, to spread the lie that he has poisoned him in
order that his name be linked to Mozart's, if only by this infamy.
Hickey attempts the conversion of Hope's derelicts to his philosophy of peace by forcing each to face some personal truth. In
the end, the verdict of the world is that both protagonists are
deranged, and so their intricate plotting comes to nought.

However, just before the final curtain, Hickey learns a terrible truth about himself. He makes the momentous discovery
that he killed Evelyn not out of pity but deep hatred: "I remember I heard myself speaking to her, as if it was something I'd
always wanted to say: 'Well, you know what you can do with
your pipe dream now, you damned bitch!' *(He stops with a
horrified start, as if shocked out of a nightmare, as if he couldn't
believe he heard what he had just said. He stammers)* No! I
never—!" (IV, pp. 241-42). Upon this marvelous spring, held
coiled until the last moment of the play, depends O'Neill's entire
plot. It is perhaps his finest moment in the theater. Salieri in
Amadeus has no comparable discovery to make, and indeed,
this poses something of a problem. For all his verbal wizardry,
Salieri increasingly reveals himself to be a static character, one
who is unable to learn during the course of the action because
he knows everything from the start. His omniscience sets a
constraint upon his monologues from the perspective of internal
growth.

The problem becomes noticeable shortly after the beginning
of the second act. Not only does Salieri fail in his self-disclosures
to keep pace with the extraordinary revelations in Act I, but
in addition he is permitted to accomplish Mozart's ruin with far
too great an ease. He is left without an obstacle; there is in effect
no barrier to his will. Shaffer invents all manner of stage business
to distract the audience from this perception, and it is clear that

he has worried over it. He informs us that he has revised the
act considerably:

One of the faults which I believe existed in the London version
was simply that Salieri had too little to do with Mozart's ruin. In
the second act he was too often reduced to prowling hungrily
around the outside of the composer's apartment, watching his
decline without sufficiently contributing to it. Dramatically speaking, Salieri seemed to me to be too much the observer of the
calamities he should have been causing. Now, in this new version,
he seems to me to stand where he properly belongs—at the wicked
center of the action."16

Yet the revision is only partly successful. We do have much
delightful business: the opera rehearsal, the impersonation of
Mozart's father, the plan to discredit him with the Freemasons,
and the Messenger of Death. But all of this concerns the plotter
in Salieri, his histrionic flair and zest for machination, not the
emotional center of his character. Here he is like Hickey only
in Act III of *Iceman,* working on others, not himself. Salieri
glides through *Amadeus* relying on that splendid instrument, his
voice, and the fact remains that the second half of the play is
simply not as engaging as the first.

By contrast, *Iceman* builds throughout the final act, and
Hickey's monologue comes as a rocking explosion, not an atten-
uation. Earlier I argued that *Equus,* in comparison with *The
Great God Brown,* succeeds in providing a concrete psychological dimension to an abstract metaphysical theme. Here the
reverse is true: O'Neill creates a personal dimension for Hickey
that somehow seems lacking in Salieri. It is true that Salieri is
a witty man, and it would be wrong to confuse his coolness
with a lack of feeling; certainly, he suffers grievously from
wounded pride. Nevertheless, at times there is a hollowness
about him, a disembodied eloquence floating on a cushion of
wind. Salieri's real passion (aside from sweets) is an *idea* about
God and his relationship to man. In *Iceman* the metaphysical
idea stays in the background, and Hickey's human anguish, his
love-hate relationship with Evelyn, vivifies his character and
makes him convincing as a human being. There is, perhaps, a
conclusion to be drawn from this. It is that, while ordinarily
drama cannot afford much indirect conversation, the rule might
be inverted whenever playwrights talk to God.

Throughout most of Shaffer's work there is in fact a certain
slickness, which is the negative aspect of his admirable facility.

One would never dream of lodging such a complaint against O'Neill. Clumsy and ham-fisted, O'Neill struggled toward eloquence only on the rare occasion. Yet he had greater range than Shaffer and greater depth of feeling—an ability to live _within_ his characters and to twist them inside-out on stage. Shaffer seems always to be holding back, transmuting passion into rhetoric and smoothing out some inner turmoil by a flow of words. Of course, Shaffer is still in mid-career, and there is every indication that he is growing. Despite the reservations voiced above, _Amadeus_ is a stimulating work and a welcome addition to the modern repertoire. Together with _Equus_, the play suggests that Shaffer will continue to transform O'Neill's theatrical bequest of technical experiment and high seriousness as he enlarges a body of work that already is impressive in its scope. And if the comparison between the two playwrights holds any predictive value, then Peter Shaffer's best years as a dramatist still lie ahead.

16:1 (Spring 1982)

NOTES

1 Quoted by Joseph Wood Krutch, "Introduction" to _Nine Plays by Eugene O'Neill_ (New York: Random House, 1954), p. xvii.

2 Shaffer, who prefers living in New York to London, sometimes thinks of himself as more of an American dramatist than a British one. In his own estimation, he is drawn to the broad canvas, which seems to him an American trait: "English dramatic taste rather deplores the large theme, largely broached: it tends to prefer—sometimes with good sense, but often with a really dangerous fear of grossness—the minute fragment, minutely observed" (Prefatory Note to _Shrivings, Equus and Shrivings_ [New York: Atheneum, 1961], p. 115).

3 Eugene O'Neill, _Long Day's Journey Into Night_ (New Haven: Yale Univ. Press, 1955), IV, p. 153.

4 Peter Shaffer, _The Royal Hunt of the Sun_ (New York: Stein and Day, 1964), I.x; p. 31.

5 Quoted by Krutch, _op. cit._, p. xvii.

6 Quoted by Brian Connell, as cited by C. J. Gianakaris, "A Playwright Looks at Mozart: Peter Shaffer's _Amadeus_," _Comparative Drama_, 15 (Spring 1981), 46. Gianakaris is right to treat as a side issue the historical accuracy of Shaffer's portrayal of Mozart. His essay demonstrates convincingly that the main concern of _Amadeus_ is Salieri's relationship with God.

7 Kenneth Macgowan, "The O'Neill Soliloquy," _O'Neill and His Plays_, ed. Oscar Cargill _et al._ (New York: New York Univ. Press, 1963), p. 449.

8 Several critics have contributed detailed analyses of O'Neill's soliloquies and monologues, categorizing their general structure and various functions. See for example Egil Tornqvist, *A Drama of Souls: Studies in O'Neill's Supernaturalistic Technique* (New Haven: Yale Univ. Press, 1969), pp. 199-216; also, Timo Tiusanen, *O'Neill's Scenic Images* (Princeton: Princeton Univ. Press, 1968), pp. 207-17.

9 Peter Shaffer, *Equus* (New York: Avon Books, 1975), I.21; p. 85. Subsequent references are cited in the text.

10 Eugene O'Neill, *The Great God Brown*, in *Nine Plays by Eugene O'Neill*, "Prologue," p. 318. Subsequent references are cited in the text.

11 Quoted in Arthur and Barbara Gelb, *O'Neill* (New York: Delta, 1964), p. 580.

12 *Ibid.*

13 I cover some of this ground in *"The Birth of Tragedy* and *The Great God Brown,"* *Modern Drama*, 16 (September 1973), 129-40. Shaffer demonstrates his familiarity with Nietzsche's terminology in the following quotation: "There is in me a continuous tension between what I suppose I could loosely call the Apollonian and the Dionysiac sides of interpreting life . . ." (Cited by Gianakaris, p. 45).

14 Peter Shaffer, *Amadeus* (New York: Harper and Row, 1981), II.9; p. 70. Subsequent references are cited in the text.

15 Eugene O'Neill, *The Iceman Cometh* (New York: Vintage, 1946), IV, p. 239. Subsequent references are cited in the text.

16 "Preface," *Amadeus*, pp. ix-x.

Index